That's Me in the Closet

That's Me in the Closet

A SPIRITUAL MEMOIR

Steven Andrews

RESOURCE *Publications* • Eugene, Oregon

THAT'S ME IN THE CLOSET
A Spiritual Memoir

Copyright © 2023 Steven Andrews. All rights reserved. Except for brief quotations in critical publications or reviews, no part of this book may be reproduced in any manner without prior written permission from the publisher. Write: Permissions, Wipf and Stock Publishers, 199 W. 8th Ave., Suite 3, Eugene, OR 97401.

Resource Publications
An Imprint of Wipf and Stock Publishers
199 W. 8th Ave., Suite 3
Eugene, OR 97401

www.wipfandstock.com

PAPERBACK ISBN: 978-1-6667-7053-7
HARDCOVER ISBN: 978-1-6667-7054-4
EBOOK ISBN: 978-1-6667-7055-1

07/11/23

The events portrayed here are events the author believes are true. The author admits he could be mistaken. Where possible, names and identifying details of other characters have been changed.

Scripture quotations are from the New Revised Standard Version (NRSV) Bible, copyright © 1989 National Council of the Churches of Christ in the United States of America. Used by permission. All rights reserved worldwide.

that's me in the closet was edited by Amy Reed (amyreedfiction.com). The author did not take all her suggestions. Perhaps he should have. Any remaining errors are his own.

to Kari, Brenda, Nicole,
and all the strong women who made me who I am,
supported this writing,
and paved the way

Contents

The Past is Prologue — ix
1. Old Stories and Early Memories — 1
2. The Conflagration — 8
3. Paradise — 20
4. Almost Oddly Normal — 35
5. Atheism, Comedy, and Becoming an Outsider — 46
6. Feeling, Thinking, Connecting — 61
7. Fighting at Home and Abroad — 72
8. Trying on Faith — 84
9. Romantic Affinities — 98
10. What it Takes to See the Light — 110
11. I Believe in Something — 119
12. Spiritual but Not Religious — 132
13. All My Heart — 143
14. With Me All Along — 154
15. Life Ever After — 165

Epilogue: Being Yourself at Church — 179

The Past is Prologue

What I wanted, more than anything, was a book. Books had been with me every step of the way until now. Here, on the bottom floor of my college library, in a quiet, secluded corner, I should have been able to find a book.

By fourth grade, I was a committed atheist. In middle school and high school, I was an anti-religious evangelist—and all that was in the early 90s, before it was cool. However, toward the end of high school and the beginning of college, as the old millennium was fading and the new was emerging, I had been slowly converted from atheism, to agnosticism, to 'spiritual but not religious,' and a book was always there to help me jump from one metaphysical lily pad to another.

Now, it is deep into the fall of sophomore year. The Indiana air is crisp on your skin. The leaves crunch beneath your boots. I am hunkered down inside for a night of study. I have been dating an evangelical Christian, Dani, and even through the fog of hormones that cloud my sophomoric mind, I am on the verge of another leap of faith: ready to believe in a Christian God and accept Jesus Christ as my personal Lord and Savior. I wanted a book. I needed something clear. Something rational. Something that could provide intellectual cover. How could I, of all people, become, of all things, a Christian? The very thought arose in defiance of everything I held rational and holy.

At that moment, I thought about Dani and all the things that led me here—all the twists of fate that brought me to this strange, all-male college; to the fraternity I reluctantly joined; to the young men who helped me meet the young woman who evangelized me. It had been quite a journey to this library, to this moment. It all felt like too much.

I thought about the journey to the books that thawed my atheism—*The Art of Happiness* by the Dalai Lama, and *The Perennial Philosophy* by Aldous Huxley—and how, through them, I embraced a spiritual vision of the world and an inchoate vision of God. I thought about the Christians I had met who helped me see that there was some good in this faith, that you could be an intelligent person and a person of faith, and that religion could help people become better versions of themselves. Through them, I came to grudgingly admit that faith could, in a limited way, be a force for good in the world.

Most of all, overshadowing the books and the people, there were those twists of fate that shaped my path. All the relationships that didn't work out the way I'd hoped, clearing the way for Dani. The crushed academic aspirations and disappointed literary expectations that led to a college that was better for me than I could have dreamed.

I didn't expect to be here, on the cusp of a faith I never wanted, but somehow, it all made sense. It was like the larger hand of an author was guiding the story and had arranged the twists of fate that were, in fact, neither twists nor fate.

In the end, I didn't need a book. My life was a book. The direction it had taken was evidence of the author of the story, and I was now ready to get to know that author. I thought to myself, using the language of the evangelical church I'd been attending, *I accept Jesus Christ as my personal Lord and Savior.*

For all the things that led to that moment, I cry and curse and thank God.

For all the things that followed from that moment, I do the same.

I am queer. I use the label 'bisexual.' I was a foster child. I survived childhood trauma and am in the process of healing from that trauma, but the healing is never complete, and the scars remain visible. I am strange looking. A bit on the small side, with thick, reddish lips and eyes shaped differently from each other.

Above all else, or perhaps because of all else, I am weird. I have been an odd duck in every context I have ever been in, from schools to families to churches to cocktail parties. I am an odd person, and I want to help other people, and all the Christians in the world, embrace their inner oddness.

I am an ordained Presbyterian pastor, and I have offered ministry in a lot of places. I have lived in intentional Christian communities, worked in trauma hospitals and correctional facilities, and I've also worked for a bright, shiny, suburban church. The church had a formal brick facade. It had a prominent place near the downtown of a respectable suburb. The people were also bright and shiny and resplendent in their facades. Behind the masks people usually wore, there were stories of pain and redemption, stories of cowardice and heroism, stories of trauma and triumph. On the inside, there was an authenticity far more beautiful than the facade.

Too often, the institutional church constrains people, crushing the creativity of leaders and leading its people to hide behind a false veneer.

"What is the institutional church?" you may ask. It's the part of the church that pays bills, maintains a building, and manages a staff. It's the part of the church that worries about losing people, and then strives to hold onto those people by undermining the fullness of who they are, by repressing their creativity and striving for homogeneity. The institutional church does not, by its nature, take chances. It does not pursue its passions. It doesn't even pursue Jesus' passions. It doesn't express itself in authentic ways. It is afraid that if it were truly authentic, it would lose everything that keeps it alive.

The church and Jesus are different. The church and Jesus are different. Every time I am hurt by the church, I say this to myself again.

The church and Jesus are also the same. The church is the body of Christ. The Bible says that we are his hands and feet, that we have a mystical connection with him such that the church is an extension of him, a physical representation of him. For some reason, Jesus chose to throw in his lot with the church. What a holy fool! Either his judgment is poor, or we need to do more to live like him.

And it is "we." The church, I mean. "We," not "them." No matter how much I sometimes wish there was a separation. I am a follower of Jesus and I am part of the church. I offer myself as a critic of the church, calling for reform, but I am also a member, and I am also guilty of its characteristic sins. I have hidden behind my own false veneers. I have clipped the wings of other people. I cannot present myself as a holier-than-thou critic of others because I need to be reformed as much as anyone.

What I can do is offer the gift of my oddness. Because I did not grow up in the faith, I have a fresh perspective on the practices of the church. Just as a fish often does not think about the water because it has always been the unquestioned element of reality, church insiders live in an ecclesial reality that is often unexamined. But an outsider can see it all with fresh eyes. Because I have been the pastor of an institutional church, I have also seen beneath the surface. Like a marine biologist in her scuba gear, though I grew up on land, I have spent some time in the water. I have learned to understand it, as best I can from the safety of my wetsuit, and I love the water. I love it so much, in fact, that I want to work for a cleaner ocean. As a scuba diver rather than a fish, I have a view of the water that the fish might not see. Therefore, I offer the gift of my vision to the fish.

The institutional church is full of beautiful people, followers of Jesus, walkers of the Way, who were made in the image of God and instilled with their own divine, creative thumbprint. We were made to be like God and to be uniquely ourselves all at once.

The basic sin of the institutional church is limitation. An authentic community of Christ would help us to be who we are, to shed the false selves imposed by the world and accepted by us as a means of survival. This is what Jesus meant when he said, "For those who want to save their life will lose it, and those who lose their life for my sake, and for the sake of the gospel, will save it" (Mark 8:35). The self we need to lose is our false self, the persona created by what other people want to see and by our assumptions about what they want to see. Shedding that, we can find and express the true self at the core of who we are. (Fun fact: this piece of ancient wisdom corresponds with insights from Jungian psychology, Buddhism, the Enneagram, and Internal Family Systems. All these intellectual strata recognize the need to engage in personal work to move through a false self—imposed from the outside—to the real self that lies within.)

In this book, I am sharing my story, my personal narrative of adopting, befriending, and moving beyond a false self. I hope that my story inspires other people to go on a similar journey, and I hope it inspires all the congregations in the United States to become incubators of people giving birth to their authentic selves, then finding and expressing who they are through the power of narrative, so that we can all be our most divine selves as we seek after God together. I think a movement like this—where authentic, vulnerable people create spaces that allow the tremulous expression of personal truth—could spark a revival in America. Even if it doesn't, it could at least bring the people who encounter it closer to Jesus.

Toward that end, I offer my odd story, knowing that we are all odd in our own ways, though we are often afraid of embracing that inner uniqueness. This is not just an issue in the church. In all kinds of cultural spaces, we are afraid of expressing our true selves out of fear of rejection or punishment.

In an ideal world, the church would be the space where we do not have to be afraid, where we are empowered to be bold elsewhere in the great, wide world. Too often, though, the institutional church reinforces our fear and stands in the way of our journeys toward authenticity.

Why is that? What is it about the presence of an institution that leads to falseness and fear? When I look around the institutional church, I see the building, the professional staff, the curriculum, the furniture—all the things that cost money. Unfortunately, these are also the things that bring out the worst part of our false selves. Church members who invest money and time in the institution want to make good on that investment. They desire to "fix" the staff and change their personalities so that their employees can present a winning image to the wider community. That way, the congregation can bring in more people—to help pay for the staff, the stuff, and the building.

And speaking of that building, the members of the church will incessantly fight over it, especially if it, too, does not present a winning image to the proverbial "community."

But what community, exactly, are they talking about? The truth is, most of the time, when church members speak of community, it does not extend to people outside the church. We make it sound like it does. Some of us genuinely believe that we are trying to communicate with a community of people who are not yet members of the church. Generally, though, the things we think this community wants—or *should* want—are remarkably the same as the things we want.

All this image-conscious concern and anxiety serves a role for us. The more we focus our attention on fixing the church, the less we need to worry about fixing ourselves.

Thus, the drama of preserving the institutional church becomes a way for us to avoid doing what Jesus wants us to do: find and express our authentic selves. As we seek prestige, power, and popularity for the church, our desires for the institution stand in for the desires of our false selves—the lust for pyrite success that does not need to be gold because it glitters.

I seem to remember Jesus getting by just fine without this institutional stuff. Well, I mean, he had money, don't get me wrong. There were wealthy women who funded his ministry (Luke 8:1–3). There were people who made decisions about how the money was spent (John 12:4–6). And yes, there were institutional forces trying to keep Jesus from being who he truly was: There was his biological family, who wanted him to come home and take up carpentry and cool it on all the ministry business that made him look like a crazy person (Matthew 12:46). There were all the times the disciples sought prestige or respectability over authenticity (Mark 10:37, John 13:8, Luke 22:60). There was the apostle Peter specifically, who would have prevented Jesus from living his mission because of his own desire for a more respectable Messiah (Matthew 16:21–22).

So alright, I guess Jesus knew a little something about the weight of institutions. I guess he recognized the need for some structure, for a modicum of clear channels of leadership, and some level of organization. But he didn't let it stop him from authentically being who he was called to be. Because he was not entrenched in the institutional weight of the modern American church, there was a lot more room in his movement for people to take risks, to express their authentic selves, and to love themselves and others with wild abandon. What I think we need, most of all, is to recapture that.

We need to shed the institutional burdens. We need to liberate ourselves from all our money and give it to the poor. I think Jesus himself might have said something about that (Luke 18:22). He recognized that the longer you hold on to money, the more you fear losing it, and the more your false self becomes your dominant state of being. So let's live less like an institution and more like Jesus.

Thus freed, we can be less concerned about appearances. We can spend less time maintaining the false veneer of our stately brick facades and more time designing the eclectic mélange of our odd and wonderful church parlor. We can spend less time being afraid of how we might look to other people in the "community," and we can spend more time being our wonderful, weird, authentic selves. We can bring in other people who want to live in a space like that. We can embrace people who used to inspire fear in us because of their oddness—people in ratty clothes, people with lisps, people with calloused hands, people with accents—people with stories to tell and journeys to walk, and we can integrate their streams with ours.

For the church to be a physical representation of Christ, to be his very hands and feet, it needs to have his heart and mind, and that means embracing all people fully as who they are.

In this book, I share who I really am, as best as I can, and narrate my sideways journey from atheism to the church. Perhaps, because I came here sideways, I can name dynamics others fail to see or tremble to name. Perhaps, by giving full expression to the odd and beautiful creature I am, I will free you to do the same, and we can liberate the church together.

1

Old Stories and Early Memories

THE STORY BEGINS IN Indiana, with two star-crossed parents and a child they didn't expect.

My mother could never rest easy, no matter when and where she was. My father left before I had a chance to get to know him, but I know he was tall and had a beard and rode a motorcycle. Both he and my mother had daughters from previous relationships. We lived in a farmhouse near Columbia City, Indiana. Yes, *that* Columbia City.

(I'm kidding. You've never heard of it. Unless you're a member of my family or someone who's probably a not-too-distant relation.)

My earliest memory is of a cat outside a window. Beyond that, I have only scattered memories of the inside of the farmhouse. I don't know what's genuine, what's based on the photographs that remain of this time, or what was evoked while walking through the ruins of the house many years later, that hull of burnt wood and ancient fear. Human brains are constantly grasping for scattered details and weaving them together into the narrative we call memory. Who knows what's real? All I know is that if it lives in your brain, it's real to you.

I have a clear first memory of that cat, and even if it didn't happen, it still means something to me. I was almost three years old, in the living room with Mom, Dad, and my sisters. The television was on. Through the sounds of talking and people laughing, I was the only one who could hear the kitten outside the window, meowing and tapping her paw against the glass. I was alone in my own reality with the kitten. No one else could see her, and I could not look away.

The farmhouse sat on several acres of good land, on which we grew our own fruits and vegetables and raised animals for eggs and butchering.

There were cats all over the property, so many that my mom once accidently put a litter of kittens into the washing machine and killed them, not knowing their mother had hidden them in the laundry hamper.

Sometimes, a mother makes a decision she believes to be in the best interest of her children, and she never suspects that the poor things are going to be thrown into a washing machine.

In my earliest memory, I see this kitten outside the window. I tried to get my mom's attention to tell her that the cat needed to be let inside. At first, she didn't pay me any mind, but eventually she said I could open the window. But I was three, and I did not know how to open a window. The kitten gave up and so did I.

In our house, kids were expected to do things long before they were ready. Oftentimes, we were invisible, hurting in ways that the grown-ups couldn't see.

I don't have a clear memory of the neglect, but I feel the reverberations of it etched on my heart and soul. According to my mom, when I was an infant and a toddler, my father would put me down for my afternoon nap, then leave the house to go spend time with his girlfriend. He would just leave me there alone while he was off betraying his marriage. When my older sisters came home from school—two young girls in kindergarten and second grade—they knew it was "our job to take care of the baby."

Though I cannot remember them, those lonely afternoons would alter the course of my life. How many times did I cry out between the moment my father left and the moment my sisters came home? At what age did I learn to stop crying? When did I realize that no one could help, and no one was coming?

I am told that my father did not work during this time; instead, he "stayed home" with me. My mother was busy working as a nurse at the hospital, so she was not aware that he left me during the day, nor was she aware of his girlfriend. But one afternoon, my uncle came to the house to get a log splitter our families shared, and he discovered the arrangement: two little girls coming home from school to take care of a baby who had been left on his own. My uncle told my aunt, and my aunt told my grandparents. Everyone assumed that Mom already knew. The girls seemed to feel so natural about it all. They figured she must have known.

When she was growing up, Mom had been one part model child and one part rolling stone. In high school, she was a cheerleader and the salutatorian of her class. A local doctor had offered to pay her way through a bachelor's degree at DePauw University and a medical degree from Indiana University—if she would take over his practice in South Whitley, Indiana.

My mom turned down this offer. At eighteen years old, she wasn't sure she wanted to be tied down. After graduating high school in Larwill, an even smaller town near Columbia City, she traveled. She considered joining the Air Force. Eventually, at age twenty-one, she moved to the shining metropolis of Fort Wayne, Indiana, the seventy-second largest city in the country, where she waitressed her way to a nursing degree from a regional branch of Purdue University.

Before kids came into the picture, she had some wild experiences. She told me once that she'd never tried cocaine. Marijuana, yes, but never cocaine, and certainly not crack. She had definitely never tried crack. But heroin? Oh, right, she remembered—she had done heroin.

But she didn't just have wild experiences. She also had the wherewithal to hold down jobs and make what passed for decent money in the 1970s, especially compared to the family she'd left behind in rural Indiana. When my mom's nieces and nephews came to visit her, their parents told them to ask Aunt Brenda for the expensive things they wanted. After all, they thought, she could afford it.

It is no stretch to say my mother was exceptional. She was the one who broke out of the family pattern in so many ways. She was the first in the family to earn a college degree. She was living a glamorous life in Fort Wayne. She hadn't been tied down too young to maternal responsibilities and the staid expectations of rural womanhood. She was a model child and a rolling stone.

Eventually, a kid came: my older sister Nicole. At twenty-six, Mom had already married and divorced once, but her ex-husband wasn't the father.

You see, her first husband had been her parents' choice, not hers. Having grown up in a small town in Indiana, as one of the few young women who graduated from high school without an engagement ring on her finger, my mom did not know there were other options in life, so she didn't protest. Her parents drove the couple to Michigan to get married, because they were both under twenty-one and could not wed in Indiana without the groom's parents' consent. When they arrived in Michigan, marital arrangements had already been made, and my mother's grandmother was ready to serve as her maid of honor. What choice did she have?

Three years later, my mother's aunt got a divorce, and it opened the floodgates for others in the family. Across generations, my relatives started leaving bad marriages and seeking something better. With all her courage, my great-aunt saved them all.

I once asked for the story of my sister Nicole's father, this other man who was not my mother's ex-husband from an arranged marriage, but Mom wishes to hold that story in a vault for safekeeping, and there it will remain.

As a twenty-six-year-old divorcee expecting a child, at the tail end of a relationship that had run its course, the rolling stone that was my mother rolled away. She rolled to Atlanta, Georgia. A friend of hers had moved there, and on a whim, Mom decided to move to the same city and neighborhood. Thirty-five years later, as a young adult, I would live in Atlanta and go to church in that very same neighborhood. It wasn't intentional. It's just a small world.

As a registered nurse, Mom could get a job anywhere she wanted, and Atlanta seemed like a worthy adventure. But she had no idea how many things she would be unable to do in Georgia in 1978. She could not start a bank account—unless her father drove from Indiana to co-sign the papers on her behalf. She could not register to vote as a Republican because the Democrats dominated local politics and all the action was in their primaries; whether or not it was actually legal, the county clerk wouldn't allow her to waste her vote by registering as a Republican. And there was one more thing: no one would give her renters' insurance unless she bought a gun. "Why should I protect your things when you won't?" they asked.

Still, she lived a decent life in Atlanta, starting over and raising her daughter as a single mom. She didn't need the first man. She didn't need the second man. But who did she need when she was down there? Who did she connect with? Who helped her raise Nicole? Surely, she couldn't have done it all on her own. But this, like so much of my mom's story, is cloaked in shadows.

Two years later, she moved back to her home state and the glamorous city of Fort Wayne. The reason she has given me was that she realized that if she stayed in Atlanta, Nicole would have grown up with a Southern accent, and that was unacceptable.

Shortly after she returned to Fort Wayne, my mom and dad met in a bar. Dad was tall and had a beard and rode a motorcycle, which is a bit of a theme.

Not long after they met, I was conceived.

Not long after that, Mom and Dad got married.

My dad adopted Nicole, age five at the time, and claimed her as his own. He also brought his own seven-year-old daughter, Betty, into the relationship—and my fragile first family came together.

Eventually, we moved into a farmhouse near Columbia City, Indiana, close to my mom's parents and the rest of her family. My dad's dad lived up the road from us.

This is where I begin: Birthed by a loving mother. Nurtured by two older sisters. Neglected by my dad, with everyone in the extended family knowing, with everyone deciding not to say anything—because of course Mom must have known. What did these close, but distant relations think about her? What impressions did they have of this rapidly rolling stone? I imagine they must have envied her education, her income, her free spirit—even as they looked down their noses and resented her for the very same things. What made them look the other way when they knew I was being abandoned, when they knew I was being cared for by children not much older than myself? What made them think this was all okay with her?

Here are some things I think I know. When my mom was pregnant with me, she liked rhubarb pie, and my dad could make an excellent rhubarb pie. I think I have a memory of riding on my dad's motorcycle, safely held between his long legs as we zipped up and down the country road outside our house. My mom says the motorcycle memory can't be true, but she also says the kitten outside the window can't be true. There were so many other things happening in that house that she did not—or chose not—to see. In this season, and the ones before, and the ones that followed, how many things did she not know?

The last thing I think I know is that I didn't talk until I was three, which I have learned is common for kids who are neglected. But once I started, I was talking in full sentences, a sign of natural, unearned intelligence. My mom says she thought I was "retarded," to use her word, for waiting so long to talk. Even still, she makes fun of me for grunting when I was a toddler, saying I would grunt and point when she was trying to sleep, grunt and point and my older sisters would come running and get me what I wanted. Mom thinks I was spoiled by my older sisters, who loved taking care of the baby and rushed to meet my needs. For my part, I think Nicole and Betty's love saved me from a complete mistrust of human beings and from a complete inability, later in life, to trust and have faith in God.

When I was around eighteen months old, before Dad left, my mom saved enough money to take six months off work. She had missed a lot of moments from Nicole's early years and didn't want to miss as many with me. In addition to the caring I received from my sisters, these six months must have been a huge part of the positive side of my development ledger, the part that helped me survive and become who I am, the part that became trusting enough to not be ruined by the world.

Aside from this six-month sabbatical, my mother worked a lot during those years. She was the main source of financial support in our home, and she also had to do most of the cleaning and a lot of the farm work. If she was too tired to notice kittens in a laundry hamper, or kittens outside the window pawing to get in, or a kid who isn't crying because he doesn't think there's any reason to tap on the glass and ask to come inside—I can forgive her for that. I really can. I think she did better by her kids than her parents did by her, and for most of us, that's the best we can do.

I don't know exactly what this time in my life was like. I am piecing together a hypothetical childhood from stories told by others, shards of memories, and the evidence of who I am today. I am trying to fill in the shadows by reading the scars on my heart.

According to developmental psychologist Erick Erickson, the first stage of psychosocial development occurs from a child's birth until eighteen months. This stage is defined by trust versus mistrust, and the relationship with the mother is crucial in developing a healthy sense of trust. The focus of the next stage, from eighteen months to age three, is autonomy versus shame. Here, a child learns to be independent, to be a capable director of at least some aspects of their life. Looking back and guessing about my hypothetical toddlerdom, I must have been encouraged enough to develop some sense of autonomy—despite the shame and doubt that, even still, can burn like a wildfire across my cheeks—just as I was loved enough to not devolve into complete distrust of the world.

But development is a mixed bag for me. In this second stage, healthy kids develop a strong sense of will, coupled with an ability to think of themselves as strong and capable and worthy. But to this day, my will is not as strong as others. Apathy is a strong compulsion that I am constantly working to overcome. I am more than happy to work, but I feel a constant shame around my work because a part of me is sure that no one wants what I have to offer.

Today, I am a functioning pastor, a caring counselor, and a loving father. I have endured the pain of coming out of my shell, recognizing that this pain is far more tolerable than the crucible of remaining inside. In this book, I am sharing my story with anyone who has the faith to listen—even though I'm not built for this kind of sharing. I'm built for staying in the shadows and keeping it all to myself. Today, I am changing and growing—and it hurts, but in a better way.

There are moments when I long to be with other people, but I can't muster the courage to ask them to be with me. There are moments when I don't even think to ask for help because I thoroughly, instinctually, believe no one is coming.

There are times when my emotions are numb, when my body, mind, and soul are disconnected. Everyone has moments of numbness, but traumatized people tend to have them more often; the numbing of all emotions, both positive and negative, is a shield against heartache. Many survivors of trauma withdraw from the best relationships in their lives, in the most toxic ways they can—because, like numbness, withdrawal is a shield.

These are the just some of the ways trauma has been scarred into my heart.

These mark the birth of the false self who is still trying to reclaim my life in a misguided attempt to shield the real me from being hurt again.

These are my first closet—and part of me wants to stay in there for protection. The rest of me is writing.

Today, I am learning new ways to engage with the world, and I love that, but it's a struggle. It would be so much easier to retreat. I was built for retreat. My life has taught me to be a boy in a closet. However, a loving God and loving people continue to draw me out of that fortress—into a vulnerable, terrifying, life-giving authenticity. And I have chosen to be drawn out, to keep working against all the forces trying to drag me back in.

2

The Conflagration

"I wasn't there," I can imagine my father saying with a deadpan voice and soulless eyes. "That night, I placed a collect call to the house from North Carolina. See, I have an alibi. I couldn't have been there."

Could he really prove he wasn't there on the night of the fire?

As my parents' marriage was going down in flames, he had threatened several times to burn down the farmhouse. "It would be so easy," he told my mother. "One night, I could do it, with you and the kids inside. It will take hours for the firefighters to get there. No one would ever know it was me. There would be no way out."

His stated intent was to kill. "No one else lives nearby," he said. "I could burn it down with the three of you in it, and no one would ever know."

My father had raided the joint checking accounts and had taken all the money he could. He had filed for divorce, and he wasn't traceable. Mail sent to and from him was filtered through his mother in Indianapolis so we couldn't know where he was.

There are many unanswered questions about that night. When he called from North Carolina, who answered the phone? It was a collect call, so there was a verified record. Someone called from his number. Someone answered at our house. But who? It wasn't Mom, my sisters, or me. My dad's dad lived up the road—was Grandpa at our house to receive the call? Was he in on the whole thing? Did Grandpa burn down the house himself? Where *was* my father that night?

Three things are certain: Mom wasn't there. Nicole wasn't there. I wasn't there. In response to the threats, my mom had us sleeping at her parent's house. She was working at the hospital that night. At the very least, we were not killed in a farmhouse inferno.

Of course, I didn't know about my dad's murderous rage at the time. I was three years old. I must have had some awareness that our house had burnt down, some awareness that my toys were gone, but all I really knew for sure was that everything had changed. Dad and my sister Betty were gone. Nicole and I were living with our grandparents. Mom and Dad were no longer an item.

I didn't know, until many years later, about the time my father rammed his speeding truck into my mom's car and tried to run her off the road. What emotional kindling leads a man to this kind of combustion?

I know one thing: there was a disease running through the genes of the men who came before me. They were compulsively unable to respect women, and they were compulsive abusers.

Many years later, as a teenager, I had a long conversation with my father's father, where he extolled his regrets. Throughout his life, he had been a womanizer and an abuser. He regretted leaving women and hurting them.

He remembered one clear moment: when a young woman who had been a friend of his granddaughter's, whom he had treated kindly when she was a girl, gave him a pass on his vision test at the DMV—even though his aging eyes weren't up for the tasks being demanded of them. On his deathbed, speaking to the grandson he had not spoken to in ten years, he offered this story to me—as a lesson in being kind to others because you never know when they might repay you.

Grandpa Brock was capable of kindness, especially if he knew it might benefit him. He was nice enough to his grandkids, but he had not been kind to the women in his life. And neither had my father. When he was around, my father was often kind to me; he was clearly proud to have a son. He was, perhaps, happy at times with the life he and my mother were building in rural Indiana. But he cheated on her, and he neglected me in order to do it. He was abusive toward Mom, Betty, and Nicole.

I do not have memories of this abuse. I do not have memories of the house burning down, of saying goodbye to Betty or my dad—if I ever did—or of what my mother must have said to Nicole and me to explain all the changes.

All I knew was that everything had changed.

The first three years of my life were a whirlwind of pain and neglect, but as I grew up, my mom told me only good things about my father. As much as he hurt her, she did not want to defame him in absentia. She also did not want to answer too many questions about her own past. By weaving a simple and positive narrative about him, she strove to protect me from the truth and to guard her own thoughts and feelings.

Years later, when I was in my mid-twenties, I learned about my real father, about the character of this man who passed his genes onto me. In piecing together the details, I discovered the short biography of a sociopath.

For much of his adult life, my dad told everyone he had been wounded in Vietnam. No one had any reason to question him. Everyone believed it. My mom believed it, even after the divorce—until she learned it wasn't true.

As it turns out, he joined the Army as a young man, but when it came time for him to deploy to Vietnam, a knee injury he'd had since high school "suddenly acted up." He needed the Army to pay for his surgery, so he managed to get discharged as a service-related disabled veteran with all the privileges thereof.

The scar on his knee was a souvenir of his time in the Army, and so too was his first wife. As it turns out, he had spent some time in Korea, where he raped a woman. In the eyes of their culture, she was now disgraced by his actions and no honorable man would marry her. Her family agreed not to press charges against him if he would marry her. I doubt anyone ever asked her what she wanted.

So he married the woman he'd assaulted and brought her back to the United States, where he systematically isolated and abused her. For a year and a half, her family believed she was dead, because he had told them she was. She also believed her parents were dead—because he had told her they were.

Eventually, she broke free of the lies and escaped his abusive clutches. But it wasn't easy.

When he married my mom, he did everything he could to keep his first wife away from his second. He made up all kinds of stories about his first wife, about her hatred of my mom and her skill with deadly weapons, and he did the same about my mom toward her. The last thing he needed was for the two of them to talk and see through all the deception together.

Like many sociopathic people, my father could be charming. When he first met my mother, he was charming. And he was able to keep that charm going for a few years, as cover for the lies, the pain, and the constant betrayal.

After the divorce, Mom looked up his records through the VA and discovered the truth about his military career. While she was there, a VA counselor suggested she meet the first wife. In response to my mom's fear of her, and her fear of my mom, the counselor offered to mediate the first meeting.

They were surprised to discover the truth about each other. Perhaps even more surprisingly, they became friends. They even went clubbing together.

Still, the connection would not last long. My mom was ready for her next adventure, ready to change her life again, and ours along with it. If she was going to be a single mother, then she wanted to make enough money to do it in style and make a difference for sick people along the way. At age 35, my mother, who had once turned down the opportunity to become a doctor because it would have tied her down, enrolled in the Master of Public Health program at Harvard. Here, she believed, she would finally fulfill her academic promise. Here, she believed, she would craft a new and better life for herself and for us.

She found a job at a VA Hospital in New Hampshire, because she was a registered nurse and could get a job wherever she wanted. She was prepared to move Nicole and me to the East Coast, to start a new life in a new place, free from a strained extended family and the memories of a marriage doused in flames.

But my father would not give permission for us to go. Because he had adopted Nicole, he was legally her father, and neither of us were allowed to leave the state without his permission.

As far as I know, he never made any attempt to visit us. I don't have any memory of him being present at all, aside from sending the proverbial birthday card with a five-dollar bill. But he'd be damned if he passed up a chance to mess up my mom's life.

Again, I didn't know any of this at the time. As a kid, I just knew that Nicole and I were settling in with our grandparents, that we were moving in this time and not just staying there for the night. My mom decided to move to New Hampshire on her own, continue her education, and come back for us in two years. In the meantime, she would send money. She would visit when she could. We would stay in Indiana and her parents would take care of us.

Even today, I continue to look back on this season with Grandma and Grandpa as the closest thing I had to a normal childhood. Given everything that happened after we left our grandparents' home, there was never a possibility of returning to normal after this short respite from chaos. Later in life, even when events were not occurring at a breakneck speed, even when caregivers were not coming and going like waves—I would be so scarred by what happened next and next and next that there would never again be a possibility of me being anything like normal.

But for these two years, there was a period of calm upon the ocean. For now—after the boat caught on fire, and the lifeboat slipped away, and we somehow managed to swim to the island oasis of our grandparents' home—everything was fine.

During these years, life revolved around scooters and kittens, bologna and French toast.

My grandparents found kittens for my sister and me. Mine was white and brown and named Tiny, and he was not ironically named. My sister's cat was a big, grey tomcat named Tom. Our grandparents suggested both names. Depth of imagination was not among their strengths.

A few months after his short life began, my cat lived up to his name by contracting worms and dying of starvation. My sister's cat grew into a large, affectionate feline who survived for many years. I don't remember being terribly affected by the death of Tiny, even though it must have been my first experience of death. I don't want to overanalyze the emotional life of a three-year-old, but I think I was already numb to emotions. I had already learned that relationships come into your life and then leave again, that attachments should be light because parting is inevitable. After all, so many people had just departed from my young life. The death of a cat was one more drop in a deep, heart-numbing bucket.

By this time, I think I had learned not to claim too much for myself and to be satisfied with the small scraps of what life would give me—to not try to eat too much because the metaphorical worms would inevitably claim any excess nourishment as their own. For me, the scraps were enough, because they had to be. I had some scraps of joy with Tiny, and now Tom belonged to all of us, and that would have to be enough.

I still had French toast and bologna.

Like many children, I was a picky eater, craving the familiar and rejecting the unfamiliar. But I was definitely pickier than most, and I wonder if this was heightened by an unconscious sense of all the chaos, an unconscious desire to assert familiarity and exercise agency in at least one realm of my life.

None of us were psychologists in that house, least of all a grandpa who was retired from factory work and a grandma who had never retired from domestic work. None of us analyzed my pickiness; we just dealt with it. For food, they always gave me the choice of opting out of a meal in favor of bologna. I had to take one bite. If I didn't like it, I could make myself a bologna sandwich. In those days, there were many dinners I rejected in favor of bologna. I also came to rely on French toast as the meal I would eat after a long morning in the Missouri Synod Lutheran preschool.

One day, I came home and Grandpa was in charge, not Grandma. Before I could even ask, he told me the culinary import of this news: "I can't make your French toast, Stevie. I'm sorry."

"It's okay, Grandpa," I responded. "I know how to make it."

I could tell he was skeptical. I was only three, after all. But I had watched my grandmother do this countless times, and after some persuasion, I convinced Grandpa to let me lead him. We cracked and beat the eggs, added vanilla and cinnamon and nutmeg, coated the bread, and then fried it up. We used his hands because he wouldn't let me cook on my own, but I gave the instructions. I knew what I was doing in the kitchen. Grandpa was surprised by my budding culinary intellect and delighted to tell Grandma about our accomplishment.

My precocity was apparent both at home and at school. In preschool, we memorized Bible verses, and we took them home so we could practice. One day, I came home without a Bible verse, and my concerned grandmother called the church. They explained that I had already memorized all the Bible verses. Not that I had memorized the whole Bible, of course, but I had memorized all the sanitized verses pre-approved for preschoolers. We weren't reading 2 Kings 2:24 or anything.

I should mention here that I'm not trying to brag. When I act like an obnoxious know-it-all, it's not because I think I'm better than you. It's because part of me is thoroughly convinced that I'm worse, that intelligence is my one redeeming grace and I desperately need to prove it.

That was life back then. Just normal kid stuff and funny little stories.

Maybe the only abnormal kid thing is that I did not learn to ride a bike in this season.

I was captivated by a tricycle and a scooter. An intrepid, small-town reporter took a picture of me riding the scooter around our little neighborhood. It appeared in the local paper next to the weather report: "Little Stevie Andrews enjoys the sunshine on a cool spring day."

Everyone called me Stevie back then. When Grandpa took me to Mike's Barber Shop, Mike and the other regulars called me Stevie. Grandma, Grandpa, and Nicole called me by that name. When I was granted the immense privilege of accompanying Grandpa to the truck stop, where I could have a delicious glass of chocolate milk and a few quarters for video games—the regulars knew me as Stevie as well. "That's Gene Kile's grandkid," they would say. "Brenda's boy," some might add, though she was less well-known than her father.

More than anything, I loved tormenting my older sister. It was mostly not deliberate, but I enjoyed doing the things she was doing. She was getting into music, so I asked for and received a small record player. She enjoyed going with Grandpa to the truck stop—until I started coming and ruined that for her. She got a special dispensation to stay up late and watch the Adam West *Batman* on Nick at Nite; it was one of her favorite things—until I got permission to do it too.

She was a tomboy, as befits a girl with a tomcat. She played baseball, so I played t-ball. She loved fishing with Grandpa—until I started going and ruined that for her. Once, when we were out on a local pond, she made a big deal of teaching me to fish. However, by the luck of the cast, I wound up with the first big fish of the day, and as Nicole and Grandpa helped me haul it in, I turned to her and said, "That's how you catch a fish!" She was mad. We went home after that.

There was a certain cat-and-mouse game throughout this season of life, where she would gain an interest in something, I would tag along, and then she would move onto something else.

Once, Grandpa dug clay out of the garden. He made a big deal out of it. Maybe it was a favorite childhood activity of his. We could play with the clay as long as we wore old clothes and settled ourselves on the picnic table on the front lawn. I spent many hours sitting at that table, alone, playing imaginative games with clay. Sometimes, I would invite other people to join me, but eventually I understood that no one would. Eventually, I gave up on including other people and went back to shaping an imaginary world with an unfinished substance on my own. It was like I was back in the closet again.

This part of my childhood was a happy one, but a lonely one. I loved my grandparents and I loved my big sister, even if she constantly evaded my mental grasp. But I spent a lot of time on my own. I didn't have many friends in preschool. I enjoyed Tom the tomcat and Buffy the golden retriever—but my life was short on people.

At the time, I didn't really notice my solitude, and I didn't really mind. I accepted the scraps of what life would give me. But the loneliness seems so clear now when I look back—through a lens of clay and maple syrup, through a lens of psychology and all the things I must have subconsciously known.

While I was living with my grandparents, I discovered my love of learning. On PBS, I enjoyed watching *Math Blaster* and other educational shows. As I moved through preschool and into kindergarten, I loved encountering new challenges in math and reading, absorbing new information, and showing off my learning like the good little know-it-all I was becoming.

However, I did not find kindergarten all that challenging. By the time I got there, I had already mastered all the lessons through a combination of preschool and workbooks and television learning. Every assignment was easy, and I was bored. So one day, I refused to do the work. I went on strike. My teacher allowed my rebellion to persist in the classroom, but at recess, the hammer came down: students with incomplete assignments could not go outside.

Even at the time, I remember feeling amused. Did my teacher expect me to be motivated by slides and teeter-totters? I did not find recess especially fun. Still, it was a break in the monotony of the day, and I felt annoyed at having to remain in the classroom with students who couldn't complete their work on time. So, because I wanted the diversion, and because I wanted to show my teacher what I could do, I completed the entire day's assignments in a few minutes.

Looking back on this moment now, I know that my childhood self felt some arrogance. I thought I was better than those other kids stuck inside during recess, at least academically, and I had a desire to show off. But even more than that, I had a need for recognition and praise. During the rare moments when I saw my mom, she always commented on how smart I was. Other people seemed to like it, too. I was learning quickly that this was my calling card in life. This trait was my ticket to appreciation. If I could show my teacher how smart I was, if I could prove to her that I was special, I would be worthy of love.

Again, none of us had studied psychology back then, but it's clear in retrospect that I had been deprived of love by that point in my five-year-old life. Not starved entirely, but deprived. I wasn't emotionally emaciated—there had been some affection, some nurturing, some warmth, and some of it had been really deep. But it was not as much as a five-year-old needs and deserves. It wasn't as much as I deserved.

I needed more, and I knew that if there was one way I could get even a scrap of it, it would be through intelligence.

In terms of psychosocial development, I had earned a clear sense of autonomy alongside a heavy dose of shame and doubt. Those traits were already etched into my soul by the age of three. In this current stage, the stage of initiative versus guilt, I once again learned that I deserved to be left alone—in my own little mental closet.

To the point where it was almost conscious, I learned that I was unworthy of the company of others, but that I also enjoyed being alone because I liked blazing my own trail. I deserved only the scraps of life, but I also enjoyed the scraps of life.

These were the signposts of my inconsistent development roadmap. Through my preternatural intelligence (See? See? See how smart I am? I don't know why my older sister found me annoying. . .), I had a source of esteem, a source of confidence, a source of internal strength to counteract the shame and doubt.

These were the nascent forms of the shell that would protect and surround me. Buried beneath these defense mechanisms, there was an authentic self, a person God made to thrive in community, enjoy the company of others, love and serve other people, and shine forth with creativity and inventiveness. But that authentic self was hidden under layers of shame, doubt, showing-off, and the assertion that I was content to be alone. These were the nascent forms of the false self I needed in this and other childhood seasons—the false self I would need to befriend and set aside as an adult.

In my little-kid heart, how did I process the rapid changes in my life? What rationalization did my little-kid mind find for all the people who had come and gone? How did I explain my changing sister, who was still here but pulling away, as she desperately tried to establish an adolescent identity and live her own life?

And how must I have felt when everything changed yet again, when I was ripped from my grandparents and the most stable home I'd ever known, and taken to a new place? I remember feeling almost nothing—perhaps surprise, perhaps uncertainty, but not sadness or fear or anger, none of the emotions I can imagine other children feel when their whole life is upended.

One day, during kindergarten, my mom showed up and pulled me out of school. There was a man with her, a Missouri Synod Lutheran pastor named Joshua Lawrence. Mom had come to take both Nicole and me out of school, and she felt she needed a man by her side for support; if he was a member of the clergy, all the better. Joshua was the husband of Emily Lawrence, a coworker of my mom who had become a good friend. Mom and Emily worked together at the VA Hospital in New Hampshire, and Joshua was the self-proclaimed "handsomest Lutheran pastor in Maine." There were two. Joshua had come all the way to Indiana with my mother.

Mom came back because my grandparents had filed for custody of Nicole and me. They claimed our mother had abandoned us, that when ambition and adventure had taken her off to the East Coast, she had left us suddenly and without support.

She did not believe she had abandoned us.

The plan had been for her to send money, which I believe she did. The plan had also been for her to visit. She told me years later that she visited us every weekend, but I do not remember these visits. I have a vague memory of Mom's presence on holidays and at other special moments, and I remember a time when Nicole, me, my grandma, and one of our cousins visited her in New Hampshire. But I do not remember these regular weekend visits.

At any rate, Mom was not able to finish her degree at Harvard. Instead, she came back to Indiana and promptly married again.

Bill was another tall man with a beard who rode a motorcycle. While they probably would not have rushed into marriage in other circumstances, Mom felt it would help to have a man by her side when she stepped into court with her parents. After all, in a small town in Indiana, what chance did a single, twice-divorced woman have against two model citizens with standing in the community?

Of course, my grandparents were not saints. Years later, I learned the details of their biographies. For most of our childhood, my mom did the best she could to preserve the memories Nicole and I held of her parents. Whatever her feelings about them, regardless of how much they hurt her by trying to take us away, Mom still strained to not let us think ill of them, to maintain a family relationship that included weekend visits for us kids and holiday meals with the extended family. But years later, after they had died, when I was a young adult and kept pushing for answers, the truth came out.

My grandparents married each other when they were young and foolish. Almost immediately, my grandmother wanted out of the marriage, but her father made it clear that she could not return home if she left. During the early years of that unhappy marriage, my grandfather was not a kind man. He was wounded, physically and emotionally, and from the depth of his wounds, he wounded others.

My grandfather's childhood dream had been to follow his father into farming, but his new wife was not cut out for that life, so they moved into town, and he never stopped resenting her. He was an insecure man, perhaps because he qualified for disability after a finger was chopped off in a factory accident and it shamed him to accept the small government handout—rather than working full-time to make a living.

He drank beer. He smoked. He was prone to fits of rage, and neither his wife nor his daughters could avoid becoming victims of that rage. He had more than one affair. Like all the men in my family, on both sides, he had that compulsive disease.

My grandmother, for her part, did the best she could in these times that were both financially and emotionally trying. She ran a small hamburger shop for a while and brought in some income that way. But mostly, she made do with the income that came through him.

To cope with the emotional strain, she became a steady churchgoer and a vicious gossip. She kept a calendar to note the dates of every wedding in town and then the date when the first child was born, making a hobby out of calculating whose children were conceived out of wedlock. My grandmother was a woman who had small kingdoms and ruled over them with an iron fist. She did not hurt her daughters physically, but on an emotional level, she cut them down a thousand times.

I have no doubt that if we continued to look back in the family tree, we would find that my grandparents, and likely their parents before them, have plenty of their own painful stories to tell, their own stories of abuse and neglect and being hurt by those who should have loved them. This is one reason why I do not blame my grandparents for their sudden claim of custody. That, and the fact that they could not have known how much pain would result from their actions.

It is also worth saying that knowing who my grandparents are helps me understand and forgive my mother. Looking back, I do not think she expressed her love to me in a way that a child needs to be loved, in a way that was full and unconditional and present when I needed her the most, but I believe she loved me as well as she knew how, and that her love was deeper than what she knew as a child.

As for my grandparents, they were kind and loving toward us during this brief childhood oasis. In fact, I wonder if the chance to raise Nicole and me was an opportunity for absolution, to do what they wished they could have done for their own children. Now that they were retired and had the accumulated wealth of inheritance and a lifetime of work, they could give us things they could not have given their own children. We were their second chance.

I think they loved giving us kittens, and they loved giving us scooters, and they loved buying a house in the country with more room to run around, with a ping pong table in the basement and a golden retriever to boot. I think Grandpa loved taking us fishing and showing us off at the barber shop and truck stop, and Grandma loved being able to cook for us on a modern stove and range—one that cooked food evenly, unlike the broken stove she had used to cook for her own kids.

During the trial, while my grandparents, mom, and new stepdad were in the courtroom, Nicole and I were watched by Grandpa Brock, my father's father, the guy who may have burnt down our farmhouse. Apparently, he was the best we could do. My father, of course, was nowhere to be found.

As for me, I was once again learning the same old lesson: people come and go. Attachments should be light because parting is inevitable. My mom won custody of us, and I remember being happy for her, in the way that you might be happy for a work colleague who won a raffle for a new boat. I'm happy that you got a thing that you're excited about.

For me, it was goodbye to Grandma and Grandpa—goodbye to Tom and Buffy—goodbye to my kindergarten teacher and the shallow friendships I had managed to make—goodbye to the life I had known—and hello to once again starting over.

I did not know how much of my world had been burned physically and emotionally, how much had already been devoured by the flames. I did not know what to expect from Bill, this new man who had suddenly entered our lives. I did not yet know how much deeper the scars could go.

3

Paradise

WE MOVED TO THE shining metropolis of Fort Wayne, Indiana, a nascent family of mom, stepdad Bill, sister, and brother. Bill's parents lived in Fort Wayne, and for several weeks, we stayed with them.

One of the features of the house was a trophy room full of impressive trophies that were taller than me. The participation trophies I won in tee-ball were nothing compared to Bill's motocross trophies, and this one room was overflowing with them all. You opened the door and it would hit a trophy. You could barely walk in the room for all the trophies covering the floor, creating a canopy above me and a forest floor below. Some were for stunts, others for racing, and all were stunning.

Like my father, Bill was a tall, bearded man who drove a motorcycle, but he was taller and his beard was thicker and he was a more accomplished rider. He could not make a rhubarb pie better than my father, but he exceeded him in everything else, both positive and negative.

It was wonderful to get to know Bill. He showed me the places that were special to him when he was a kid. He and I walked on the railroad tracks he used to walk and we played in the same park. He walked me to the neighborhood elementary school where I continued kindergarten.

Some days, we would go to the farmhouse that had likely been burned down my father—or at least the hulking frame of what the farmhouse used to be. While Mom and Bill surveyed the property and thought about rebuilding, my sister and I explored the grounds.

Everything was okay during this time in Fort Wayne. I made friends in our new neighborhood and at school. Bill's parents were kind and his mom was a good cook. A new nuclear family was forming in the wake of another one's explosion.

Bill was aware of the physical similarities between him and my father, of the phenotype that had been passed on to me by another man. Once, he looked at me, then turned to my mother and said, "He should have been my kid." He appreciated me and I appreciated him. I wonder how he felt about my sister. I suspect he did not feel as connected to her as he did to me. Still, it was nice to be appreciated.

However, the good times didn't last long. My grandparents kept appealing the custody decision, appealing to higher courts to claim custody of Nicole and me. To escape this legal morass, Mom's lawyer advised her to move somewhere remote, suggesting either London or Hawaii. And well, my mom was a registered nurse, so she could get a job wherever she wanted. She found work at a hospital in Honolulu, a good position with relocation assistance from the hospital.

And just like that, we were moving again. First, we drove from Indiana to California. From the backseat, I counted. As we travelled through the desert of the southwestern United States, I counted constantly and drove everyone crazy. I counted by one into the ten-thousands. I multiplied by two into the millions and billions. Numbers and cacti dotted the landscape.

In California, we put our car on a boat and sent it to Honolulu. A few days later, we flew to the city of pineapples and palm trees.

We would stay in Hawaii for exactly one year and one day, long enough for me to finish kindergarten, but not long enough to complete first grade. In the end, Hawaii would be a place of abuse, learning, family chaos, and resilience. But in the beginning, things were good. We lived in paradise, after all. The weather was incredible, the perfect temperature all the time. Our school had palm trees and the hallways were outside—to get from one room to another, we walked outside to get there! As a family, we went to the beach and collected hermit crab shells. We ate Hawaiian lunch plates and enjoyed the general vibe.

At first, we lived in a transitional apartment provided by the hospital. There was a TV with cable, and Bill noticed a channel, ESPN, that played exercise shows in the morning. He encouraged us to watch these shows and exercise in the morning before school. Bill thought exercise in the morning was important. After all, Bill's dad had been in the military, and when Bill was a kid, his dad had made him do exercises in the morning. Bill was encouraging and inviting in his approach to this. He even joined along with us.

But everything changed when we moved into our own apartment. By then, Bill had found work as an electrician with a construction company. He was a provider now. He was the head of the household.

The move and the work must have been liberating for him. He was no longer living under the thumb of his parents in the home he grew up in. He was no longer living in a transitional space provided by his wife's employer. Now, he was an equal partner. It was his place as much as hers. Nicole and I belonged to him as much as her, and he was free to raise us as he saw fit. So he imposed military-style discipline on our lives, like the discipline imposed on him when he was a child—the kind of regimen that he knew would be the best and most thorough way to raise a healthy child.

In the dark corners of my memory, there is a faded Polaroid of the first conversation about this new regime.

"You will address me as 'sir,' and you will address your mother as 'ma'am,'" he said.

"What if we forget?" I asked.

"'Sir, what if we forget?'" he corrected me.

"Sir, what if we forget?" I asked again.

"You will be punished," he told us. And then he continued: "Your daily schedule is posted on the refrigerator. You will wake up every morning at five a.m. sharp. No excuses. You each have alarm clocks you can set each night. And your first duty is exercise. Jumping jacks, push-ups, sit-ups, crunches, running in place. Numbers and times are posted on the schedule. Keep on track, and I'll know if you're lying."

"Sir, can we watch exercise shows like in the old apartment?" my sister asked.

"No," he said. "We don't have a TV here."

I asked, "Sir, can we get one?"

"No!" He raised his voice. "We're not getting a television. It rots your brain."

I was confused. "Sir, what about Saturday morning cartoons?" I used to love Saturday morning cartoons. When we lived with our grandparents, I watched He-Man, G.I. Joe, and the Real Ghostbusters.

"Here. Right here!" he said, with a rustle of papers. "There are Saturday morning cartoons in the newspaper."

My toys—the box that had been driven from Indiana and flown across the ocean and now resided here in this stucco-walled, faux-coral apartment—went up on a high shelf in a hall closet. They were not to be touched.

Do you know of any other five-year-old who doesn't have a toy?

"When you want to play, you can play outside, or do something educational," Bill said.

We had an Apple II GS computer at the time. There were math games I could play. There was *Where in the World is Carmen Sandiego?* and *Where in Europe is Carmen Sandiego?*

But there was not much time to play. In the morning, there were exercises. There were hand weights. Once I learned how to swim, we swam laps in our apartment's swimming pool. After that, there was school. After school, there were chores. After chores, there was more work to do. Bill would go to teachers' stores and buy us workbooks in math, reading, and writing. My sister was five years older than me, but soon enough, I was excelling at the same math that she was struggling with. Bill realized I needed to be challenged more thoroughly, so when we went to the public library, he assigned me topics to read about and book reports to write.

When was the last time you heard a six-year-old ask a librarian, "Do you have any books on the Monitor and the Merrimack?" But this was the sort of thing I would do. And yes, by the way. They did.

As my knowledge of US history, world geography, science, and mathematics went from zero to sixty in seconds, I was particularly drawn to biographies of US presidents. At the library, I found a series of biographies designed for middle school readers, and I promptly devoured them. I was intrigued by the paths the presidents followed to that high position, by the policies they enacted once in office, by the praise and adulation they received. Because presidential biographies for kids are hagiographical, I came to think of the US as a meritocracy and a president as the person who has the most merit.

I thought I might have that kind of merit one day. I wanted to grow up and become President. But first, of course, I would serve three terms in Congress and then two terms as a Governor. Either that, or I would be a museum curator.

I would grow up to become something that would show off my intelligence. Demonstrating intelligence, after all, was the only way I knew to win attention and receive love. At the age of five, I was full of self-doubt about a lot of things. But I knew I was smart, and that was something the adults in my life seemed to like about me.

In fact, by the time I was six, I could name every US President in order—from George Washington to George Herbert Walker Bush. (I mention this so that maybe you'll like me.)

My mom says I knew all the vice-presidents and first ladies in order, as well, but I don't think that's true. Or if it's true, it was just for a moment of memorization and then it faded away. My mom has always been a good storyteller, but not necessarily a reliable narrator.

But speaking of narration, the narrative of our time in Hawaii was painful and arduous. It was a short period of life-defining trauma spiced with moments of amazing. In a few beats, I'll say more about the hard things, but let's dwell for a moment in the amazing.

We lived in an island paradise!

We made frequent trips to the Bishop Museum, which I loved, and I had a t-shirt from there devoted to the state fish, a trigger fish called the humuhumunukunukuapua`a. We went to the observatory at night and learned the constellations.

We sampled good food throughout Honolulu. I tried shark and mahi mahi. I loved lemon meringue pie from Marie Callender's fine restaurant.

When my sister and I had free time, we went everywhere on bare feet. All the kids did. We went to the corner store on bare feet, where we would buy packets of Ramen, spread the powder on the hard squares of uncooked noodles, and eat them as a raw, crispy snack. We even went to school on bare feet. The dress code at school was, "If we're going on a field trip, wear shoes."

I tagged along with my sister as much as I could when she hung out with kids in the neighborhood. At school, I palled around with Maynard, a Malaysian boy whose dorky sense of humor was aligned with my own.

All that was good. In some ways, even Bill's military-style discipline was at least partially good, because I thrived academically under his regime. The problem came when we stepped out of line. When a chore was done incorrectly in Bill's estimation, or when I committed the cardinal sin of wetting the bed, or when my sister snuck candy into the house—at those times, there would be hell to pay.

Spankings, I often hear, have the potential to save the world. If only we devoted more time to hitting children, the way we were hit when we were young, they would be disciplined and respectful, like we were. If we hit them more, they would honor us, obey us, enthusiastically carry on our traditions, and adopt a moral code more like our own. This is not my viewpoint, of course. This is a version of what people have said throughout centuries, throughout millenia, in cultures across the world—that the wounds we bear should be borne by our children, who should be initiated into the world with the same pain we felt, because that pain will make them more like us.

Today, as a father, I know there are better ways to enact boundaries and help children grow. As a father, I believe in conscious discipline and nonviolent intervention.

But Bill didn't.

He thought that pain was the best way to teach.

He took a sadistic pleasure in hitting us. When we made a mistake cleaning the toilet, when we were lax in our jumping jacks, when he had a bad day at work, our pants came down and we went over his knee. Most of the time, he smacked us with the large, calloused hands of a construction worker, propelled by the muscles of a man who could work wonders on a motorcycle. The belt was reserved for particularly egregious offenses—or for when he chose to feel particularly offended.

He left marks on our bodies. Our asses were red. They had welts. They had bruises. At one point, when we lived in Hawaii, I developed hemorrhoids.

What kind of a six-year-old has hemorrhoids?

It would almost be comical—if it weren't a sign of how much stress I was living under, how much anxiety I felt, and perhaps, if bodies behave in psychosomatic ways, how much my body was straining to protect me from the torture.

With Bill, physical assault came with verbal assault. He called us weak and soft. He made fun of us if we cried. I felt like a worthless worm, with my pants at my ankles, my ass in the air, and his hand coming down like a hammer. My face would be red and wrinkled in anguish. It hurt even more when he laughed while I cried.

"Sir—please. It was an accident!" I must have shouted dozens of times, and the response was always the same: "You were an accident!"

"I'm sorry, sir! Please! It was a mistake!" I shouted, only to hear the rote response: "You were a mistake!"

He made me feel like nothing.

There was something in the way he said what he said, an ever-present snarl inherent in the yelling, a viciousness that cut to the bone. I know spanking is a common experience, that many people reading these words have been hit by their parents in ways that left bruises and made them cry. If you're one of those people, I don't think it's okay that you went through that. But if you turned out okay despite that, it's because when you went through it, you still knew you were loved.

I did not.

Bill was capable of expressing pride. He would sometimes offer praise for my academic accomplishments, but that wasn't love. He would brag about me to people he met, and I felt good in those moments, but I didn't feel love.

He never apologized to us, not even when the hitting was clearly about his frustrations and not about what we had done. He never came back in an attempt to teach or repair the damage. There were good moments with him, but my memory of them is overshadowed by the hitting.

I don't have words to explain how degraded I felt, how ashamed and hopeless, how much joy was sucked out of my young life with every lash of his tongue, hand, and belt.

There was nothing redeemable about this. Even the development of my young bright mind, from which I could pull out little slivers of self-worth, became a reason for Bill to frequently beat, berate, and insult my sister. There were moments when she was compared to me and found wanting, when my success became a lash against her. I enjoyed doing well, but when my accomplishments were turned against Nicole, they became sour—even the one lovable thing about me became one more reason to hate myself.

Why did I hate myself and not him? Because that is so often the case with abuser and abused. Bill was my provider. He fed me. He clothed me. He provided the scraps of parental attention on which I had learned to subsist. If I hated him, I would lose even that. This is how I learned to survive the abuse—by loving my abuser and hating myself, by loving my abuser and convincing myself I deserved it.

It's simple, really. If you believe you deserve it, then you have an explanation for why it's happening. If you did something wrong, then all the pain makes sense. If it's just the random lashing out of an insecure and erratic sociopath, then that means the world is chaos and out of control, and that feels even more insecure. If the fault is not his, but yours, then at least you can convince yourself you have some sliver of control.

Another means of survival, for me, was emotional detachment. Emotional detachment was already part of the closet in which I dwelt, already part of the shell that made up the false, survival-oriented self that protected my authenticity from the world. In this situation, it came in handy.

There were brief moments of joy, but joy can be dashed and disappointed. It is better to suppress it. Joy is a cousin of hope, which is similarly foolish to hold.

I learned to avoid emotion—and attention. While praise felt good, I learned that the safest strategy was to be invisible. Both negative and positive attention could lead to pain at the snap of a belt. The real world hurt and was best avoided, so I used my imagination to make new worlds out of books and computer games, to lose myself in those realities, to slip away in my mind—so that at least mentally I would remain unseen.

In this cruel world, my mind and body had a job to do: to protect the truest part of myself, the part that persisted deep down below the surface. Through a combination of shame, imagination, detachment, and avoidance, I could protect an authentic portion of my soul.

In Hawaii, rent is impossibly high and furniture is expensive. Virtually everything has to be imported, sent by boat or plane thousands of miles across the ocean, and the goods produced in Hawaii are overpriced because of tourists. As a result of all this, many Hawaiians lead a minimalist life. Life is better spent outside than inside, anyway. In our family, the cost of rent, the cost of furniture, and the cost of living, meant that my sister slept on a couch and I slept on a loveseat in the living room of our one-bedroom apartment.

One night, I appeared in Mom and Bill's room, where they slept on an air mattress on the floor. "Excuse me, sir," I said quietly, meekly announcing my presence. "Bill?" I asked into the darkness. My mother laid beside him, but she was not the one I asked for.

My mom worked at the hospital most nights and slept during the days. Thus, whether it was day or night, whether she was gone or present, she was distant in one way or another, and Bill was the person I was learning to ask for, even when she was there.

"Bill?" I pressed again. His eyes opened—like a long-slumbering dragon in a cave. "Sir, Bill, I wet the bed." I began to tear up, anticipating his anger. I stuttered, "And—and—and—it soaked through the blanket, and—"

I didn't want to tell him about the awful thing I had done. I didn't want to wake him up. But the pee had soaked through the blanket and onto the loveseat, and I didn't know how to clean it on my own, and there was nowhere else to sleep.

He exploded in anger and sprang from the bed. He pulled down my pants and spanked me, hard. I made the usual, plaintive plea, "It was a mistake!" only to hear him roar that I was a mistake.

He woke Nicole up to make her clean the loveseat, so she would have to suffer alongside me. The loveseat was one of our few pieces of furniture. It was a precious item, so it had to be cleaned right away. But I was dirty too, and Bill had a solution for that.

He made me take off the rest of my clothes. He grabbed me by the wrist and dragged me to the shower. Usually, I took a bath. But tonight, in the middle of the night, it was the shower. Bill knew I was afraid of the shower. He turned the faucets on brutally cold and had me sit down under the water. The water hit my skin like cascading shards of ice.

We had just seen *Arachnophobia* at the drive-in movie theater, a film that no parent should ever show to a six-year-old, and I was terrified of spiders. I cried as I looked at the drain in the middle of the shower. I shrunk my freezing, naked body back as far as I could from that drain. I asked Bill, "Can spiders come up through there?"

"No," he said, "Not regular spiders. Just tarantulas." For all of his earlier rage, he was cold and quiet with these words. "Tarantulas are sturdy enough to live in the sewer and strong enough to push the drain open. They love moisture, and they love the dark."

He turned off the lights, stepped out of the bathroom, and closed the door. There were no windows. I was left in the pitch-black night, cold water beating down like his relentless hands, with imaginary tarantulas pushing through the grate over the drainpipe. I cried like I'd never cried before.

Outside the bathroom door, I heard my mom talking to Bill. I heard a smack. Eventually, Mom came into the bathroom with me. She was unable to change what was happening, but at least she was there.

I do not remember what she said or did during that time. I just remember the terror and the anguish of the night—and her being there. Eventually it was over, and no more was said.

My sister was my hero during this chapter of our lives. She let me tag along when she hung out with neighborhood kids—surreptitiously on the weekdays and with permission on the weekends, when our schedule allowed for free time. We'd stomp around the neighborhood on our bare feet like the other kids, and we'd play in the park and on the playground, and in those moments, I could almost believe we were like all the other kids.

When Nicole had the chance to sleep over at a friend's house, she would bring her annoying little brother along with her. She knew that I needed to get out of that place as much as she did, and she had grace enough to allow me to annoy her, even in those treasured moments of freedom.

She also arranged for us to spend a few nights at Mom's hospital. Mom worked in the ICU and we could sleep in the ICU waiting room. Nicole convinced Bill and Mom that we needed to see her more often, that she worked so hard and had to sleep during the day and we missed her. These things were true, but more than anything, it was a ploy to get out of that brutal environment.

Imagine—an ICU waiting room being a less brutal environment than a home.

One of the unexpected joys of nights at the hospital was Filipino food. Hawaii is a fusion of cultures—with Native Hawaiians, mainland whites (*haoles*, we were called, pronounced like 'howlies'), and people whose ancestors had lived in Thailand, Malaysia, Vietnam, China, Japan, Samoa, Korea, Tahiti, the Philippines, and more.

When there was a Filipino person in the ICU, their whole family came to the waiting room, and this was not the kind of waiting room you see in the mainland. This was a waiting room in the tropics—palm trees in planters everywhere, opaque walls replaced with transparent glass. It was more like an atrium. There was an outside platform, perched upon what must have been the roof of other parts of the sprawling building, where the inviting darkness of a cool-breeze-tropical-night would wrap you in its arms like a blanket.

On this large porch, the Filipino families would set up their buffets, and everyone in the ICU waiting room, including the two *haole* kids, was invited to a grab a plate. We enjoyed lumpia, pancit, and barbecued meat, and there was always plenty of rice.

In Hawaii, I learned to have an adventurous palate. As I said before, I ate shark and mahi-mahi. I also ate fried fruit. I ate fruits and vegetables that I had never heard of before, and they were delicious, like guava on a warm spring day.

However, at home, there was one food that was not for me—guacamole. I could not stomach even the idea of it. It was green. It was slimy. Bill and Mom were excited to have it, perhaps because it was a rare treat to discover affordable avocadoes in the expensive produce markets of Honolulu. But I did not like the way it smelled. Or the way it looked. Or the way it felt. I didn't want to try it, but one day, Mom and Bill forced me. Trembling, I put it into my mouth, and I immediately gagged. The guacamole flew out of my mouth onto the breakfast counter where we ate our family meals.

Mom and Bill made me eat what I had spit up. I gagged again, as the smell of my own saliva mingled with the unpleasant smell of the food. It came up again, this time as vomit, with guacamole and whatever else was in my stomach splashing across the counter.

And I had to eat it again. I knew that if I threw it up again, this cycle would continue, so I somehow found a way to get it down.

Swallow it. Stomach it. Try not to cry. In so many ways, these were the refrains of my youth.

My sister was my hero, not just because she found opportunities to get us out of the house, but because she stood up for me. She took the blame—and the punishment—for things we had both done. She even took the blame and punishment for things I had done on my own.

Under Bill's regime, I was young enough and detached enough to accept the brutal world in which we were living, to comply with the demands, keep my head down, and survive. But Nicole was old enough to feel the injustice, and brave enough to fight against the cruelty of it all.

She found opportunities for small rebellions. She snuck candy into the house, contraband, less because she wanted it and more because it was a way to defy Bill.

When she was spanked, she cried as little as possible, refusing to give him the satisfaction of her tears. She was strong, both physically and emotionally. She was engaged in a war of wills with him, and she was determined to win.

But Bill had more machinations up his sleeve. When physical pain no longer worked as it should, he found new ways to humiliate her. On many occasions, he would force her to take off her clothes. He would send her into the one bedroom of our apartment and force her to stand, naked, in the corner, with her face pressed against the wall.

This was during the daytime. Our mother must have been working the day shift on these days or sleeping on the couch. I don't know where she was. I know Bill would leave the windows in the room open, telling my sister that everyone driving by our apartment would see her and gaze upon her body. He wanted the world to see how wrong she was. And if she moved, he would hit me.

Standing there in her pubescent nakedness, Bill could finally make my sister cry.

Finally, as the height of her humiliation, he would send me into the room and force me to see her.

It was my job to tell her that her punishment was over and she could put her clothes back on. When I came into the room, she cried more than ever.

My sister, of course, was scarred the most by these incidents, and I will never truly know the depth of her suffering. I can only know my own scars from being exposed to something clearly wrong in ways I couldn't name—and being required once again to participate in my sister's pain.

That feeling of guilt persists, even today, as one more aspect of the closet where I hid. Intellectually, I know I should not feel guilty about this or anything else she endured in Hawaii, but trauma has a way of bypassing thought. It works on emotions, creating feelings that persist beyond the moment, emotions that endure beyond logic and reason.

I am proud to say that Nicole remained a freedom fighter. Even in the face of the worst that Bill could do, she was the one who finally ended our nightmare. She spoke to a counselor at her middle school. From there, Child Protective Services was alerted. We were taken from the faux-coral apartment on an emergency basis and placed in a shelter home in the suburbs of Honolulu.

I was given what I now know to be a forensic interview. I was asked to identify male and female genitalia as observers looked on from the other side of a two-way mirror. I am sure they asked many other questions, but I specifically remember the questions about genitalia and how I was happy to show off my knowledge of the scientific names for these body parts.

It was with this same show-off spirit that I nodded knowingly when the "mother" in our shelter home explained that this was different from a foster home, that this was short-term and not long-term. I didn't know anything about the child protection system, but pretending to know was a comfort in the face of sudden change.

Fear and grief might have overwhelmed other children in my situation, but I was detached and protected from these emotions. People come and people go, after all. Things change. You adapt.

Again, my imagination was a shield and a guardian. At age six, I was not creating fantastic worlds with their own maps, histories, and languages, like C.S. Lewis and his brother, but my imagination wrapped a protective bubble around the worlds I inhabited, segmenting the world of play from the world of school from the world of family, so that one thing could be enjoyed while everything else was falling apart. For another child, it might have been too much. For me, it was another day in another place.

As an adult, looking back on this, I am glad my heart and mind were able to devise these mechanisms of survival, to save some part of my soul, to prevent me from becoming a bitter vial of acid—angry, closed-off beyond repair, depressed beyond salvation. I was scarred by this time in paradise, but not as scarred as I could have been, and I thank God for the defenses that saw me through. But my adult self has needed these fortifications to come down—so I can befriend this false persona and move beyond it to the authentic self who has been yearning to live.

As much as I am glad for the armor I was privileged to wear, these protectors have left scars of their own, and I thank God for helping me heal from them. But that is a story for later.

When my sister and I returned to our faux-coral apartment from the shelter home, everything had changed again. Bill was no longer around. A protective order had been filed against him and a trial date to determine Mom's fitness for custody was on the horizon.

I did not know it, but Mom and Bill had made arrangements. He had bought a one-way plane ticket out of Hawaii and was set to fly on the day after the hearing. He had also given my mom $3,000 to help us make it through the rest of the year. Mom had six months left on her contract with the hospital, and there were six months left on the lease. With the cost of living in Honolulu, she did not believe she made enough to support two kids on her own, so Bill arranged to help on his way out of the door. This, at least, was a positive contrast between him and my father.

And here's another positive contrast: he didn't interfere with us anymore after that. He didn't say a word when Mom, Nicole, and I took a family vacation to the Big Island of Hawaii. In the midst of a tense situation, as a sort of reward for surviving what we had survived so far, we stayed in a resort on an active volcano. We walked on slowly cooling lava. We took some of the volcanic rocks, known locally as Pele's tears, even though we were warned about the curse. In retrospect, maybe we should have listened to those warnings.

When we returned to Oahu, we got a small TV that sat on the breakfast counter. We went to TCBY and ate frozen yogurt. We were no longer required to wake up at 5:00 am, no longer required to complete an exercise regimen and turn in book reports on top of our schoolwork. Triumphantly, my mom brought the box of toys down from the top shelf in the hall closet. I remember sitting on the floor with this box in front of me, staring at my old Ghostbusters, He-Man figures, and G.I. Joes. Mom sat at the breakfast counter, encouraging me. "Play with your toys," she said. "Go on and play."

She could see I was struggling. I was not sure what to do. "Go ahead," she said, tears forming in her eyes. "Be like a real boy."

I had a sense of how important this moment was to my mother. I had a sense of what I was supposed to do, and I tried to meet her expectations. I picked up some toys. I made noises and mimicked actions. I feigned the feints of toy-based combat. I tried to play. I really did.

My mom was crying. She encouraged me again: "It's okay. You can be a little boy now."

But I didn't want to be a little boy—not in this way. I wanted to read. I wanted to fire up the computer. I wanted to play math games and *Where in Europe is Carmen Sandiego?*

She cried more. Eventually, she gave up, and so did I.

One day, everything changed again. I came home from school, and there was Mom, sitting in the living room with one suitcase packed for each of us. We had already left belongings behind in Indiana, and now we were leaving more behind in Hawaii. In my suitcase were clothes, one book about the Presidents, and one toy—a Donald Duck stuffed animal I had slept with at my grandparents'.

I didn't know it at the time, but Mom had learned that the upcoming hearing could spell trouble. Even if she were deemed fit as a mother and retained custody of her kids, they would have to keep tabs on us for the next year and a half—but we couldn't afford to stay for a year and a half.

An attorney advised her that if she had not yet been served with formal papers, the year and a half of scrutiny was not yet in effect. Equipped with this knowledge, she decided we would leave the state before the hearing.

I clung to Donald Duck as we drove to the airport. I clung even tighter as we got onto the plane for the first stage of our journey, flying from Honolulu to Atlanta, where we then caught our connection to Cleveland.

From Cleveland, we got a ride to Willowick, Ohio, where we would be staying with Emily and Joshua Lawrence, the nurse and Lutheran pastor my mother had known in New Hampshire. Mom had leaned on Emily's moral support and Joshua's clergy-like authority when he accompanied her to Indiana one-and-a-half years earlier, and now we would count on them again, this time for a safe place to stay and shelter from the storm.

The Lawrences had three sons—one in high school; one who was in middle school, like Nicole; and one who was my age, Jason. Since I was going to stay in Jason's room and, presumably, spend a lot of time with him, Mom and Emily tried to help us bond by telling us different facts about the armpit. I suppose they thought we would share them with each other while giggling like little boys and making noises with our armpits, and then we would be friends forever.

But I didn't go for those kinds of little boy things. I was more interested in William Henry Harrison than armpits.

At the Lawrences' house, we played in the backyard, all of us kids together. It was so close to the end of the school year, and Nicole and I had been through so much, that we were given a choice about whether we wanted to enroll in school or wait until the fall and start the next grade then. We chose to wait. During the day, while the Lawrence boys were at school, I read books. I watched Emily cook. I played computer games. I played with Jason's toys. Perhaps I was becoming a real boy again, after all.

I don't remember exactly how long we were there, or what I thought or felt about yet another transition in my life. What I knew by that age was that my family moves. The shape of it changes. We live in different houses and different people take care of us. This is the way things are. I do not think or feel about things I cannot control.

What I remember most about this time is the day my grandpa tried to abduct us. Nicole and I were in the backyard when he rolled into the Lawrences' driveway and told us to get into his minivan. As usual, I was the compliant one, so I got in. I remember sitting in that van while the grown-ups talked angrily in the driveway—Mom, Emily, Joshua, and Grandpa. He told me to lock the doors, and the others told me not to, and I was paralyzed. My normal approach to life was to please the grown-ups, to meet their expectations and avoid their wrath. What do you do when different grown-ups want different things? I couldn't move, and I didn't lock the doors. Eventually, I was taken out of the van, and we remained with the Lawrences.

It was not long after that when we came to the attention of Child Protective Services in Ohio. The situation did not look good in their eyes. We had been abused in Hawaii. Our mother was thought to be complicit in our abuse. We had fled the state to avoid a hearing. And then we had suddenly shown up in Ohio, where we weren't living on our own and weren't even going to school.

But wait. It gets worse. Mom thought we left the state of Hawaii free and clear, but the state claimed otherwise. Mom said we were never served the papers that would have set into motion the year-and-a-half of investigation and scrutiny, but the state said she was.

But wait. It gets worse. There were court records from Indiana, exaggerated claims about my mother made by my grandparents and their allies during the custody proceedings that had taken place in Columbia City. My mom was said to be a gun owner because she had a bought a gun in Georgia to protect her apartment, a condition for receiving renter's insurance. She was also labeled as erratic, violent, and unpredictable. The state of Ohio thought she might kill in defense of her kids.

When the state came for us, they came with multiple police cars and sirens blazing, like we were criminals to be apprehended.

We spent our first night as wards of the state of Ohio in the town lockup. It was a small jail, not the large, industrial-type jails you see in metropolitan areas. This had more of an Andy Griffith feel to it. But it was still jail.

Another kid might have been frightened, but I was fascinated by the novelty of the place, like it was a museum full of artifacts worth studying.

We were behind bars, all three of us. The doors were locked and the police were there. Mom was terrified. She clung to us that night, and I clung back, not because I felt the same urge, but because I had a sense that she needed me to. My heart was hidden in the closet, or in this case, locked up in a jail cell.

4

Almost Oddly Normal

When I was almost seven years old, I entered the foster care system. Initially, my sister and I were placed in different homes, with two different families, each in the town of Wickliffe. I was with the Benes family and my sister was with the Russos.

Lydia Benes and her husband had been unable to conceive children of their own, but they had a lot of love to give, and they opened their home to many children over the years. When I lived with them, there was a teenage girl in the house. We rarely saw her, between school, after-school activities, and her room. There were twin boys who were close to my age, both intellectually disabled. And I was the fourth kid. The house was big enough for me to have my own room, a privilege I had not enjoyed since living with Grandma and Grandpa.

Living with the Beneses was an adjustment, but I was used to adjusting.

Lydia's husband owned a convenience store. I don't think they were rich beyond anyone's wildest dreams, but I don't remember money being an issue.

What I do remember is relishing the attention. In this home, attention was almost entirely positive, and there was no abuse or hint of abuse. I was praised and affirmed often, and I almost came to appreciate being seen.

There was a relative of the Benes clan, a cousin who was about my age, who visited from time to time. I remember thinking he was not a kind person, but he was smart and funny, and I didn't mind spending time with him. Once, this cousin handed me a stuffed animal and dared me to hit one of the boys on the head with it. I was reluctant, but he had me feel how soft it was on the outside to convince me that it wouldn't hurt him, that he would like it. I believed the cousin, so I hit the kid, not knowing that he had stuffed a softball inside the stuffed animal.

As Lydia untangled this situation, she comforted the kid who was crying, punished the cousin and me with time outs, and made the cousin's punishment last longer. When he protested, she told him that she believed me, that she knew the cousin had been the protagonist in this story, and that I hadn't known what I was doing. I was so gratified by that. I appreciated being seen, heard, and believed. I had experienced more than my fair share of parental injustice at that point, and it was nice to have a feeling of justice being done.

Life in the Benes household was great in a lot of ways, but also a bit lonely. My best friend was Wally, a stuffed purple bear. He was a gift from Nicole's father's parents, two people who wanted to be grandparents to Nicole and me. Even though Nicole's father wasn't a father to her, his parents had always thought of themselves as grandparents to both of us. Driving from Indiana to visit us was not in the cards for them at their age, but they sent me a stuffed purple bear wearing sunglasses and checkered overalls. I clung to him at night, even as I also wondered if I was too old for him—even as I also wondered what force compelled me to cling.

I don't remember much about these grandparents, before or after foster care. I have a vague image of them—but I don't remember the where, when, or why of that memory. But I remember Wally.

During those days, I only saw my sister through the fence that separated the elementary school from the middle school. At her school, they would give the kids outside time after lunch, and my sister would walk around the track talking to the new friends she was making. One day, we discovered that her time outside coincided with my recess, and that the track on her side came close to the playground on my side. We talked. We briefly touched fingers. My sister.

I saw my mom through supervised visits in a small room with a large mirror. I'll say more about those visits later.

My overwhelming reality was the Beneses, their house, and their boys—boys who were not biologically theirs but who were theirs in spirit. As a family, we shared meals. We watched the Indians and Browns on TV. There were Saturday morning cartoons, which I had missed and which I loved. Together, we played. Individually, I read books. Life was good.

One day, I noticed Lydia at the dining room table, talking with a woman I had never met before. They were talking about me, wondering if the Benes home was right for me. Lydia was talking about how smart I was, which was loving music to my know-it-all-ears, and how there really wasn't a peer for me in their house, between the intellectually-disabled boys and an often-absent teen.

I'm not sure what compelled me to do what I did next—perhaps a return to an old habit as a means of comfort in the face of transition, or perhaps a chance to show off, to prove the kind words Lydia was saying about me. I began multiplying by two, as I had on the car ride from Indiana to California, which felt like a lifetime ago. I made my way into the thousands. I stopped well before I could have. I was ready to name the Presidents in order, one to forty-one, as well, if they had asked.

"See?" Lydia said to the woman. "This is what I mean. He's wonderful. We love him. But I wonder if we're the right fit for him."

Soon after, I was told that a place had opened in the home where my sister was staying, with the Russos. I was asked if I wanted to move and I said yes. And so there was another transition. So it goes.

This was just a move across town. I packed up the few things I called my own and moved into another room in another home. I stayed in the same elementary school and the same classroom, but with a new bus route. And it was on that new bus that I met Mike Kaminksi, a kid who was smart, kind, and fun to be around. We traded baseball cards with each other. He became a good friend.

My sister and I lived with the Russos, Ava and Frank, the matriarch and patriarch of a decidedly Italian family. They had three kids who were married and living on their own. Their fourth child, Deanna, lived at home, waiting to be married to her fiancée, Nick.

Nicole shared a room with Dana, another foster child, a teenage girl who had decided not to return home. Dana had decided to live until the age of majority with the Russos, and the state of Ohio had granted her wish. Unbeknownst to me, my sister wanted the same thing for herself. That was why I didn't see Nicole in the tiny rooms with the two-way mirrors where Mom and I had supervised visits. That was why my only contact with her had been through the fence between our schools. She was pulling away from Mom. She was angry with her. She saw the Russos as a lifeline and she wanted to remain with them.

I didn't know it at the time, but she hadn't wanted me to move in with her. For her, I was the one person she would miss, the one person she hated to leave behind, and she didn't want me around all the time, reminding her that leaving Mom also meant leaving me.

But I was glad to be close to my sister. She was the person who had been there for me all along, the one who cared for me as an infant, who shielded me from abuse with her own body and soul.

Once, around her birthday, I bought a shell in a gift shop. It had orange-yellow coloring and black stripes. I was excited about giving it to her. My sister loved tigers, or at least she had at one point in her life, and I was excited to give her this tiger-colored shell as a birthday gift.

But one of the Russos' grandchildren ruined the surprise. Marie was a little younger than me. During the sprawling extended-family visits enjoyed by the Russo clan, I was expected to play with her and spend time with her.

When Marie told Nicole about the shell, I was so angry. I knew it wasn't a huge gift. I knew it wasn't the most special thing in the world. The main thing it had going for it was that it was a surprise. It would tell her I had been thinking about her, that I appreciated her. The gesture mattered more than the gift, but without the element of surprise, it didn't feel like much of a gesture.

I was so upset that I tried to lock myself in my room with my Encyclopedia Brown books. I didn't want to talk to Marie anymore. I didn't want to play with her. I didn't want to be forced to act like a kid to appease her.

This is not an uncommon pattern for those who are emotionally detached—to cut off people and retreat into a world of our own imagination. But Ava Russo wasn't having it. She knew that isolation was the last thing I needed, and she forced me to come out of my room and play with Marie.

In the short-term, I was mad about being forced out. But in the long term, this was good for me. I needed people to make me stay in relationships. Left to my own devices, I would run away from the world like a miniature Henry Bemis.

From a less dramatic perspective, there's something kind of exciting about this little event: what a thing to be upset about! After all we had endured in Indiana and Hawaii, this was an oddly normal moment in an oddly normal life. A kid gets mad at another kid over a little thing, a thing that doesn't mean much to one kid and means a lot to the other kid, but he doesn't know how to say it. There is a minor conflict over this ultimately little thing. The parents help resolve it. Is that how it's supposed to work within a family?

With the Russos, in an oddly normal way, I did chores and earned an allowance. I took the money to the corner store, where I bought candy and baseball cards. Is that what normal kids did too? With Frank, I watched the Indians, Browns, and Cavs—just like a normal boy—and I became a fan of Cleveland sports. With Mike Kaminski and another friend, Johnny Duval, I played baseball in various front yards and traded cards.

With Dana and Nicole, I walked to the park and the pool, and watched MTV. I wondered why Prince wanted to buy diamonds and pearls to make someone a "happy boy or a girl." What did that mean? They laughed—my sister and this new sister—and told me I would understand when I was older. Looking back, I wonder if they knew more about my future romantic affinity than I did.

Eventually, I was eight years old, and I had a sudden realization: I had never learned to ride a bike. I wanted to, or at least I felt like I was supposed to want to. Mike and Johnny had bikes. Clearly, we should ride our bikes together. That's what boys my age were supposed to do. But how could I learn? The Russos had an older, adult bike I was welcome to use, but it was ugly and big, and I felt awkward trying to ride it.

How had I never learned to ride a bike? How had I missed that normal childhood initiation? I had no interest in bikes when we lived with our grandparents. Back then, I was still graduating from a tricycle to a scooter. And none of the kids rode bikes in Hawaii. It just wasn't part of the culture there. Our bare feet were good enough to get us around.

If I was going to learn to ride a bike now, I would need one of my own—something I could learn how to tame and ride off into the sunset. But here's something you might not know about foster care: no one could give me a bicycle or anything like it. As a foster kid, no one who is a viable option for custody is allowed to give you a gift of any value. No one can shower you with gifts that might influence your custodial desires. I've been told that my dad wanted to buy me a bike at this time, but he couldn't, and it wasn't an option for Mom, grandparents, or foster parents. None of the people who wanted to do this for me could.

But Nicole decided to come to my rescue. One day, she came home with a bike that was just the right size for me, which she claimed she had "found" at the local park. It was just sitting there, she said. Someone had left it, she said. I felt a bit uneasy about this, but I appreciated the gesture. Eventually, the boy who belonged to the bike came to our house and confronted my sister, but she dismissed him. Then the police showed up, and the bike was returned to its rightful owner. Concern was expressed about Nicole, about how she was behaving and the people she was spending time with. Unfortunately, this would not be her last encounter with the police.

It was also not the last time Nicole would try to protect me, nor the last time she would try to provide for me. It may have been a misguided, adolescent attempt to provide, but there was love in that stolen bike.

Still, at the end of the day, a bike was something I could live without. Mike and Johnny were nice kids, and they weren't going to leave me out because of something I had to do without.

In a similar way, they almost never said anything about me not wearing my glasses. Back then, if I could have chosen something for Nicole to steal for me, something I really felt I needed, it would have been a different pair of glasses.

I was in third grade when I learned I needed them. It was the classic story of a teacher noticing a kid having trouble seeing the blackboard. (They still used blackboards back then, if you can believe it.) Like many kids, I didn't notice I was having trouble seeing because I was used to taking the world as it is, and I thought the world was supposed to be a bit blurry.

In general, I was trained to accept the scraps of what life could offer. But even I was unprepared for the ugliness of my first pair of glasses.

Again, as a foster child, no one who could potentially be a custodian could purchase anything of value for me, so I was limited to the glasses Medicaid would provide. At the optometrist's office, the choices were dismal. They handed me a tray with four ugly frames. I chose a pair that was large and block-shaped, poop brown, with two plastic rods holding the lenses together above my nose. They were the least ugly pair I could have chosen.

I am a nerd at heart, and I was destined for glasses. But this pair embarrassed me, and the other kids at school knew it. When I could get away with it, I would take them off and hide them in my pocket—otherwise, I would be ridiculed. And even at my new home, with Mike and Johnny, I was too embarrassed to wear them. The fact that I had to, at least part of the time, was just one more marker of difference, one more signal that I was not like the bike-riding kids who lived with their parents.

My mom was eventually allowed to see me without supervision. At first, we had to stay near CPS property. The Child Protective Services building was next to a park with forested areas, a stream, and a playground. Mom and I walked in the woods near the stream. She showed me how to skip flat stones across the water. Eventually, she was allowed to take me off site. We went to see movies—like *My Girl*, *Curly Sue*, and *An American Tail: Fievel Goes West*.

Mom and I had seen the original *American Tail* at some point in my young life, before foster care, and we both remembered the song at the center of the movie. In plaintive tones, a lost boy and his mother sing to one another: "And even though I know how very far apart we are, it helps to think we might be wishin' on the same bright star. . ."

The memory of this song brought Mom to tears. It was a song that gave her hope, that through all the fear, red tape, and double-sided glass, we were sleeping under the same sky, and we would find one another. Through love, we would be reunited.

I was moved by her pain, which she tried to keep hidden, but there were times when she couldn't contain it. How could I not be moved? In those moments, I almost loved her.

Looking back, I wish I had felt the same feelings she did, the same kind of grief and longing, the same kind of sadness a normal kid might have felt. But that wasn't my reality. In any given situation, I could generally discern the words, gestures, and actions expected of me and try to offer them to the world. But a lot of the time, I was acting.

My longings were different. At the core, what I desired most was privacy. I just wanted people to leave me alone so I could read Encyclopedia Brown in peace. I wanted to not be scrutinized, to not feel like I had to perform a gesture or an emotion.

In the Russos' backyard, I used concrete blocks to build a wall around a corner of the yard, an isolated pocket between a bush and a fence. It was my territory and no one else could come in. I made my proclamation about this territory clear. I told Ava that this was my private space and walked her through the limited conditions in which I could be disturbed.

I desperately wanted to be in places where I wouldn't be observed and didn't have to perform. Every so often, I could feel like that around Mike, Johnny, or Nicole. Sometimes, I could even feel that way around Ava, Frank, or my mom, but those moments were few and far between. For the most part, I wanted to be alone. This was a further contour of the false self that was forming its protective shell around me, a shell I would eventually need to break through to expose the authentic little hermit crab inside.

Between my mom and my foster home, it was like I was living a double life. With the Russos, there were cookouts and family gatherings and the annual family trip to Cedar Point. There were large pasta dinners where Ava lived up to the Italian mother stereotype, giving you a full, heaping plate of food if you dared to ask for "a little more."

At the Russos, there was my sister, my friends, my books, my baseball cards. There was school and the school library. There were pickup games of baseball on the front yard or in the park.

With my mom, there were movies, games, walks in the woods, and the simple pleasure of being nurtured one-on-one. It was a rare experience, something I'd not experienced for years, to have a safe grown-up all to myself.

For a few weeks, during our visits, we tried therapy. Mom discovered that a benefit of the foster care system was free therapy for Nicole and me. It was something CPS would pay for, and I think, more than anything, Mom sought it out for me as a way of sticking it to them, a way of extracting something from the foster care system that had taken her children.

I was not very good at therapy. Each week, my mom would take me to the counseling center. While we waited for our turn, I would play with puzzle toys in the large indoor play area or swing and slide on the playground outside. When it was my turn for therapy, I saw a relatively young woman with short, black hair, and she just didn't get me.

We did the play therapy thing. Unstructured play—under observation—and I was always aware of being observed. As a subject of play therapy, I was supposed to reveal my inner life through play, and I was supposed to become comfortable with the therapist, so I could verbalize the unspoken feelings I was enacting with the toys. But the problem was that I was always aware of being observed, which meant that I was always at least somewhat aware of the expectations the therapist had for me. I did not have the ability to become comfortable. Real, authentic play requires that a child be uninhibited and spontaneous, and that was impossible for me when I knew I was being watched.

The therapist asked me questions about our experience in Hawaii, and I answered as well as I could. At one point, she gave me a doll and told me to pretend it was my stepfather. I felt no emotions toward it, and I felt no emotions toward him. I just looked at the doll. When the therapist invited me to, I picked it up and looked at it more closely. She encouraged me to access my feelings and do to the doll what I wanted to do to Bill. So I halfheartedly hit it, less because I wanted to and more because I was trying to meet her expectations, trying to perform the emotions and gestures I was expected to display.

I heard her sigh in exasperation. I think she could tell I was faking it.

After the experiment with the doll, she asked me what I wanted to do, how I wanted to spend this time in therapy, and I told her I wanted to go outside and play. So that's what we did. Outside, it was easier to ignore her and imagine I was alone, free to play without being judged or observed.

I don't know if the therapist really was frustrated with me. On one hand, I was prone to feeling judged. On the other, I had a heightened sense of the dangers adults could pose, and a heightened sensitivity to their gestures and expressions. Perhaps this therapist's affect was in fact neutral, and I imagined the feelings I projected onto her. Maybe I couldn't read her the way I could read everyone else, and onto the blank therapeutic canvas, I projected my fear of being hurt for not being enough.

What if both theories are true? What if my perceptions were accurate, and I was also projecting? Maybe she saw me emotionally running from her, and that was why she gave me the freedom of the playground and, from there, tried to encourage me to come back to the office, to go back in and do the therapeutic work. Maybe I wanted to keep running from her, so I insisted on staying on the playground and tuning her out, and maybe that left her feeling genuinely bored and frustrated.

Looking back, I wonder what would have happened if she had recognized my intellectual maturity. What if she had treated me more like an adult client, or at least an adolescent? What if she had explained her theories and therapeutic interventions and involved me in the process? I wonder if I would have responded to these confidences and done more to access the emotions that were buried inside.

Whatever the reason really was, we didn't connect, this black-haired therapist and me. I thought I had to keep going to therapy, so I kept trying to have whatever fun I could—to make the best of a bad situation. But when my mom asked me if I wanted to keep going, and I realized I had an actual choice, I chose not to go. Movies, games, and time with Mom were a lot better. They were maybe even therapeutic.

Eventually, Mom was able to visit for a whole weekend. She would rent hotel rooms and we would spend our nights there. Eventually, Nicole started coming to visits too, or at least to parts of them, if for no other reason than to see movies she wanted to see.

Eventually, I saw the inside of a courthouse for the second time. I remember how sleek and modern and smooth it was, more like the corridors of a mall than the marble halls of the classical construction in Columbia City. I remember meeting my mom's lawyer, and she seemed nice. But most of all, I remember the judge's chambers—a large, clean room with high bookshelves—where I sat in a high-backed, leather chair and the judge asked me questions.

"Tell me about your mom," he said. "How do you feel when you're with her?"

"Tell me about your foster parents," he said. "How do you feel about living with them?"

I did my best to answer. He was a new adult, and it was my job to meet his expectations—but I couldn't read him very well. I didn't know what he wanted. As it turns out, all he expected was honesty and authenticity. All he wanted was *me*.

"What we're trying to do in the courtroom is to decide who you're going to live with. Now, you're not yet old enough to decide, 'I want this,' and poof!—that happens. But you are old enough to tell me what you think. What is it that you want, Steve? Who do you want to live with?"

My dad was never really an option—for the judge or for me. The state of Ohio had been in contact with my dad. He had come once to visit me, at the same child protective services center where Mom's supervised visits had taken place. A social worker was with us the whole time. Knowing what I now know about him, I am very glad for that layer of protection.

When we played outside, I remember asking him about his favorite vegetables.

"I like tomatoes," Dad told me. "Not when they're cooked, but when they're raw."

"You're a good climber," I remember telling him, when his long legs spanned the metal bars on the geodesic climber.

"That's from experience," he said. "From working construction."

This was the first time I had seen him since I was three, and it was the last time I would ever see him.

I wondered about my grandparents. They had come to visit us once in foster care, with a van load of cousins and even our old golden retriever, Buffy. Nicole and I spent a long afternoon with them, at the same CPS center next to the park.

In his chambers, the judge watched me, waiting for my answer. I squirmed in the too-tall leather chair. What I remember feeling was a desire not to let anyone down.

"What are the choices?" I asked.

"You don't have to worry about that. Your only job is to tell me what you think."

"Where will Nicole live?" I wondered.

"That, too, is one of the things we have to decide. Do you like being with your sister?"

"Yeah," I said, and then I was quiet for a long time. I thought about my mom and I thought about the Russos. I thought about Mike and Johnny, and how I would miss them if I had to go away. I thought about Nicole, and I had some level of awareness that she wanted to remain with the Russos.

I had a sense that the Russos wanted to keep us both, and I had a sense that my mom desperately wanted to have us back. I felt no particular pull one way or the other. Whoever I lived with, I would adjust to the situation and make the best of it. I just didn't want to let anybody down. I didn't want anyone to be upset with me or disappointed by my choice.

"I think we should live with our grandparents," I finally offered. I wanted a compromise. I didn't want anyone to be upset because I didn't pick them. I thought I could accomplish this by choosing neither of the main options. I thought I could find a third option that would be okay for both Nicole and me.

"You love your grandparents," the judge said. "Of course. But they are not an option right now. Your mom is one possibility, and your foster parents are another."

So there it was. I had to pick. I couldn't compromise my way out of it.

"What are you thinking about?" the judge asked.

"I don't want anyone to feel sad or upset because I didn't pick them."

"You don't have to worry about that," the judge said. "No one will be upset."

Again, I was silent for a long time—or maybe it just felt like a long time to me. As the silence continued, I stopped thinking about life with the Russos and the parts of it I liked. I stopped thinking about saying goodbye to Mike and Johnny. I tried to put aside Nicole and her desires. In whatever place I chose, Nicole would live with me or she wouldn't, and I would adjust like I always did.

For me, the deciding factor was this: between these two parental units, Mom wanted me the most. She would be more hurt if I didn't choose her. She had more at stake than any other stakeholder. It never occurred to me to think of myself as a stakeholder.

"Then I choose my mom," I said. "I want to live with my mom."

The judge thanked me for my help, and I was allowed to leave his chambers.

5

Atheism, Comedy, and Becoming an Outsider

By the time I was out of third grade and about to enter the fourth, everything changed again. The judge awarded custody of my sister and me to our mother, and we moved to the shining metropolis of Fort Wayne, Indiana. Mom had set up an apartment for us there. She bought waterbeds for all three of us. In this new apartment, we each had our own rooms. Soon enough, I met new kids in the apartment complex, and Johnny and Mike were replaced by David, Scott, and James. I made friends at school too. Life in this place was starting to feel good.

But there was a specter hanging over us. Even though we had physically left foster care, it still haunted us.

I was glad for this bright new life in this shining metropolis, this fresh start. Things were finally settling down and I thought we might actually experience some stability. But it was hard for my sister. She tried to make the best of it, but she had wanted to stay in Ohio with the Russos. Nicole blamed Mom for the abuse we experienced—I can't blame her for that—and she didn't want to live with us anymore.

Through all we'd been through together, Nicole had been through more of it. She was abused by both my father and our stepfather. For me, it was only our stepfather. How many times did she take the blame and offer herself to Bill as a sacrifice on my behalf? It was natural that she would resent our mother, the woman who brought these abusive men into our lives, the woman who had failed to protect us from them.

Was Mom complicit in the abuse? As a kid, I always thought of her as a victim of Bill like me and Nicole. But she must have approved of the schedule on the refrigerator, the military-style regimen of chores and exercises, and the academic work. With me, she was on Bill's side in the guacamole incident. With my sister, she didn't believe everything Nicole told the authorities about what happened to us. Those were all choices Mom made.

So it was natural that Nicole resented our mother. It was natural that she wanted to stay in Ohio with the Russos and her friends. At that time, Nicole was about to enter high school. Now, she would have to do so without her closest friends, living in yet another new place. This would be a crushing blow to any teenager under any circumstance.

Of course, Mom was scarred by her experience of foster care, as well. She still complains about the day she was deemed too late for a visit with me. After a night at work, she had driven several hours from Fort Wayne to Willoughby, Ohio, to have her visit. She was tired—so she slept in her car until it was time to go in. Back then, Indiana was not on daylight saving's time, so she wasn't thinking about the time difference. She wound up sleeping through the appointed hour. When she woke up, she was turned away.

For her, this was one more bead in the abacus of injustice. Why couldn't they have made an exception for her? She showed up like she was supposed to. She was there, in the parking lot. Why didn't they wake her up? Why didn't they move our visit an hour back? Why did she drive all that way for nothing? Why did they take her son away?

My mom felt unjustly judged by the system, and she sought subtle ways to fight back, to undermine the state and the Russos. For example, she was not allowed to give gifts of great value to either of us, but she could give small ones—like little hand-held video games, those old four-bit, two-dimensional, single-game handheld devices with titles like *Top Gun* and *Teenage Mutant Ninja Turtles*. When I played those games, the Russos would ask me to turn down or mute the sound, but I never could. I would press the button and nothing would happen. I didn't like the sounds either, if for no other reason than that they drew attention to me, but I liked the games.

Little did I know, Mom had a coworker who could disable the mute buttons on these addictive little devices, and she always looked for the ones that made the most annoying sounds.

In a similar way, I was baptized into the Christian faith. During one of our visits, Mom asked, "What would you think about being baptized?"

"What's that?" I asked.

"It's a way of saying you believe in God. You stand on a stage with a pastor and he pours water on you. It's a symbol of what you believe."

"Oh," I said, and it seemed reasonable enough at the time. When we lived with Grandma and Grandpa, I had gone to church with them. I had no conception of not believing the things I learned in Sunday School—or not believing the Bible verses I had memorized at the Missouri Synod Lutheran pre-school.

Our friend Joshua Lawrence had offered to baptize me. Was it something I wanted? It wasn't something I understood. But it seemed fine. From what Mom said, baptism sounded like a natural thing to do, like going to the dentist to get your teeth cleaned, so I agreed to have my spiritual teeth cleaned. Pastor Lawrence baptized me during a small private ceremony arranged during one of Mom's visits.

As it turns out, she encouraged religiosity in me as another way of annoying our foster parents. By law, they would have had to accommodate any religious preferences I had. Mom was hoping I would be moved by the baptismal experience and by further encouragement to engage with Joshua and his church—so that I would want to go there on Sunday morning and Ava and Frank would have to take me—week after week.

But I was not moved. I had little frame of reference for the experience. When I had gone to church with my grandparents, I don't remember seeing anyone baptized. I don't remember ever being taught about baptism. These things may have happened, but they didn't leave an impression.

For me, baptism was just one more thing for Mom and me to do on our visits. It was nice to see Joshua. I remembered him. But the ceremony didn't mean much to me. Still, it did plant a seed—a seed of atheism.

Before I go further, I should be clear that I am convinced of the efficacy of my baptism. I am convinced that, in that moment, even with mixed motives and half-hearted beliefs, God made a claim on me: that I belong to the Lord and the Lord belongs to me. I believe that claim is eternally significant and cannot be revoked. Even if the humans involved, including me, are broken and impure, God is not—and this baptism forged a bond between God and me.

But in the short-term, there is a through-line from third-grade baptism to fourth-grade atheism.

Looking back on it, I am not completely sure where I first heard the word "atheist" or how I came to believe this label applied to me. I simply know that by fourth grade, this is what I was, and I was convinced enough to argue about religion with my friends.

During that moment of baptism with Joshua, I was disconnected from religion, but I didn't yet consider myself a non-believer. So what happened between one point in the narrative and the other?

I internalized my mother's logic: You believe in God, so you should be baptized.

It made sense in the moment.

But did I believe in God?

What did it mean to "believe" "in God?"

I asked questions—of Mom, of Nicole, of Ava and Frank Russo. Who is God? What is belief? These are questions I had never thought to ask before. But now that I had proclaimed through baptism that I believed in God, I began to wonder if that was actually true.

What did I actually know of religion at that point in my life? I was there when the Russos' daughter, Deanna, married her boyfriend, Nick, and that was a religious ceremony, but what did it mean? I knew enough about geography and history to know that other regions of the world hold to other faiths. But what were those other faiths? And if there is one true God, then why are there different religions?

I was a well-read kid. Between US history and adolescent literature, I must have encountered the word "atheism" somewhere. But what was atheism? At some point, I came to understand that Christians believed in a heaven and hell, and that the only way to get to heaven was through belief in God—and that seemed completely wrong to me. After all, there were other people born in other lands with other faiths, and they seemed to believe the same things about their religion—that only *they* held the key to salvation, that only *they* would be getting into some eternal place of pleasure. I thought about all this in the context of world history. What about the Egyptians and their pyramids? What about the Vikings and their legends? Surely, they had once believed in the superiority of their respective faiths, and now they were just a whisper of a memory.

Somewhere around age nine I adopted the idea that all religions were made up, that they were all attempts by primitive people to understand the world and promote their tribal interests. From there, I began to see religion as ridiculous. I thought of it as savage, foolish, and unbelievably beneath my superior intellect. Once this idea took hold, how could God mean anything to me? How could I believe in any imaginary human construction of a god?

In a hypothetical world, I might have encountered these thoughts and expressed these doubts without becoming an atheist. But I was missing that one essential ingredient that could have made a difference: love. If I had a relationship with this God, if I felt in my heart the love of this God, if I felt the love of other people who talked to me about God and embodied her in my young life, that might have made a difference. But how could that happen when I did not know what love was?

I thought I knew what love was. I knew as much about it as I could at the time. While its expression had certainly been inconsistent throughout my young life, I wasn't utterly maladjusted from lack of love; I wasn't so numb to the world and closed off to natural affection that it raised alarm bells for anyone. I could hug. I could be held. I could make friends. I could care about the feelings of others and respond with empathy. I cared about the proverbial kitten tapping on the window. I noticed kids who stood out from the crowd and I tried to bring them inside. Love lived somewhere inside me, pushing me toward connection.

At school, I looked out for other weirdos like me. In the fourth grade classroom at a school within walking distance from our new apartment, Trent was my first friend. Then a new kid came into our class in the middle of the school year, a kid who had moved from New York to Fort Wayne. He often sat on his own, without any friends. So I made sure that Trent and me became friends with him. At first, Trent was unsure. During recess, he wanted us to do our own thing and not worry about the new kid, no matter how lonely he seemed. But I insisted, and we became friends with Gerald for years to come.

When I was in fourth grade, I was sensitive to the needs of the world, and I had empathy. But love? That was different. In the judge's chambers, in a whole other world a whole other lifetime ago, I expressed a desire to live with my mom—not because it was a burning hope of mine, but because I understood how important it was for her. It wasn't an act of love. It was empathy.

Love is different.

Empathy is a one-way street, an impulse that doesn't require the consent or participation of the other. But love is a relational connection, a gift that is both given and received. As a young empath, I could see myself in others and feel some level of understanding about their loneliness, their desires, their joys, their struggles. And I believed in myself enough to think I could help. But did I allow myself to be loved? Could anyone break into my heart and love me?

That was why I couldn't believe in God. If I had felt God's love in my life, I might have given the Lord a chance. I might have asked more questions. I might have held onto the dim sparks of faith long enough to keep asking the questions and see the answers spark a flame.

Maybe, if I had felt God's love, either through religious experience or the embodied, evangelical love of a church, the intellectual objections would not have loomed so large. The questions would have appeared within the context of a relationship. And you don't give up on a relationship just because your ideas change.

But without love, without a relationship, and with the best knowledge I could muster about this faith and this God—what else was there? By the time I was in fourth grade, how could I have been anything but an atheist?

While I tried to philosophize through the pain of transition, chaos, and abuse, Nicole struggled in more noticeable ways.

She missed her friends in Ohio. She missed her friends in Hawaii. She was about to start high school. Instead of doing that with a group of friends who were ready to conquer the world together, she was in yet another new place, alone. It had only been three-and-a-half years since we lived with our grandparents—a relatively short amount of time since we had enjoyed a relatively normal life in smalltown USA. But it felt like a lifetime ago. I could barely remember how many times everything had changed since then, and I accepted the reality that people come and people go. But for my sister, it was different. She was in love.

I don't mean the romantic kind of love, though there was some of that in her adolescent life. I mean *philia*, the affectionate love one feels for friends, and *storge*, the protective, kinship-based love one might feel for their dorky younger brother. The difference between Nicole and me was that she had a deep reservoir of intense emotions, a capacity to feel passionate feelings, both positive and negative. Joy and anger, fear and sadness, love and hate.

And did I mention hate?

Because she hated our mom. She tried to keep it down as best she could, tried not to express the lava of hate that was erupting from her heart. But she was a warrior, and in Ohio, she'd glimpsed the possibility of putting down her armor, of living a life where she wasn't being constantly attacked by a tall, angry man, where she didn't have to defend anyone from anything, a life where she could live—and be herself—with her friends.

Mom took that away from her. The same mom whose lack of awareness led to a kindergartener taking care of an infant. The same mom who had failed to protect Nicole from all those harsh words and painful hands and stripped-down humiliation. The same mom who hadn't stood in the way of, and who sometimes actively took part in, the abuse.

Mom and Nicole fought all the time, with the largest and smallest provocation. Nicole placed expensive long-distance calls to her old friends in Ohio, in Hawaii, and in Samoa. She also found a new set of friends, people who were bad influences, kids who were involved with gangs and drugs, like the people she knew in Ohio.

One day, I remember being home with Nicole while Mom was at work, and she took me on a long walk. We walked a few miles into downtown, as we often had in Hawaii, but this was on much less pedestrian-friendly streets than the ones in Honolulu. We walked to the economically wounded neighborhood where Nicole's boyfriend lived, and we spent the day there. I played with his younger sisters, one slightly older than me and one a bit younger. They whispered about which one of them "liked" me and who would "date" me. That made me smile. I liked them too.

Still, for all the diversity I had known in my young life, I had never been in a neighborhood like this one. There were rundown houses in Hawaii, but there was a certain intentionality and almost charm to it there, a carelessness with one's home that enabled a life lived outside. This place felt different. There was a sense of hopelessness here, a sense of despair, as if everyone had given up on wanting anything more because there was no point. The homes were dilapidated. The grass was overgrown. The people talked with an accent I had started hearing in the voice of my sister, a tough kind of accent with an edge to it, an accent that was new to me.

What I most remember is the strange-smelling smoke. I had seen and smelled tobacco smoke before. That was what Mom smoked. This was something different, something I wasn't supposed to talk about.

I wonder if this field trip is one of the reasons Mom became okay with the idea of me being alone, of me being home by myself without the need for a babysitter—because that now seemed safer than being with my sister. When we lived in that apartment, there were a lot of times when I was alone. Nicole would be off with who-knows-who doing who knows what, and Mom would be at work. She would leave money on the table so I could buy fast food. This was all new to me—being home by myself, walking to a restaurant by myself, ordering by myself. But I was fine. It was fine. Really.

Arby's was my favorite.

I had to cross a busy, non-pedestrian-friendly street to get there—but I was fine.

Mom worked a lot. She worked per diem for a nursing agency, which meant that she picked up shifts when she could at any hospital where there was need. She often worked at night or in the evening, and she was paid more per hour than if she worked for a single employer. This suited her; she was skilled enough to step into different roles as needed, and she was willing to trade consistency for income and flexibility.

For one thing, she needed the money. She still had legal debt. Her legal bills had become credit card bills when she had used credit cards to pay them. Winning our custody had cost around twenty-thousand dollars. She needed the money.

While Mom worked and slept, and Nicole did what teenagers do, I spent a lot of time alone. I read. I watched TV. The early-morning exercise shows I was forced to watch in Hawaii had been replaced by *Sportscenter* on ESPN, and I liked this show and its cheeky humor better than the exercise. I enjoyed the narrative of sports, the way you can get to know an athlete and then see their mettle tested in a kind of live metallurgy. I still liked the teams from Cleveland, because that's what you do when you're a sports fan: You don't just ditch your team when you move or they're awful. You stick with your team through thick and thin.

After school, I watched kid shows like *Animaniacs* and *Power Rangers*. On Saturday morning, it was *Darkwing Duck*, *Doug*, and *Ren and Stimpy*. Later in the day, I found standup comics, *Seinfeld* reruns, and my personal favorite, *Beavis and Butthead*. In fourth grade, before puberty changed my voice, I could do a spot-on impression of Beavis, and it amused my sister to no end.

Some of these shows may seem a bit too adult for a nine-year old, but I was a smart, perceptive kid. There was a direct throughline from *Animaniacs*—with Slappy Squirrel's perpetual line, "That's comedy!"—to curiosity about comedy. What was it? How did it function? What could you learn from it?

In front of the TV, I absorbed information with a critical eye. While I took many things with a grain of salt, I also recognized that television offered an education on cultural norms and expectations, on the fantasies and foibles of life. By learning about the things that make people laugh, you also learn what's considered normal and what isn't.

I needed that education, because I struggled to understand the world. Sometimes, I felt like an alien standing on the outside of human life, trying to categorize foreign terms so I could comprehend this strange and mysterious culture.

I analyzed sports like an anthropologist. Why do I like this? Because of the drama. How is this experience optimized? Through team loyalty: Your loyalty enhances the joy of every win and the agony of every defeat.

I started to develop a taxonomy of humor. I decided jokes are funny if they are either true or absurd—if an observation is true in a way the audience has not heard before, or if a joke or situation is so untrue that it exposes the truth, as in sarcasm or physical comedy.

I had it all figured out. The whole world. Or at least the limited slice I encountered.

Meanwhile, they started to recognize me at Arby's. I think they pitied me a bit. Once, when I came in for my usual roast beef sandwich, curly fries, and chocolate shake, the girl behind the counter stopped me for a moment.

"Hey," she said. "I see you in here a lot."

"Yeah. My mom has to work. We get money to buy our own dinner."

"Oh, wow. You do that all by yourself?"

I didn't know this was a weird thing. But I was starting to suspect it might be. Perhaps a nine-year-old coming alone to the Arby's on the other side of a busy four-lane street was not a normal thing. Perhaps a kid sitting in a fast-food joint reading a book and eating curly fries was a bit out of the ordinary.

I was alone a lot, and that was okay for the most part. But there was also some family bonding. Mom took us to Foster Park, where we could play on playgrounds and hike on trails. She bought us cats, like the ones we had when we first lived with our grandparents.

Mom even tried to convene a celebration of Groundhog's Day. This evolved from a conversation about holidays that never get celebrated. Somewhere in there was the idea that we were a new family, starting a new life, in need of new traditions, and here was a tradition we could adopt. We wore hats and exchanged cards. To this day, Nicole and I halfheartedly compete to be the first to wish Mom a Happy Groundhog's Day.

Mom often took us out to eat. She presented this as a special treat, but Nicole and I didn't really know what to do with it. Looking back as an adult, I have done this in my own parenting: presenting a convenience for the parent as a special treat for the kids, and then trying to make the kids appreciate something they never asked for in the first place. My mom was an indebted, overworked single mother, and she liked the idea of gathering with us around a table where she didn't have to cook the dinner. As a parent, you think you're scoring two goals with one kick, giving yourself a rest while the kids get something special. But the kids see through it. They know when a gift is meant for them and when it isn't.

I think this is why I began to sabotage these dinners.

I also loved making my sister laugh. I could execute a well-timed quip. I was mature enough to play with words, create puns, and craft jokes in the middle of a conversation, but Nicole's sense of humor tended more toward *Beavis and Butthead*, more toward the crude and explicit. And that was alright with me. I had developed a whole taxonomy of humor, after all, and I knew there were many ways to elicit a laugh.

One night, when we were out at a restaurant, I had the sudden urge to re-create a scene from *Seinfeld*. In the scene, Jerry and George believe a woman in a restaurant is spying on them, so they fake an elaborate conversation about how gay they are and how they must hide it from the world. I don't know why I thought it would be a good idea for a nine-year-old to mimic this in a public place, but I thought it would make Nicole laugh—and, as I said, I believe there was a part of me that wanted to sabotage the dinner, a part of me that wanted to declare, "This is not what family togetherness looks like. I've seen quality time in other families. This isn't it."

I had noticed some older adults at a nearby table who would look at us from time to time, and I directed the *Seinfeld* bit toward them, declaring to our table that they were eavesdropping on us, then declaring to the world, "Well, you know how incredibly gay I am!"

Nicole laughed. I kept going. Eventually, the other diners moved to another table. Mom told me to leave the restaurant and wait outside, and that was fine with me. From the hood of our car, I could observe the world. I could do some reading. I could make toll-free prank phone calls on the payphone by the door of the restaurant (because they used to have payphones back then); I had watched enough TV on my own to memorize several 1-800 numbers.

After this, I made a deliberate effort to get kicked out of whatever restaurant we were in. I made rude noises. I told jokes. Sometimes, the jokes were borrowed from the comedians and sitcoms I was watching. Other times, I made them up as I went. I loved making Nicole laugh. Sometimes, Mom would laugh too. But inevitably, Mom would send me outside and I would entertain myself instead of them.

It's not that I didn't know how to behave in a restaurant. I was just fine at Arby's, alone with whatever book I was reading—but here, I had a platform, and I was using that platform to reach out to Nicole. I wanted to be something in her eyes. In those moments, I was a cool, funny rebel, joining her in her perpetual quest to stick it to authority.

This was my act of rebellion, and if I were to analyze it—which I tend to do—I would say it meant several things all at once.

For one thing, I think it's kind of cool that I felt safe enough to rebel. For all I'd been through, I think it's amazing that I felt secure enough to put down my shield of compliance, violate the sanctity of dinner, and still trust that our relationship would remain intact. I think that says a lot about my mom.

For another thing, I enjoyed the performance. This was a new way to use my intelligence to win approval. Rather than showing off with facts I memorized or thoughts I conceived, I was using my brain to create a crude, absurd character at the dinner table. When I performed the character, the laughter I won was the applause I needed. Being asked to leave was the standing ovation.

More than all that, though, I wanted my mom's attention. I wanted my mom to notice me, to react to me, even if the reaction was negative. I wanted to make her care.

After all, I had been through a lot in the last three-and-a-half years, and no one was talking about it. No one was telling the story, much less making sense of all the emotions. I could barely feel the emotions anyway. They were buried so far down below the surface. It was not like my heart was just going to crack open if you gave me a little attention. If someone wanted to know what all this meant to me, they would have to be devoted. It would take time, energy, and creativity to help me feel safe enough to feel. But who has that kind of time?

So I expressed my feelings through comic acts of rebellion. Nicole expressed hers through outrage over curfews, friends, and who knows what else. Mom's feelings tended toward a combination of quiet despair and loud disgust. None of us talked about the things we needed to talk about. None of us knew where to begin.

A lot of the time during this chapter of life, I was alone, just like I thought I wanted to be.

But deep down, I wanted them. I wanted my family, or whatever shabby, angry shell of it was left. But the only way I could have them, albeit briefly, was to create a situation where I would eventually be alone, kicked outside to the car. Subconsciously, I was acting out my place in the family: a performer who can hold everyone's attention when he works for it, but who always, inevitably, ends the night alone.

Years later, I would recognize a companion who had been with me all along. I would realize that God had been after me the whole time. I would relent and embrace the Lord in my heart, and then start to recognize the embrace of the one who had held my hand all along. But God had a lot of hurdles to overcome to get to this heart. Trauma had cast a thick plate of armor around my soul, and it didn't just go away when foster care ended.

Given all this, I felt a vast canyon of difference between me and my peers.

The "atheist" label was a useful marker of difference, a neat shorthand for me not fitting in. Today, a fourth-grade atheist is not as strange as it was in 1992. The world has changed so much since then. US religiosity, which had already been on the decline for decades, took an even sharper turn from the early nineties onward, and for a time I was part of that decline—but in 1992, in Fort Wayne, Indiana, most of the kids were at least nominally religious, and a lot more families were more than nominally religious.

I remember arguing with my friend David's older sister. "Have you ever read the Bible?" she asked. She was a teenager, a little younger than my sister.

"No, but I don't need to," I said.

"Then how do you even know what it is you don't believe?"

"I know because the whole idea of religion doesn't make sense. Every culture has come up with its own set of beliefs. They all believe they're the only ones who got it right. It's not like one makes more sense than the other."

I know it sounds strange, but this was me as a fourth grader. This is how I talked.

"But how can you know that?" she asked. "If you haven't read the book, you don't know if it makes sense or if it doesn't. You haven't seen the deeper meaning. You don't know the way it makes you feel."

"Look, there are things in this world we can see. My hand. That countertop. Those things exist. But every culture in the world has made up stories about things they can't see, things that don't exist, to try to explain what they can't explain. Why is there lightning? Zeus sends thunderbolts from the sky. Why are there rainbows? It's a sign of peace from God. These days, we have science. We know more. We don't need those stories."

"But again," she insisted. "You don't know anything about those stories. You don't know what value they might have. You don't know what you think you're rejecting by saying they were completely made up."

"But I do know how unfair all this is. If you really believe there's a heaven and hell, and people only get into heaven if they believe in Jesus, what about all the people in India? What about the Vikings?"

"I don't know about that. Those are God's decisions. Not mine. I do think everyone has a chance to hear the Gospel. Maybe this is yours. What do you have to lose by reading the book? The worst that can happen is you learn something. Don't you like to learn?"

"Yes. But a person born here is going to be a lot more likely to pick up that book than a person born in India, and why should it matter where you're born? If God is all-loving and all-powerful, why should some people have more of a chance just because of where they were born? Where's the fairness in that?"

"I don't know," she said. "Like I said, those decisions are up to God. I just know that faith in God matters in my life."

"The Vikings had a belief system, too," I responded. "They had faith in Odin. And they thought their faith would get them to Valhalla. What makes their belief any less true than yours?"

"I think if you read the Bible, you'll know."

"Well, I still don't think I need to, not to know what I need to know."

As we argued, David looked back and forth between us, fascinated. We were both calm. There was no yelling, no hitting, no hurt feelings. She was surprised to hear big words and weighty arguments coming from the lips of a fourth grader, but she wasn't going to remain silent in the face of her surprise. For my part, I loved the intellectual back and forth, the contest of ideas and the wider search for truth. We ended the conversation with a sense of mutual appreciation—for a civil conversation about matters of great importance. As for David, he enjoyed seeing his friend match wits with his older sister.

When I could, I had conversations like this one. I enjoyed them. I was becoming a sort of atheistic evangelist. It's not that I sought people out in order to convert them to atheism, but when the subject came up, I enjoyed talking about these ultimate questions. I had a thirst for figuring out the world and unearthing the truth.

One of the ways I learned about faith was through Religious Education. In Fort Wayne, this was a formal program made available by the public school system. Our elementary school had a trailer in the parking lot where the class was held. When my family happened to drive by other schools, probably on our way to a restaurant, I saw the trailers outside other schools as well.

Religious Education was basically Sunday School for public school kids whose parents might not be taking them to church. It was an evangelical tool to reach the unreached—to attempt to strike a spark and save a few souls.

It was an hour each week on a weekday afternoon. And why did they hold it in a trailer? It was an attempt to avoid a lawsuit (though the class was still being held on school property even if it wasn't technically inside a school building). Here's how it worked: a permission form was sent home with each kid. If you wanted to opt your child out of Religious Education, you checked a box and signed the paper and sent it back. If the school system didn't hear from you, they assumed you were okay with it.

When I first heard about this whole trailer thing, I wanted to opt out. It seemed wrong to me. It felt like Christian faith was being pushed on us. I was already developing a sense of injustice about evangelism, a sense that Christians were aggressive about their faith, and the rest of us were victims of that aggression. I was already thinking in terms of "us" versus "them," and I was often among the "them."

My outsider identity was nurtured by atheistic evangelism—and by the books I'd been reading at the school library. In particular, I'd been checking out books about Native Americans, and those books were shaping my ideas about the history and character of Christianity. Reading about how Christian faith had been foisted upon Native Americans, how it had been used as a tool to extinguish their culture, how it had been forced by gunpoint onto so many innocent people, and how the necessities of life were used as a bribe for Jesus—I was primed to be offended by the attempted evangelism of Religious Education.

I wanted to opt out of the class, to protest the injustice of it all. But Trent appealed to me. He wanted me to join him. He and I had bonded over humor, and we shared an off-beat view of the world. He liked making fun of Religious Education, and he wanted to make fun of it with me.

So I went to the trailer. I sat in the back with Trent, where we rolled our eyes at the stories of the Bible and mocked the eccentricities of the poor woman trying to teach us.

She would play songs for us, and we enjoyed the ones that had a rock and roll flair. There was one song, "Emmanuel," that was fast paced and fun to listen to, as it extolled the names of the messiah unveiled in chapter nine of Isaiah. When we had a chance to request songs, we requested this one again and again. Our Religious Education teacher would sigh, exasperated. At first, she liked our enthusiasm for the song, but in the end, I think she knew our souls were not being saved.

For my part, I had heard religious people described as "sheep," and everything I encountered in Religious Education seemed to confirm it. The Biblical stories were obvious myths, exploring primitive themes in childlike ways, just like all the other myths from all the other ancient cultures. The claims made were fantastic. The stories were absurd. Most of the kids in the trailer seemed to believe them, but the more I heard, the more I felt affirmed in my convictions.

They were wrong and I was right. They were foolish and I was intelligent. They were blindly affirming family tradition, following the bloodless inertia of past generations; I had the courage to stand up, to stand out, to think for myself.

I liked being known as an "atheist." I liked that claiming the label was shocking to people. I liked what the label said about me.

Little did I know that as I grew up, anti-religious sentiment would become the unthinking norm in my generation. By the time I was an adult, the freethinkers would be the people who could calmly and rationally regard tradition, rethink what needed to be rethought, and set aside what needed to be set aside, rather than blindly rejecting the old ways out of hand.

But for me, as a nine-year old in 1992, I was a rebel. I was safe and secure enough to be a rebel—to stand out from the crowd in a way that no one could see unless I showed it to them—but I was a rebel. For those I chose to show it to, the "atheist" card was a way of announcing who I was: smart, unique, willing to swim against the tide. I often felt out of place in the world. This was a quick and easy way for me to say it.

At school, I had a couple of close friends. There was Trent, and the new kid, Gerald. Together, we developed a Power Rangers parody that we enacted in imaginative games on the playground. When we activated our powers, we became the Super Chunks! Trent and I also enjoyed drawing comics. We invented two characters, Bob and Marc, two fools who sometimes stumbled into accidental profundity, who enjoyed life despite the heights of their own hurdles.

Aside from Trent and Gerald, I didn't fit in with my classmates. I felt this in my bones. And my peers confirmed my intuition.

When I was in fourth grade, I was standing on one side of the coat closet while a couple of my acquaintances—not Trent or Gerald, thankfully, but two other kids—sat on the other side. The rain had forced us indoors for recess. We were spread out in the classroom, talking and playing. For some reason, I was drawn toward the coat closet—and what I heard through the divider stopped me cold.

"What's wrong with Steve?" one of them asked.

"What do you mean?" asked the other.

"I mean, he tries to be cool. He seems like he should be. His clothes are in. He's funny."

"Right," the other agreed. "But it's just—I don't know."

"There's just. . ." The first kid hesitated. "Just something about him,"

"Yeah, something," the other agreed, chewing slowly on the words as he contemplated this obvious reality.

"I don't know what it is," responded the first kid. "It's like, everything about him says he should be cool, but he isn't."

I swallowed. Part of me felt like I'd been punched in the stomach. Part of me shrugged it off. On one hand, I hated that there was nothing I could do to overcome whatever impenetrable wall stood between me and my peers. But on the other hand, they were right: There was just something about me. It hurt and it was a badge of honor all at once.

I had already experienced more of the world than most of my peers could imagine. I had already grown up in ways that would elude the rest of them for years. I felt like I was twice as old, mentally, as any of them.

Given all this, I found myself drawn to Native American history and identifying with their stories. I know I am not them. I know their historical oppression has been systematic and cruel, and that their continued struggles are tangible and tragic. Their stories are beautiful and terrible and not mine to claim.

Still, there's something about them rebelling against a larger group, showing courage in the face of insurmountable odds, and asserting their identity in the face of sharp headwinds. I identified with that. When I read about them, I cheered them on.

For a kid like me who had cut his teeth on presidential history, memorizing the hagiographical stories of great white figures, it was a privilege to learn some of the other side of the American story. It was also a bit jarring, and a bit gratifying, to learn that I could identify with the people on the other side.

6

Feeling, Thinking, Connecting

"You don't listen!" Mom shouted.

"Fuck you!" Nicole fired back. "You don't give a shit about me!"

"Do you know what I've been through for you? Do you have any idea?"

My mother and sister had been screaming at each other all year. There were bad grades, long-distance (and sometimes international) phone calls, threats to run away, attempts to run away. There were drugs in the apartment. Nicole's boyfriend was a drug dealer. Was she hiding something for him? Was she using?

"You have no idea what I went through to get you back, and this is the thanks I get!" Mom yelled.

"Fuck you!" my sister responded. "I didn't want this shit! I don't want to be here!"

When it came to bids for attention, Nicole and I were both making them, but she was better at it than I was.

"I want to hang out with my friends! That's it! It's not a big fucking deal."

"It's a huge deal, Nicole! I've seen what those people are like!"

"Those people! I can't—I can't deal with this shit. I'm outta here!"

My mother and sister had been screaming at each other all year, but this one was different. Glass was broken. All the neighbors heard the shouting. I don't remember the issue, but my sister's boyfriend and his father came to our apartment. They were prepared to take her home with them.

I was sent across the hall to our neighbor's apartment. She was a kind old lady who lived on her own. That night, she let me watch whatever I wanted on the TV in her living room, and I chose a Cleveland Indians game on ESPN.

I don't know if the neighbors complained to the owners of our complex, if there was a noise violation, but the police were called. Nicole had already spent some time in juvenile detention. She had been stealing from Mom. She had placed keys to our apartment up for sale on her high school's black market. Whatever brought the police there, it would not be her first or last encounter with them.

Often, when Mom and Nicole fought, I would go outside and play with a friend, or play on my own in the wooded creek or the one-hoop basketball court. If it was late at night and outside wasn't an option, I would go to my room, sit on the waterbed, and read. I would do whatever I could to tune them out.

I didn't care about the content of the fights. I just knew that my mom and sister were constantly on edge around each other, that they could blow at any time, and I knew to hide from it all. I did not want to be involved. It was not my job to take a side or try to mediate, despite the attempts they both made to pull me in. I just wanted it all to go away.

Soon after that, we were looking for another place to rent. The apartment owner didn't formally kick us out. They simply did not give us the option of renewing our lease and invited us to find another place to live. And so it goes.

For all the drama, solitude, and open emotional wounds, there had been some real joy in that apartment.

For one thing, there was the money. Mom was able to sell the farmhouse in the country near Columbia City, the one my father burned down, the one Bill had considered rebuilding. The acres around that house had lain fallow for five years. One day, a man drove past the property and fell in love with it. It was just the kind of place he'd been looking for—the kind of place where he could build a house and raise his boys. He inquired about the property, found our mother, and offered to buy it. With the proceeds, we were able to climb out of debt.

Another positive development was the boyfriend. Now that she was out of debt, Mom could afford to work less and be present more. She took a regular job with daytime hours at a mental health center. It didn't pay nearly as much as her previous role, but she could be home a whole lot more. And one of the perks of the job is that it came with friends and suitors. Now that she was settled into a workplace, she could meet people, like the coworker whose Super Bowl party we attended, and another coworker: Kyle.

Kyle was a social worker at the center. My mom had an aversion to social workers, driven by her experience of them when we were in foster care. Recently, I asked her how she felt about Kyle having the job he had, and she said, "He wasn't much of a social worker!" She recalled a group therapy session at their workplace where everyone gathered in a circle, staff and patients alike, and they all went around and introduced themselves. When Kyle said he was a counselor, the patients responded, "Woah! We just thought you were one of us!"

Kyle was tall, like a lot of the other men my mom had loved, but he was also kind. He did not have a beard or drive a motorcycle. He was a vegetarian. He listened to indie rock. He liked The Flaming Lips several years before you even thought about hearing of them, and he had a signed poster of The Cynics in his living room.

He liked sports. He was a Cleveland Browns fan, so we connected over that. He liked gambling on sports, too, but don't worry. This isn't one of those tragic stories where his gambling debts drag us back into financial hell and familial chaos. He knew his limits and kept it under control. It was just a hobby.

Mom was careful with the introduction of this man. She knew we had been through a lot of change and didn't know how we would respond, in this year of transition, to the introduction of another someone new. When Kyle came over for the first time, he and I played basketball—real basketball on the one-hoop court in the parking lot, and virtual basketball on the Sega Genesis. We even gambled to make it interesting—five dollars a game. It was fun. He was a good guy.

During this time, another positive development was occurring—my sexual awakening. It came through a strange encounter, in a series of moments that are hard to explain and embarrassing to write about, but I do not want to be embarrassed. I would like to recount the odd parenting choices that led to this awakening without feeling shame about my own behavior. I want to be able to talk about this in a way that allows others with similar stories to share theirs, in a way that makes sexuality less taboo and more natural.

In the church more broadly, I want more people to feel comfortable sharing the timid and tenuous parts of their stories, the timid and tenuous parts of themselves. In that spirit, I share this story. It is a positive one. I'm not sure I would have said that before writing it down, but here I am, trying to be unafraid.

A younger sister of a friend of Nicole's needed a place to stay. She lived with her grandmother, who was suddenly hospitalized. The mom was in jail, and the dad was long out of the picture, so she didn't have any other stable place to go. We were the same age, both in fourth grade, and her name was Aaliyah. She had cocoa-colored skin and voluminous black hair.

Rather than giving Aaliyah a couch to sleep on or putting her in my bed while I slept somewhere else, Mom thought it would be fun to set up a tent in the living room for us to sleep in together. After all, if we were going to have an extra kid in the house, why not make it fun for both of us?

In that tent, Aaliyah and I explored one another in a way that blurred the boundaries between innocence and adolescence. When she first suggested the game we played, I wasn't sure what to do. I had never done anything like it. She wanted me to press my body against hers. She wanted our genitals to touch. She wanted us to "hump" each other, as she said. I only had a nascent understanding of even imagining something like this. I had seen sexuality portrayed on TV and I knew what it felt like to get an erection. At the apartment complex swimming pool, there were young women who undid the straps of their bikini tops and gingerly laid face-down to sunbathe. I knew what it felt like to get an erection.

But Aaliyah wanted my penis pressed against her, and I didn't know how to do that. I hesitated.

She pouted her lower lip. "Don't you think I'm pretty?" she asked.

"I do," I said. "You're very pretty."

"Don't you want to know what it feels like?"

I didn't until she suggested it, but now I was curious.

"This wouldn't be sex," she said. "It's dry-humping."

Where had she learned those terms?

We did it at first with our clothes on, but then she wanted me to take off my clothes, and I did. She would wear her swimsuit.

Looking back as an adult, I wonder if Aaliyah suffered abuse in her young life, or if she was exposed to something she shouldn't have been. But she may not have. Grownups have a way of pathologizing child behavior, making natural curiosity into a universal symptom of childhood trauma. What we did was not necessarily abnormal for kids our age, but the duration and intensity of it was.

Was there anything out of the ordinary about her awareness of her body? About her interest in playing with mine? Her commanding direction of our play? Or the way it all accelerated from touching to humping to moaning? Perhaps. But it all felt natural at the time. And wonderful.

For several days, we had a relationship. I enjoyed talking to her and playing non-sexual games with her. And I enjoyed when she directed us toward activities that we both knew we needed to keep hidden, activities we both knew we couldn't talk about with grown-ups, which we both enjoyed for reasons we couldn't understand or wouldn't name.

"What if your mom finds out?" Aaliyah would whisper.

"Don't worry about that," I would say. "She's too stupid to find out."

Aaliyah laughed. I was bold in that tent.

My mom would not discover the furtive sexual games we were playing in that tent, as far as I know, though I'm not sure we were particularly skilled at hiding them. Our games became rather steamy. Our breathing was heavy. We made sounds. The humping was vigorous. If we were truly never discovered while doing this, I do not know how.

One night, we were by ourselves in the apartment complex swimming pool, and we decided to skinny dip. I don't remember whose idea it was. I know she initiated the games in the tent, but I might have initiated this one in the pool. We let her swimsuit and my swim shorts sink to the bottom of our personal ocean. We splashed each other. We laughed. We felt each other's bodies. At night, the pool was all lit up, and I loved seeing her body glisten above and beneath the water.

Before we met each other, we had both seen the movie *The Bodyguard*. It seemed natural for a little white boy and a little black girl with a budding romance to pretend to be Kevin Costner and Whitney Houston. It was especially fun to do so in the pool, where I could dive in front of an incoming bullet, and we could crash into each other's pre-pubescent bodies.

I was not expecting anyone else to show up at the pool, so we got lost in the games we were playing—until we heard approaching voices. Luckily, it was nothing malevolent. Looking back now, I can see how it could have been. We not only risked being seen, but in this case, we risked being seriously hurt. Thankfully, though, the approaching voices were my friend Scott and his older sister, coming to enjoy the water in the moonlight.

I sucked air into my lungs so I could swim down to the bottom for my trunks and Aaliyah's bathing suit. She swam to a far corner of the pool. I treaded water in front of her while she furtively put her suit back on, and then we traded places while I did the same. We laughed! The game of almost being caught delighted us both.

I don't remember how many days we had her with us, but soon enough, Aaliyah was gone. I never saw her again.

I am not sure what combination of genes and social development lead to the gift of bisexuality for other people, but I can speak to the emergence and expression of sexual identity in my life. For me, it was partly about the natural gifts of my body and brain—such as my full, red lips, intuitive way of thinking, and love for poetry—and partly about social development. A physically absent father and emotionally absent mother left me with a variety of yearnings for male and female intimacy. And this encounter with Aaliyah may have been part of it, too. Perhaps an early experience with a commanding girl nurtured a penchant for strong women, for people who embody traditionally masculine features and traditionally feminine features all at once. There is something vaguely bisexual about all of that.

Looking back as an adult, I wonder why Aaliyah left so soon—and why I never asked questions about her or strove to see her again. Some part of me was connected enough and emotionally mature enough to carry on this brief, prepubescent love affair in the first place. At the same time, I detached myself from her quickly. What part of me, in my too-often-solitary life, did not even miss this beautiful person with whom I shared my body, mind, and soul? Perhaps I had already known more intimacy with her than I could bear, and I did not want to let her or anyone else to get close enough to hurt me. Or perhaps I had learned not to ask questions about people and their parting. After all, people come and go, and that is life.

Looking back now, I wonder where the adults were. What was going on with Aaliyah's caretakers? Why did sending her to strangers seem better than sending her to anyone they knew? And where was my mother? I know there were times when Aaliyah and I were playing with each other, when Mom was asleep in her room. Did she have any awareness of what we were doing, what our giggling meant, what the rustling of the tent signaled? Did she even conceive of the possibility that her nine-year-old son would do something like this? While exploration between children is normal, the duration and intensity of our adventure does not happen in a happy, healthy home.

During the year we spent in our apartment, I was not completely alone. Even when my mom and sister weren't there, I had friends to keep me company. Even when I went to Arby's by myself, God was with me to keep me safe, and the girl behind the counter looked out for me. For this experience with Aaliyah, I was with someone, connecting to another human being in a way that defied our respective youth. But no one really had access to my heart. Not even me. My heart was locked away in a dark closet, and even I didn't know where it was.

Soon, we had to find a new place to rent. This time, it would be a house with an independent landlord, the traditional refuge of people with poor rental histories, looking to make a deal on a handshake without anyone looking too closely at the details. Apartment complexes would be concerned about the yelling and the fighting and the calls to the police. But the owner of a house might be willing to look at our white skin and Mom's professional demeanor and feel fortunate to have us as renters. So we looked at houses, finally settling on a two-story, three-bedroom number with big closets and a semi-usable basement, a house across town on Branning Avenue.

An added bonus to the house on Branning was that Mom's boyfriend Kyle lived close by. He was becoming more and more a part of our lives. We were going to his house more often for parties and sporting events, and he came over to see us an awful lot, as well. He stayed over so often that he eventually brought his German shepherd to live at our house—partly to protect us after a break-in when the back door window was broken, and partly because he was spending more time at our house than his own.

Normally, with a move across town, I would have had to change schools, but Mom worked with my teacher and we made another arrangement. After all the change in my young life, this was one more change I wouldn't have to go through. I wouldn't have to start over at another new school. I could dance if I wanted to and leave my friends behind, but I wouldn't have to.

In the apartment complex, I had walked to school. Now, I would take the city bus. Mom gave me bus fare in the morning, then I walked to the bus stop and took it across town. When it came to getting home at the end of the day, I was let out of school early so I could catch the most convenient bus. If I missed that one, I would have to wait hours for the next one. This wasn't Chicago or anything; it's not like there was a bus coming every fifteen minutes.

I was still in the fourth grade at this point. I was nine years old and riding the city bus alone. Some people are shocked when they hear that, but it was a point of pride for me. I was different. I was smart. I could navigate this kind of thing by myself.

I made a friend on the bus. My school schedule aligned with the work schedule at Anthony Wayne Services, a company that employed intellectually disabled men and women. Through AWS, they performed menial manufacturing tasks, earned a little income, and felt a sense of accomplishment. There was a young adult named Kyle—not the boyfriend, of course, a different Kyle—who caught a different bus for the downtown central hub, but then we rode the same bus to his work and my school. Kyle and I would sit next to each other and tell jokes. He wasn't on the same intellectual level as me, but we were probably on similar emotional levels. Most of all, I enjoyed his company. It was nice to not be completely alone. In this wild world, I was glad to have someone looking out for me.

Around this time, Mom and I had an odd little spat. One night, she wanted to take me downtown to enjoy the fireworks after a local festival, but I wasn't so sure.

"Come on, Steve," she said. "We need to get you out of the house."

"But what's so great about fireworks?" I asked. "Why do people like them?"

"What?" she said. "They're fireworks."

"Right."

I was puzzled. She had a point about getting me out of the house. In our new house, I stayed inside a lot. I didn't make friends in this neighborhood the way I had in the apartment complex. The kids seemed less approachable, since we didn't have the common bond of living in the same complex or going to the same school. More than that, though, I think I was dispirited. I didn't want to approach someone, become friends again, and then leave again. I didn't want to form an attachment and then see it ripped away.

Instead, I spent my free time with family or alone. Most days, I stayed inside to watch TV or play Sega Genesis. I read history and novels and cereal boxes. I counted my baseball cards and started looking up their values in Beckett's guide—another attempt to comprehend, classify, and control the wider world.

Every week, I earned an allowance; I would walk to the corner store and buy sports cards and Borden's Dutch Chocolate Milk. This neighborhood was more walkable than the one we had left. I didn't have to cross a busy four-lane boulevard to get to the corner store, so it was more accessible than my old neighborhood haunts. But the kids were an impenetrable wall, at least to me. I left the house for cards and chocolate milk—but not to see anybody.

Back to the night of the fireworks. I knew I needed to get out of the house more, so I went with Mom to see the exploding lights. But I couldn't shake the puzzle: Why did people like this kind of display? Was it the lights? We'd seen laser lights at the art museum. I saw lights every day on TV, flashing and forming and reforming into new patterns.

I asked her about the history of fireworks. I asked her about *her* history with fireworks, what she remembered about them and why she liked them.

Mom was puzzled.

I wondered out loud, "Hundreds of years ago, when people first started with fireworks, there weren't as many light displays to catch their interest. That would make this more of a special thing. With today's technology, though, the effect is dampened.

"I suppose it's also the sound," I continued. "The banging noise. That's different from other light shows. Is it the visual and the sound put together? Is that what it is?"

"What are you talking about?" she said.

"I'm just wondering why people like fireworks. What makes this more special than other things that light up or make noise?" If my curiosity had been entertained, I might have also started thinking about the communal nature of fireworks, about how the display is connected to an event that people experience together and find meaningful.

But Mom did not indulge my questions. "Why are you ruining this?" she said, glaring at me. "What's wrong with you?"

I wasn't playing a game with her. It's not like we were in a restaurant. I just didn't feel anything. I didn't see anything special when the fireworks shot into the air and dispersed into patterns. I wondered if they were more captivating to people who were older, people who remembered when entertainment was simpler, when technology was less advanced. In asking these questions, I wasn't trying to ruin the experience. I was trying to understand it—so that I could learn to enjoy it, too.

But that's not how my questions sounded to Mom. Eventually, she was so mad that we left.

Meanwhile at school, fourth grade turned to fifth, and I continued to grow in friendship with Trent. I would sometimes walk to his house and hang out with him after school, then take the later bus home. Eventually, we had sleepovers together. In fact, it was then—in a borrowed sleeping bag in Trent's room, with the lights turned off, during the time when sleepy kids banter and fight the dying of the light—when I first tried to make sense of my childhood story.

If I had been a normal kid like Trent—normal being a relative term here; I mean, he was friends with me—with two present parents in an upper-middle-class home I had lived in all my life, I suppose we would have told ghost stories to each other. But I had my own scary story to tell, one that happened to me, one that involved abuse and foster care and a series of changes I could barely comprehend.

Telling him the story was my first attempt to make sense of it all, to think through the events and make some kind of sense of them. I was attempting to recover from the trauma by constructing a narrative. I was attempting to make sense of the world.

Trent was a sympathetic listener. He was eager to know more about my life. His curiosity inspired me to dig deeper and remember more. As he listened and responded, he helped me understand what was normal and not-so-normal in my story. He also asked questions. He stoked my curiosity to dig deeper, to talk to my mom and sister and try to discover more. Most importantly, he listened with a caring ear. He held the space and let me express the thoughts I'd been keeping inside. Eventually, through telling and retelling the story, I came to have some measure of understanding and healing.

Once, Trent and I had a massive disagreement. I can't even remember what it was about. Perhaps it was something about the Bob and Marc comics we were drawing, or the imaginative games we played at recess, or some unexplained, unintended hurt—the kind that sometimes happen among friends. Who can say? But we were upset at each other. We were determined to never speak to each other again.

Our teacher, Mr. Browne, was in the process of reorganizing our classroom. He had divided us into clusters of four; we would sit together in groups, facing each other.

"Steve, Dina, Ryan, and Trent," he called out, announcing a new cluster. The four of us headed toward our new desks.

"I don't know if that's a good idea," Ryan said to our teacher. "Steve and Trent are mad at each other. They're not friends anymore."

Mr. Browne arched his eyebrow. "Oh, really?"

"Yeah," I offered. "We do not want to sit next to each other."

"What's going on?" he asked.

Neither of us wanted to say.

"Then it's even more important that you sit here," said Mr. Browne.

We walked to our seats. I slunk down into one of the desks. Trent remained hesitant.

"Arguments come and go," Mr. Browne said. "Words can hurt. Fists can hurt. But friendships last longer than all of that. You don't throw away a friendship over an argument. Give it some time and figure it out."

Sure enough, he was right. Before long, we were drawing comics, pretending to be comedic superheroes on the playground, laughing at each other and laughing at the stories we heard in the Religious Education trailer.

For my part, I learned a lesson about resilience and connection. You don't give up on a relationship because of a momentary setback. There is so much more to the bonds that hold us together than the minor disagreements that pull us apart. And you don't just cut off the people you love when things go sour.

I was glad for this lesson later in life, when I learned to trust in people and have faith in God. When you're developing a relationship with God, your ideas about religion can change. All of a sudden, you question everything. But that doesn't mean you stop talking to God. You give it some time and figure it out. You may have intellectual reasons to doubt, but the relationship is more than intellectual assent, deeper than your momentary thoughts and beliefs.

For my part, through these childhood experiences, I was learning how to feel. How to connect. How to love. I was learning the traits I would one day need to embrace a faith in God.

In the end, faith is not entirely an act of the heart, but you need the heart to get there. It is a motion of the head and the heart combined. There is thought. There is reason. And you also need some heart to complete the action. Faith may not be a blind leap, but it is still a leap—into this half-known, rarely-seen aurora borealis. You need emotion to get there. And I was getting there.

7

Fighting at Home and Abroad

As FIFTH GRADE TURNED into sixth, I discovered a new love: *The Lion King*. After school, I would get off the bus, head home, put the VHS tape into the VCR, and commence my daily ritual of watching it. As a daily practice, this went on for several weeks. As an occasional rite, it was several months.

What did I see in this movie? Its target audience was probably younger than me. Still, day after day, I sang along with Simba, who just couldn't wait to be king! I teared up when Mufasa died, when Simba sadly expressed longing for a father who could no longer be there. Through this movie, I had access to tears that weren't coming in other arenas of my life.

Day after day, I resonated with Timon and Pumbaa and their carefree attitude. In the end, I saw the necessity of Simba returning to his home and reclaiming his throne, but part of me wished he could stay in the jungle with the two carefree kids, living a life of ease.

In our new home, my mom and sister fought all the time. Here in the house on Branning, they could battle and the neighbors wouldn't complain about the noise. When they fought, I retreated to the semi-usable basement, where I had a train set. During these retreats, I might play with it absent-mindedly, but for the most part, I either had a book or wished I did. I wished I had something other than my own thoughts to drown out the charges exploding upstairs.

The conflict scared me in a way I don't remember it scaring me at the apartment. Was it more intense during this time? Was I just home more often, and more aware of the conflagration?

I remember my sister offering me pot around this time. She was in eleventh grade by now, and I remember her getting high in her room—with friends who Mom suspected of breaking our back window and robbing us.

I remember the bloodshot eyes and the smell of smoke. I remember I did not take my sister up on her offer. I did not want to become like the people in that circle.

There were lots of people who came around to see Nicole—boyfriends, male and female friends. It was hard to keep track of who she was and wasn't dating. But it wasn't hard to imagine where she was going when she left the house. Branning Avenue was closer to the economically wounded neighborhoods of Fort Wayne, so it was easier for her to walk to the places where she felt comfortable—the places where she was finding her liberation.

One day, a guy came over, a boyfriend. We were hanging out in the living room. She asked what he wanted to drink. He named some beverage—and then he said, "And why don't you squeeze some of that v-juice in it, too?" She was thrown by this request. She told him she couldn't just produce it on command, and this was hardly the time. For goodness sake, her little brother was right there.

She had a female friend over at that time. I remember the friend brazenly flirting with the guy, bragging to him about her sexual prowess. When Nicole went to get the drinks, the friend straddled his lap. Later, when Nicole confronted her, the friend claimed she was just trying to test the guy, just trying to make sure he was one of the good ones. But it didn't look that way to me. Nicole wasn't convinced, either.

It probably wasn't great for me to see any of this, but that was part of my reality at the house on Branning Avenue.

I do have some good memories of the place. I remember watching football with Kyle. I remember playing with his dog, who once got so annoyed with my game of jumping over both the footrest and her that she bit my head and I had to get stitches in my ear. That, in one ferocious bite, defined the house on Branning: I could create diversions and carve out pockets of joy, but I spent a lot of time huddled in terror on a cold basement floor.

I was scared of the feelings my mom and sister were hurling like projectiles at each other, and I was scared of the emotions rushing through me: the fear, the anger at them both, the desperate sadness of it all. I didn't want to feel any of these things. I wanted to be alone, unnoticed, left to my own devices—without a war going on upstairs.

When I was the one upstairs, and *The Lion King* played on the VCR, that was good. In a small way, it was a moment of reconnecting the tissue that had been torn by trauma. In those moments, I connected with a lion cub who lost his dad, a little lion who grew up searching for other male figures to fill the void, and who was lucky to find Pumbaa and Timon.

I connected with a growing lion, the adolescent Simba, who wanted to hold on to the illusion of a *hakuna matata* childhood as long as he could.

He was haunted by memories of his younger days, but sometimes he could forget the pain of the past. Sometimes, he could embrace the *hakuna matata* spirit, live without a mental filter between him and the world, and experience the pleasure of the moment.

Sometimes, I could be like that.

I had some normal childhood experiences. They came in fits and starts. Kyle taught me how to ride a bike—resolving that long unfinished thread. Mom had the emotional courage to reestablish her relationship with her parents, and I would sometimes visit them on the weekend. At their house, I was a worry-free kid. Grandma made chocolate chip cookies and French toast. I played basketball on the hoop in the driveway. Grandpa and I went fishing. He would take me to the truck stop and give me chocolate milk and quarters for *Galaga*. People recognized me as little Stevie, Gene Kile's grandkid, all grown up.

Grandpa and Kyle were father-figures to me. They were both imperfect in their ways, and my love for them was imperfect, as well, but I am glad for their presence in my life.

Still, from this chapter, it's the fighting I remember most.

Once, as an alternative to punishment for some legal misdeed and as a diversion from court, Nicole was referred to a family therapy group at the YMCA. It was mainly for mom and Nicole, but I was dragged along when Kyle was unable to watch me. There, in the presence of other troubled teens and troubled parents, my mother and sister tried to resolve their differences and learn to see things from one another's perspective. When I came, I sat in the middle.

Once, the counselor asked Nicole and Mom to pretend to be each other. Perhaps, by seeing the caricatures each portrayed of the other, they might understand how they looked in each other's eyes. And they might gain some empathy for the person on the other side of all the yelling.

During this exercise, I thought I was being invited to participate, as well. The counselor said, "Kids, act like your parents; parents, act like your kids; talk to each other from the other person's shoes." He didn't specify that I wasn't one of the kids. In the exercise, I thought I was supposed to be a parent, too, and so I joined the conversation, pretending to be an absent father without a name.

At first, I joined Nicole, who was pretending to be Mom, in her crusade against Mom, who was pretending to be Nicole. I wanted the real-life Nicole to gain some perspective and make better choices. But both Nicole and Mom were unreasonable. Their portrayals of each other were ridiculous and unrealistic. In their dialogue, they weren't talking to each other at all.

They were just thinking of the next thing they could say to make the other one look ridiculous.

"Hold on," I said. "Hold on!" I said, louder. "Let's all calm down!"

At that point, the counselor stopped us. He invited Mom and Nicole to see the impact their fighting was having on me, that it put me in the middle between the two of them, that it aggravated me and caused stress for me.

When I huddled in the basement, I tried to understand the world, same as I did everywhere else. I wondered: Why did I feel compelled to leave when the fighting started? Why did I feel the emotions I felt when it was happening? Analyzing the situation, I decided that the yelling reminded me of our stepdad, that I ran from them and felt afraid of them because of him. When we lived in Hawaii, I learned that anger is dangerous and devastating, that it should be avoided it all costs lest it explode like Mauna Loa. Their anger reminded me of his, and that was why it made me feel scared and alone.

If I had been seeing a therapist at the time, the therapist might have also wondered about the anger I was feeling. It was sad, quiet anger, anger subsumed into sadness and fear—anger I could have only admitted I was feeling if I felt safe and secure enough to admit it to myself. I was angry at Mom and Nicole. Here we were, the long-promised family unit, finally together after so much struggle. We were supposed to be stable now, experiencing long-promised peace and stability. The elusive notion of everything calm. And it was torn apart with each swear word, each insult, each threat and ultimatum.

I would have liked for Mom and Nicole to see what their fighting was doing to me. I would have liked that to be motivation for them to work together and find some common ground. That is what the counselor wanted them to see, too.

But I don't think it worked, and his approach felt dehumanizing to me. The lesson I internalized was that I was not, in fact, invited to participate. I was just a cudgel to coax or crush them. I was not an overly mature kid whose grasping attempt at a childhood was torn away by eviction from a kid-friendly apartment complex and a sudden move into a lonely, hellish house. I wasn't my own person with my own response to the beating drum of trauma resounding in our family. I was a prop in the play and not an actor.

So I stopped trying to participate. Physically and emotionally, I hid in the basement.

When I made the transition from elementary school to middle, I was glad I got to attend the same school as Trent and Gerald. It was right next to our elementary school, so it was still across town for me, but now I was just in range of the school and able to ride the regular school bus. Once again, I was allowed to stay with my friends as we prepared to conquer adolescence.

However, the school bus was more intimidating than the city bus. I knew how to navigate the city bus. It was mostly full of adults, and they were inclined to be polite. Sometimes they were even downright helpful if you happened to be a kid on your own. By comparison, the school bus was a mad den of cruelty, a *Lord of the Flies* situation where I was not the lord.

With all the insecurity and awkwardness of a baby deer struggling to get on its feet, I fought to find room in a bus full of kids who had been friends with each other forever and who hated making room for me.

Middle school is often described as a fresh form of torture. I am not the first person, and I am sure I will not be the last, to have had an awkward time in middle school, but my particular awkward time was compounded by my upbringing.

Despite the elementary school affirmation that "there was just something about" me, and that I would never be cool no matter what, I still tried. Nicole told me that cool kids wore sports jerseys, so I asked Mom to buy me sports jerseys. Trent started wearing short-sleeved shirts over long-sleeved shirts, so I started wearing those, as well. He was into flannel. Coincidentally, so was I.

Trent talked about Star Wars around the lunch table. Apparently, he was really into Star Wars, which was not something I had known until then. In response, I eagerly watched the movies, and then I took it a step further and started reading Star Wars novels and sourcebooks, but when I tried to talk about it with Trent, he suddenly wasn't interested.

He was beginning to think I was weird in all the wrong ways, and he started to push me away.

In ways that I struggled to understand—though I devoted a lot of time and brain power to trying to figure it out—he began to orchestrate bullying campaigns against me at our lunch table. At lunch, it was Trent, Gerald, and me, plus a rotating cast of characters who orbited around us. One of those kids was named Jim. Jim could be smart, kind, and funny, but he also had a mean streak. Egged on by Trent, he made lunch a daily nightmare for me.

He'd throw food or he'd smear it on me, and he'd do it in small, quiet, deliberate ways. He didn't want to draw the attention of teachers. He didn't want to make it look intentional. He just wanted to elicit a response from me.

He knew that I spent time on my hair and took pride in my sports jerseys, that I was trying to be cool and never would be, and he knew how to get under my skin. He'd mess up my hair. He'd stain the jerseys. Then he'd make fun of the stains and call me dirty. And Trent would laugh and laugh.

Jim moved in the middle of the year, but another kid named Glenn took his place at our table. Again, it was the hair, the shirts, the food and stains. It was me being dirty. It was my ears and face turning bright red with embarrassment.

One of my other friends tried to get me out of this cycle of abuse. Drew and I connected over shared classes and a love of sports. We both watched ESPN a lot. He wasn't as funny as Trent, but his humor was friendly and good natured. He was just a nice guy who accepted me as I was. He invited me to his lunch table, which was already a bit crowded, but full of the kind of guys who would make room to include someone who needed to feel included.

I think I would have had a less awkward middle school experience if I had joined this new friend group—but I had been friends with Trent and Gerald for what felt like a long time, and I didn't like having to assert my way in to this new, inclusive space. So I remained inert. I stayed where I was and accepted the abuse. It was the price of friendship with Trent. Even though I could see that his friendship didn't feel right anymore, it was still something to which I clung.

This kind of clinging is not uncommon. The abused often loves the abuser. The abused may try to leave, again and again, but they often come back to the person and pattern they know. When pain is what you expect of the world and of relationships, there is comfort in the meeting of expectations.

Of course, I analyzed this the way I analyzed everything else. Why didn't I try to be accepted into the other group? Because I didn't want to loudly insist on what I wanted or needed. In many situations, I didn't want to be seen. At home, if I couldn't have friends or peace, I at least wanted space—space to read my books and watch my movie and pursue my interests. If I couldn't have what I really wanted, then I at least wanted to fly under the radar.

At the lunch table, I wanted to be accepted and loved for who I was. I wanted to sit without a fuss among kids who appreciated my unique spirit. But since I couldn't have that, I would settle for sitting without a fuss in a place that was a nightmare. Even in middle school, I was aware enough to know that this was what I was doing, that I was choosing familiarity over acceptance.

I wish I could say this was the only part of middle school that was hard. But I was made fun of in other arenas, as well. I brought a book with me to every class, to read during what would otherwise be slow or social moments. This was an odd behavior, so it quickly became a target of derision. My face and ears turned red a lot, so that was another bright, shining target.

One time, I defecated on one of my socks. I know it's weird to talk about this sort of thing. This is the kind of story you lock in your internal vault and never share with anyone, much less explore in your spiritual memoir. Still, I hope that sharing stories that are tender and tenuous encourages others to embrace vulnerability in the place where they are, to stand up and speak their truth and ask for what they need, no matter how afraid it makes them. When we open ourselves in vulnerable ways, we can be hurt, absolutely—but we can also be helped. We can open ourselves to the soaring heights of joy and community.

One afternoon after lunch, I had to leave a social studies class to go to the bathroom. I remember the class because it was one of my favorites—American History, a subject I knew well. With permission, I left the class and hurried to the restroom. When I got there, diarrhea exploded. I didn't make it all the way to the toilet before the eruption, so the fetid stuff burst out over the toilet bowl, stall, and floor. It got in my underwear. It dripped down my leg.

Frantically, I tried to clean it up, to hide the evidence of my crime. I pulled square after square of toilet paper. I wiped myself, the walls, the toilet. Sometimes, in situations like this, I threw my boxers away if I safely could, because they might be too far gone to be of any use. This day, I didn't have to do that, but I did have work to do. Alone. I wanted no one to know I had done something so socially sinful. I wanted no one to help, and the last thing I wanted was to be seen.

But I missed a spot. When I returned to class, there was feces on my sock. I hadn't noticed. One small, brown speck of gunk. I missed it.

But it didn't take long for the other kids to notice. I denied it. I tried to play it off as chocolate, some leftover detritus from the daily war at lunch, but the smell was unmistakable. More kids noticed. Comments were made. Insults were thrown.

My teacher threw me a life preserver. "Whatever it is," she said. "Go and see the school nurse. She might have some extra socks for you."

I was glad for salvation from that one, terrible moment—but it was merely a glimpse of a chronic condition. Nothing major. It's just that I was having diarrhea almost all the time, and that was not healthy. Almost no one knew. My mom suggested I might be allergic to a food, like chocolate, but I didn't want to give up eating chocolate. She said it might help if I ate more fruits and vegetables, so I tried that remedy.

Often, I had diarrhea in the morning. I would show my Mom, and she would call the school, and I would get to stay home by myself on those days while she went to work and Nicole went to school. I reveled in those days when I had the house to myself, when I could remain unnoticed, unseen.

I read. I watched TV. I listened to the radio. I played with the train set. I looked up baseball cards in the Beckett's guide. Whatever else I could find to pass the time. If it would get me out of school—given the choice between a bit of loose stool and the cruelty of my peers—I would take diarrhea any day of the week.

But this didn't happen every day. It started out as once every few weeks, and then it started happening once every couple of weeks, and then my butt was exploding once a week. The diarrhea was often short lived: two morning hours of loose releases and urgent runs to the bathroom, and then I was fine.

Eventually, my mom had a suggestion. "You know your diarrhea?" she asked.

"Um, yeah," I said, kind of embarrassed to be talking about it.

"I wonder if it's psychosomatic."

"What's that?" I asked.

"It's where your mind does something to your body. Like if you're intimidated about going to school, maybe you get sick in the morning—just long enough to get out of school."

"Oh." I blushed. "Is there anything else it could be?"

"Well, you might have some kind of intestinal disease, but we would see more than just that one symptom. Another option is that you might be lactose intolerant."

"You mean, like, allergic to milk?"

"Yeah, milk and butter and milk chocolate, maybe, anything that has milk in it. We could try to find out by cutting dairy out of your diet and seeing if you continue to have this."

What would that even be like? What would I drink with lunch at school? And what about my favorite foods? What about Borden Dutch Chocolate Milk? What about cereal? It couldn't be that.

"Well, I don't always like going to school," I admitted. "It's hard. I get made fun of a lot."

But I didn't go into detail. For example, I didn't tell my mom about how I was still drawing Bob and Marc comics with Trent, how we would both add panels to these cartoons and pass them around, and how one of the popular girls at school interrupted my reading one day to ask me about them.

"Hey, you," the girl had said. "Steve. I would love to see one of those comics you're always drawing. I just think it's so cool that you do that. Can I see one?"

"Um, I appreciate you're asking, but no thank you," I said, furrowing my eyebrows. "I don't like to share them with other people."

"Oh, come on. You and Trent are so funny. I just wanna see one."

I sensed a trap. I knew the hot cheerleader did not want to see these comics because she wanted to admire them. There was a group of boys around her, egging her on, and I could only imagine the plans they had. I quietly rested my hand on my notebook. The last thing I needed was for one of them to rip it away from my desk.

"Sorry. I don't have any on me," I said.

"Aww, why not?" she said, smiling. "Could you draw one, just for me?"

She was learning to use her feminine wiles. She knew I stared at her at times, that I "liked" her, as much as a sixth grader can "like" anyone, and she was willing to use that to get this coveted fodder for amusement. But I could also detect a note of discomfort in her. She didn't want to be doing this. It wasn't her natural inclination to torment someone. She had social pressures she was responding to, as well.

"No, I don't think so," I said. "They're just not ready to show people."

I returned to my book. She returned to her friends. My face was not as red as I thought it would be after talking to a popular girl like her.

This time, I had successfully defended myself against torment and teasing. But there were a lot of times when I couldn't—times when I faltered in gym class, when guys pushed my head against my locker as they walked by, when they knocked the books out of my hands, when they made fun of the stains Jim and Glenn made at lunch, when they called me a fag and I wondered if I really was such a dreaded thing. I hated these parts of middle school.

But I didn't say all that to my mom. To Mom, I just said, "I don't always like going to school. It's hard. I get made fun of a lot."

She didn't think there was anything special about that. "Yeah," she said. "That's part of being in middle school. It's hard for everybody."

"I guess it could be psychosomatic," I said, agreeing to this diagnosis of the diarrhea.

And I think at least part of it was. I had diarrhea less frequently after that, and when I did have it, I didn't use it as an excuse to get out of school, because I knew it would probably be gone by the time I got there.

However, I did learn as an adult that I am lactose intolerant. I probably shit on a sock in social studies because of milk in the lunchroom. I probably had diarrhea in the morning because of dairy at home. But my mom, the registered nurse, didn't feel the need to examine it further.

Of course, she had a lot on her plate back then. Nicole was a mess. We were just hoping she could get through high school without getting arrested again. I was the compliant one. I was quiet and, for the most part, I didn't complain. Together, we had reached a satisfactory explanation for the eruption of my bowels. Why check it out further? Why make the quiet, easy kid the center of your attention?

Still, if I need to say it, to spell it out for you and claim it for myself: I was emotionally repressed. I was trying hard not to be seen, not to be hurt, not to let the middle school bullying and loneliness of life affect me. And sometimes, when you prevent yourself from feeling emotions, they find ways of expressing themselves through your body. I am lactose intolerant, but at the time, I was also lonely, scared, angry, and embarrassed—and trying like hell not to feel any of it. And when you shove those feelings down, they can explode all over the walls of the bathroom, and even your best efforts to clean them up and keep them hidden will not succeed. Sometimes, a speck of emotion will remain on your sock, there for all the world to see.

There were parts of my life I liked. When I could carve out my own world and live in it, I liked that. For example, as a supplement to the comics, I started writing plays starring me, Trent, Gerald, and the celebrity crushes of our choosing. Trent liked Topanga from *Boy Meets World* and Gerald liked Alex Mack from *The Secret World of Alex Mack*. For me, it was Christine Lakin, Al on *Step by Step*, whose character was a total tomboy, and that was my kind of girl.

I liked going to the school library, where I continued to read about Native American history, especially *Bury My Heart at Wounded Knee* by Dee Brown, a book I checked out again and again.

I was also drawn to books about the paranormal: stories about Roswell, Bigfoot, Area 51, and everything else the government was keeping secret. I evaluated it all. I thought about it all. I wanted to believe it all. When *The X-Files* premiered in 1993, I could identify with Mulder—the misunderstood genius with a traumatic past, the guy who was smart enough to debunk all the mysteries if he wanted to. But he didn't want to. He wanted to believe.

Interestingly, I wanted to believe in government conspiracies, alien encounters, and a large land mammal stalking the Pacific Northwest—but I had no desire to believe in God.

For me, atheism was a continued marker of difference, a continued point of pride, especially in the awkward middle school world.

And paranormal researchers were a lot like me—skeptical of the accepted narrative, willing to follow the evidence no matter where it led, and brave enough to persist in their pursuits despite the opposition. They were misunderstood geniuses, outsiders who resisted the pull of the crowd and its inability to think with freedom. Those were the connecting points between skepticism of God and acceptance of Roswell.

Looking back on it all, I think of middle school as the continued labor of emotional birth. I still have difficulty accessing intense emotions today, and I did back then too, but some feelings were coming to the surface. I felt them when I huddled in fear in the unfinished basement—not just fear, but anger. At school, I felt anger at Jim and Glenn—and at Trent for egging them on—and at all the other kids who lashed their insecurities against the tender skin of everyone else.

Through the media I consumed, I felt all kinds of feelings. Books and movies helped me access emotions otherwise kept at bay by the breakwater.

Through history and sports, I felt a sense of connection with the underdogs. I also felt the pain of loss and the thrill of victory.

Through *The Lion King* and *Star Wars*, I identified with heroic mythology, with the well-worn narrative arc of the hero's journey, where an adventure outside of one's homeland leads to personal growth for the hero, who then uses that growth to achieve an unlikely victory back home. Through these stories, I was beginning to think that I might become a winner too, that I was not doomed to be a victim of abuse defined by childhood pain, but that this might be the tragic first act necessary to a hero's drama.

In that vein, I was able to cast myself as a hero in the plays I wrote for my friends. I may not have been a hero in real life, but I could at least be one in a world of my own creation. And I was able to be a hero to my friends, in some small way, by making them laugh and absorbing their attention with my writing.

Through all this, I was uncovering my authentic self. In Hawaii and Ohio, imaginary worlds were a means of escape, a shield between me and the reality around me. But in middle school, they became a way to dream, a way to imagine the future, a way to move forward from a stunted emotional world into the life of one who truly lives. I was befriending and moving past some of my childhood defense mechanisms. I was starting to step out of the closet and into the light.

There's a lesson for the church in all this.

For inclusive churches: Are you truly inclusive? Do you speak the language of inclusion, but fail to follow through with your actions? Is there emotional room at your metaphorical lunch table, so that new people can sit down and see the proof behind the promises? Are you willing to leave the lunch table to go out and find the lost, or will you just sit where you are and wait for them to come to you? There are inclusive churches that talk a good game—but no one knows who they are or how welcome they might be. Or maybe people try to come, but they have to work too hard to find room at the table. Or maybe they get there and they find room to sit down—but is there room for them to be their authentic selves?

Is there room for us to be who we are?

Middle school kids feel pressure to conform. The unpopular ones fear the wrath of the popular. The popular fear that one wrong move will send them hurtling down the precarious social ladder. Too often, adults re-create these conditions.

Adults form themselves into cliques. They have "in" groups and "out." They seek like-minded people who they can claim as their tribe. They form social bonds by excluding and defining themselves in contrast to all the others. In some ways, this is a natural human instinct, but according to Jesus, when we reach across the lines that might otherwise divide us, we find him on the other side (Matthew 25:31-46). There is something divine about diversity.

Like kids in middle school, adults strive to be cool, to be well-liked and well-regarded, to be on top of their particular social pyramid. But the people at the top of the social hierarchy are just as insecure as the rest of us. They look confident. They look secure. They have all the trappings of being "in" and not "out," but they are afraid of losing their place. They know their perch on the top of the pyramid rests on a precarious blend of social approval and false perception.

Can you imagine what the world might be like if we were all just ourselves? Just honestly, unabashedly ourselves? If we gave others permission to be themselves, too? We could stop judging each other for offering authentic displays of who we are. We could stop pouncing on one another's vulnerabilities. We could stop being afraid that the cracks in our own armor would be exposed. We could take off the armor altogether.

We could all be part of the "in" group, no matter who we are. And we wouldn't have to define ourselves in opposition to others—because there would be no more others anymore.

What if we made the world more like an ideal, unrealized middle school? What if room at the lunch table was limitless?

This is what the church could be like. This is what the church should be like. This is what Jesus calls us to be, and this is what we are still far away from being.

8

Trying on Faith

WE MOVED AGAIN. So it goes.

I was in seventh grade. It was 1995.

This time, our move was a shift toward stability. We were no longer renters. We were buyers. From Branning, we moved to Nuttman, a street that was still on the outer edges of the territory of my school, to a house that was nicer and a neighborhood that had a different feel.

There was a certain depressive feeling to the house on Branning. It was dark and there weren't as many windows. Outside, the pavement was cracked. There was almost never a sound of kids playing outside. While we were there, the house had been broken into, and that made the living space feel dangerous, like you could never completely relax there.

Our new neighborhood was more inviting. The lawns were manicured. The people smiled. Kids played on the street. A whole new world was opening up to us.

I knew buying a house meant we were going to be there for a while, so I felt secure enough to make friends. There was Jamal, a boy up the road who was the same age as me. He went to a different school, but he was also being raised by a single mother. We bonded over that and video games on the Sega Genesis. There were also Felix and Ella Lane, a brother and sister who were younger than Jamal and me, but Felix was fast and could keep up athletically. They were homeschooled, and their dad worked at a church. To maintain peace with them, I didn't mention I was an atheist. Other kids came in and out of our lives, but that was the core group.

As an escape from the halls of middle school, this was so much better than the isolation of the house on Branning. Here, there were people in my life.

Here, I could create a world and be a hero as before, but now I could do it with friends by my side. Felix had a fantastic supply of toy swords and other equipment for adventurers. As a group, we played at the Lanes' house, outfitting characters whose heroic base was located on the front porch. At the base, we made our plans, and at the right time, we swooped into the backyard and completed a mission that orbited around the shed.

We played football and baseball in a string of connected front yards. I had a paper route, and sometimes Jamal and others would help me with my daily duties. We would roll the newspapers and cinch them with rubber bands, then ride our bikes around delivering papers, and then ride to the corner store where we bought Airheads, Swiss Cake Rolls, and comic books.

One day, the Lanes suggested something fun we could do—we could go to church with them! I was amused by this possibility. While I was a militant atheist in some contexts, I was a secret atheist in this one, and I was open to going to church. From a cultural anthropology perspective, I was curious to analyze the experience of worship.

That Sunday, the church was having a pool party after worship. The congregation was evangelical, non-denominational, and they met in the cafeteria of a middle school—not my middle school, thankfully. That week, they had arranged with a nearby high school to use the pool on Sunday afternoon. And we kids were invited.

By going with the Lanes, we got to see behind the scenes. Felix and Ella's dad was the leader of the worship band. He, along with the other staff and hardcore volunteers of the church, came early to set up the cafeteria and transform it into a worship space. This was also the time when the band rehearsed. For us kids, we could play in the gym or on the playground.

There turned out to be one very weird thing about this church: the fact that I liked it. The music was compelling. The preacher was charismatic and articulate. The moral teachings were solid—if you stripped away all the supernatural gobbledygook.

Don't get me wrong—the main attraction was the gym before the service and playing with friends in a new space that opened up new games and new possibilities. But I could understand why people liked this worship thing. I began to develop some understanding of belief, a recognition that it might be about more than unthinking inertia and family tradition. It was still irrational, but it was no longer completely inexplicable.

On subsequent Sundays, even without the pool party, Jamal and I went with the Lanes to church. Other kids in the neighborhood sometimes joined in. And when Jamal began to lose interest, I kept going. I liked the atmosphere of the church. Maybe it was because middle school was so hard for me—I liked this other place where everyone was friendly, encouraging, and joyful.

But it was more than that. I began to look forward to what the preacher would focus on next. I particularly remember a series he did, "What would Jesus say to. . ." with the ellipses filled in by Trent Reznor, Madonna, and so on. According to the pastor, Jesus would say, "I love you," and suggest that they fill the void in their hearts with something truly fulfilling. I liked the positivity of these messages.

But it was more than that, as well. I was feeling something in worship. My heart leapt to its feet with the music. My head bowed with solemnity when we prayed. The words of the preacher had me lifting my eyes in curiosity.

One Sunday, he had us bow our heads and close our eyes. He said it was very important that we all close our eyes and keep them closed, so that everyone could feel safe from prying eyes. He asked if there was anyone in the room who wanted to pursue a personal relationship with Jesus Christ, anyone in the room who needed to commit or recommit to life with God. We could indicate our desire by raising our hand. We could trust that every eye was closed but his, that this was a private moment between him, me, and the Lord.

I raised my hand. I heard the pastor's caring voice wash over me. "I see you. Christ sees you. The Lord is with you." He said the same words to others as their hands were raised.

I couldn't believe it. I was a believer!

What next? The Lanes had never really talked to me about attending Sunday School or youth group, and I hadn't asked. Even at church, the kids my age seemed intimidating, and I almost never talked to them. When I looked at them, it seemed like they were the popular kids at their respective schools—and me and the popular kids were never a great match.

I probably could have discovered the next steps of faith if I had just asked, but I never did. I had never told the Lanes I was an atheist, which made telling them that I was now a believer seem even more treacherous.

But I felt excited about what happened. For the next few weeks, when I went to church, I hung on the preacher's words even more and tried to absorb this newfound faith like a sponge.

But it never went anywhere. It was like the seed cast on rocky ground, which springs up with enthusiasm and then, just as quickly, withers away.

As I thought about my new faith, with deliberations that were inside my own head, not supported by people or books or any new spiritual practice outside of worship, I eventually decided I had been wrong to raise my hand. That Sunday, I had just been caught up in the psychology of the moment—the warmth of the invitation, the feeling of being part of a body with other people, the momentum of the service. I had been swept up by my emotions, but that didn't change all the intellectual arguments against belief.

So I went back to being the way I was: a militant atheist in some circles and a secret one among the Lanes. I did, however, continue attending church. Even though I didn't consider myself a believer, I still liked it.

Looking back from where I am now, I can see a progression toward this flicker of belief. It began with the emotional fervor of middle school. I was growing in years, and my emotional muscles were developing as well.

Those muscles weren't perfect, of course. They still aren't. But I was feeling more than I used to. The emotional muscles that teared up when Mufasa died and felt afraid when my mom and sister were fighting are the same ones that felt inspired in that converted middle school cafeteria, the same ones that felt love emanating from the pastor.

What I didn't have back then was the intellectual component of faith. I had no resources and no response to my own arguments against religion. Because I never talked about the hand-raising moment, because I never sought any of the resources that might have been available to me, I had no fuel to sustain the fire—and the flame flickered out.

Meanwhile, at our new house on Nuttman, I developed new interests. I continued collecting sports cards, but I took it to a whole new level. With my paper route proceeds, I was able to expand my collection to basketball and football, and also to buy boxes, and to pursue rare cards and complete sets and other holy grails of the collecting community.

I also enjoyed comic books. I remember Spawn the most, and when Wolverine had his own comic, I bought those. I looked for first issues and other comics with a low cumulative count. I wanted obscure heroes where I could get in on the ground floor and like them before everyone else did.

I was also getting into music. When we moved into the new house, Mom set up half of the basement as a cool hangout for Nicole, complete with rap posters and beanbag chairs and a nice stereo. Nicole enjoyed it a bit, at first, but she spent less time in this house than she had in our old one, and the listening room soon became mine.

My love for music began with the radio. At first, I listened to Top 40 stuff. After all, when I was a very little kid, in the pre-school age range, my two favorite songs were Billy Joel's "We Didn't Start the Fire" and Van Halen's "Jump." When I was four, I remember my mom asking me if I knew what "Jump" was really about, and I said, "Yeah, Mom. It's about jumping." If you're not familiar with the song, spoiler alert: it's not about jumping.

Still, it was around this time that Billy Joel was making one of his last comebacks with "River of Dreams," and I loved that song. I liked Boyz II Men, Shai, and a few other pop mainstays. However, as I flipped around the dial in seventh grade, my heart was soon converted from pop to alternative. Alternative rock became my musical home.

I loved "Hey, Jealousy," by the Gin Blossoms, and "Good," by Better than Ezra. I dug Ben Folds Five, Weezer, Bush, and Everclear. I started making tapes of my favorite songs, running to hit record on the cassette player when the first chords of a coveted song hummed across the airwaves. I remember calling into the alternative station one night and requesting "Hey, Jealousy," a song I'd been waiting for to complete a particular anthology. The guy on the phone said, "Okay." And I said, "That's it? That's all there is to it?" And he said, "Yeah." It was a compelling dialogue.

My mom's boyfriend Kyle helped expand my music repertoire. Based on what I liked from the radio, he made me tapes from his more obscure collection of indie rock and punk, bands like Rancid, Black Sabbath, NOFX, and Pennywise. He introduced me to the movie *Mallrats*, and I told him I liked Squirtgun, a sort of pop-punk band from the *Mallrats* soundtrack. From there, I heard more Squirtgun, and also Too Much Joy and The Tragically Hip.

In the void in my soul where religion had flickered for a moment, there were cards, comics, music, and *Star Wars*—and there was a renewed affirmation of atheism. Like Trent Reznor and Madonna and the other sermon-series celebrities, I was looking for something indefinable, and I didn't know the indefinable was divine.

For a while, I was intrigued by PETA, People for the Ethical Treatment of Animals. As an adult, I can say that I'm not fully on board with their whole philosophical critique of anthropocentrism, but the important thing for middle-school-me was that Kyle was a member of PETA. That was enough to capture my attention, and once they had my attention, my natural compassion and thirst for justice held it there.

When I was doing a school report on elephants, Kyle gave me a copy of a PETA magazine with an exposé on the cruel treatment of circus elephants. That became the focus of my report—and I still today have never been to a circus with animals. I refuse to go to one.

Through the PETA magazine, I learned about foie gras and the inhumane treatment of the animals it comes from—and I still today have never eaten foie gras. Or veal, for that matter. I learned about the medication Premarin and the cruel animal practices connected to its production. After doing more research of my own, I became outraged, as well. The magazine instructed readers to call the Eli Lilly pharmaceutical company and complain, and I had enough experience making prank calls to 1–800 numbers that a protest call to Eli Lilly felt like a natural form of activism. To top it all off, for a few weeks, I was a vegetarian, just like Kyle, but I couldn't keep it up. There was bologna in the refrigerator and I was powerless to resist it. My vegetarianism was as short-lived as my personal relationship with Jesus Christ.

Meanwhile, Nicole grew up quickly, in ways that we all should have expected but no one saw coming. First of all, when I was in eighth grade and she was in twelfth, she graduated a semester early. She was eager to get out of her public school hellscape—which she would have defined in different terms than me, more of an academic hell than a social one, but hell nonetheless. Part of her escape was through vocational training, spending half the school day learning culinary arts at a vocational center downtown. Through that program, she was connected to work at the Hilton Hotel, a place where she really seemed to find her groove, and where she was recognized and affirmed.

She had her first kid two months after graduation.

I was always back and forth with Nicole. Sometimes, I wanted her to change her ways and pursue a more traditional path in life. At other times, I enjoyed being in on the secrets she carried. I liked being on her side as she subverted the customs of our middle-class world.

Back then, I may not have always liked what I saw, but I knew how to keep a secret. In fact, in the house on Nuttman, Nicole sometimes trusted me to act as a lookout, to keep an eye open for Mom and Kyle when she was up in her room with her boyfriend, practicing the act that would eventually lead to Latrell, her oldest child.

When it came to the pregnancy, Mom was unaware of it at first. She was aware that Nicole had gained weight, but she was reluctant to ask questions about it. After all, weight gain was a potential side effect of the birth control Nicole was supposed to be taking, and Mom didn't want to give her a complex about that.

Still, when the truth came out, she was supportive. She encouraged Nicole's pre-natal health and prepared herself to do what she could for her grandchild.

Latrell was born premature. He spent the first several weeks of his life in a NICU. When he came home, he still had a breathing machine to help his little lungs. Mom and Nicole attended an infant CPR class so they would be trained on what to do in case of an emergency. I was willing to go too, but Nicole's doctor thought I was too young. If something were to happen to Latrell, and I tried to save him but was unable, that might be traumatic.

Trauma? Really? You're worried about me undergoing trauma?

I loved Latrell. He was the first baby in my life. As an adult, I learned that people who had troubled childhoods are often drawn to children. We find them easier to relate to than our peers, who are always sort of a mystery to us. Also, having fun with kids helps us relive the parts of our childhood that we lost. Often, we develop a sort of protective instinct around kids, perhaps as a kind of surrogate protection to the child we once were.

Soon after Latrell was born, Nicole moved out of our house and into a new place with her boyfriend. With her job as a prep chef at the Hilton, and his job as a drug dealer, they had enough income to rent a low-budget apartment on the second floor of a house in an economically wounded neighborhood.

I should note that this drug-dealer boyfriend was different from the earlier drug-dealer boyfriend, the one whose influence had led to trouble in our first Fort Wayne apartment. I should also note that Mom and I were unaware of the drug-dealing, or perhaps "intentionally ignorant" is a better way to put it.

Kyle stepped away from our lives at this time. He was ten years younger than my mother, and he felt he was too young to be dating a grandmother. He offered to keep being around for me, and he was from time to time, but it was awkward for both of us.

People come and people go, you know? Attachment should be light because parting is inevitable. Even in this relatively stable season of life, there was still the chaos of coming and going.

When I entered ninth grade and started high school, we didn't move again, but something moved into the house that changed the whole world: a personal computer with a dial-up modem. It was 1997. America Online was in its heyday. And I was intrigued by the new worlds waiting to be discovered online.

By this time, I had already been pulling away from Jamal, Felix, and Ella. Our childlike games no longer interested me, and once I discovered alternative music, the listening room in my basement became far more compelling than church. As I began developing private interests at home, my friends didn't come with me to those new places, and I didn't go with them to the destinations that intrigued them. Even before the computer came, I was already drifting away from these connections.

With the transition to ninth grade, there was another monumental change: Gerald and Trent went to a different high school, a private Lutheran school called Concordia. Mom was happy to pay for me to go there, as well, but I recognized that I had probably outgrown the two of them—and that my friendship with Trent had taken a cruel and callous turn. I was glad to go to a different school than them.

In high school, I was captivated by poetry. It started in English class, with Phyllis Wheatley, Robert Frost, and Maya Angelou. It continued when Mom would take me to bookstores, and I discovered poets on my own. E.E. Cummings soon led to Allen Ginsberg and Lawrence Ferlinghetti. I had indeed seen "the best minds of my generation destroyed by madness, starving hysterical naked." Those words were a delightful electrical shock through my spine. I loved the off-beat Beats.

The image of the poet occupied the place in my heart that had been held by the comedian and the underdog sports team, by the tribal leader standing on the margins of "civilization." These were the outsiders. The bearers of truth whose position on the edge enabled them to see through the facade and make meaning of the madness. They made me feel less out-of-place in an off-kilter world. They gave me a literary home to call my own.

It was not too long into ninth grade before I began imagining who I would be as a grown-up. I would live the artist's life in a small apartment in New York City, writing poems and drinking coffee in eclectic cafes. My tattered notebook would be an ever-present anthology in my back pocket. The stories of Kerouac and Capote added to the vision of who I could be, to my carbonated resonance with these modern post-modernists—as they critiqued suburbia, commerce, and the chaos of modern life. I could imagine myself an off-beat, atheist outsider, scribbling profound poems, speaking truth to power, and living life with joy and freedom. In the city.

Yeah, maybe no one in my life could understand me. Yeah, maybe I was the one off-beat Beat in my culturally isolated high school. But in New York, I knew there would be more of us. In New York, I could become the person I was meant to be.

And even in ninth grade, from the top of my desk in Indiana, I could find people like me.

Through America Online, I discovered chatrooms full of people with common interests connecting with each other across spans of time and space. This was relatively early in the Age of the Internet. There was no Facebook, or anything close to what we now know as social media, where you might intentionally connect with people you know in real life. What we had were chatrooms, and they were a complete roll of the dice. Each one was a new introduction to a new community of people. Some chatrooms were based on geography. Others were based on interests, like atheism and evolution.

Online, I became an even more militant atheist. I already enjoyed intellectual sparring with people I met in person. Online, the arguments were easier to come by, and those arguments confirmed my convictions and sharpened my swords for defending them. Offline, I read books by Robert Ingersoll, Bertrand Russell, and Jean-Paul Sartre. Online, I argued with evangelicals, taking up the cause of science, evolution, and a modern approach to the great, existential questions.

Through the internet, I began tasting a flavor of atheism I had not known before: atheism in community, experienced with people who believed the same things and argued the same points until we became, in some ways, indistinguishable from one another. In our chatrooms, I think I had more pity for our Christian interlocutors than others did. I didn't like seeing anyone on any side get ganged up on. At times, the conversations felt pitiful and cruel. But at other times, it felt like I had found my tribe, like I wasn't alone in my off-beat outlook on the world.

I could see some strains of today's vitriol in these early days of the internet, but for the most part, I found the joy of discovering a community. Here were other people who employed an extensive vocabulary. Here were outsiders like me. Here were people who thought with depth, passion, and love.

"Love?" you may say, with a bit of skepticism in your voice, and it's a fair question. But please remember, our freethinking group was not the first to be cruel to outsiders out of love for insiders—or out of love for those who might be one of us one day. We were atheistic evangelists. We wanted to save young people from a life of unthinking loyalty to an imaginary being, to a human system touting ancient rules no longer suited for the modern world, to intellectual captors who wanted to capture their minds and perhaps even traumatize their hearts.

We wanted to help people unlock the secrets of reality and live each day to the fullest. After all, there was no world after this one, no life but right here, no day but today. So let's live for the moment. And if that's what you believe, isn't it the very definition of love to tell people about it, to engage in intellectual contests about it, and to strive to de-convert the believers?

The part of me that wanted to be a freedom fighter, that wanted to stand up and raise my voice and not just accept the world as it is, loved this new way of being. If I was going to be a freedom fighter, could I do it online, in a secluded corner of the house, where no one could see my beet-red face and hear my voice as it trembled?

Building this atheist community online gave me confidence to more openly express my atheistic views at school. I well remember the day in my ninth grade English class, when we were preparing to read the Book of Ruth from the Old Testament. It was one of many religious stories from one of many different traditions that appeared in our textbook. Our teacher was all too eager to have a school-sanctioned reason to take it up. But he felt the need to justify the choice first, speaking to us about the literary quality of the Book of Ruth and the Bible's place in history. He said that reading the Bible was worthwhile for us, no matter what our religious views might be, because it was regarded as a sacred text by so many.

"In fact," he said. "Who here thinks of the Bible as a sacred text? Go ahead and raise your hand if the Bible is sacred to you."

All but two of us raised our hands. The two dissenters were me and Sandy Smith.

Personally, I was offended by the question. I didn't think it was right for us to be compelled to talk about our religious views in the classroom, especially when it was obvious that he was coming from a Christian perspective. What if we were judged for what we believed? What if our grades suffered for not believing the same thing as our teacher? Still, I liked English more than any other class, and I liked this teacher more than any other teacher, and I relished the opportunity to be an atheistic evangelist.

"Okay," he said. "Most of us think of the Bible as sacred, but not everyone. Steve, why didn't you raise your hand?"

I was feeling confident that day, and I expressed myself clearly. "Because I'm an atheist," I said. "I think there are better ways to look at the world—more modern, more realistic ways to look at the world."

"Well, alright," he responded. "Yeah. That's a good reason. Sure."

And we continued our discussion.

Meanwhile, online, I continued my search for community. The atheistic evangelists were great, but there was a whole wide world waiting at my fingertips, and I was eager to explore its contours. That journey of discovery eventually led me to Rhy'Din, a chatroom-based world where players engaged in online role-playing in the spirit of Dungeons and Dragons.

Now, I know that some of your heads exploded when you read that last sentence. Role-playing? Dungeons and Dragons? What does that even mean? Let me try to explain—and let me assure you, before I do, that the explanation is going somewhere and I hope you'll do your best to follow along.

Among the various AOL-generated chatrooms of the day, there were rooms with the heading "Red Dragon Inn." They had a number attached. If a certain number of people occupied "Red Dragon Inn 1," a 2 would be created, and so on. Rhy'Din was a shortened, lyricized version of the name of the chat room, with the R sound from 'Red' and the D sound from 'Dragon' and the In sound from, well, you know. Anyway, those chatrooms were thought of as a sort of medieval tavern in an imaginary world where the mundane rules of Earth do not apply. The occupants of the chatroom all played characters in that world. Some of those characters might have magical powers and others might be elves and orcs. Some might be common human beings who just happened to pop in for a pint of ale. There were many possibilities.

Think of the room like a canvas. As players of the game, we had an implied agreement about what the space was like—about its feel and its furnishings, about its sense of being a place for travelers where anyone who makes sense in that world might come. Based on that implied agreement, we could all paint with each other on the canvas. In those roadside inns, any traveler from any land, with either magical abilities or common abilities, with as much or as little history as the traveler cared to share, might appear. Given our consensus on the construction of the canvas and the background of the painting, we could fill in the work of art with characters of our own creation—with their thoughts, dreams, actions, and interactions.

In these rooms, our characters would live their imaginary lives. Some came through the front door with their swords drawn, ready to pick a fight. Others preferred dialogue, storytelling, and simulated romance. Within this constantly changing, constantly reemerging community, there was room for many different players, many different characters, and many different ways of adding brushstrokes to the painting.

From Rhy'Din, I encountered another community. Apparently, there was a set of chatrooms where people played role-playing games centered around Star Wars. My adventure started when I met a fellow Rhy'Din player with the screen name "Jedi Mia." In the game, she was sultry and flirtatious. In her profile—every AOL screen name had a profile, where other users could click on your online moniker and learn your real name (or your fake name), your real location (or your fake location), or whatever else you wanted to announce to the world—she mentioned Star Wars "simming" as one of her interests. What was that? I wanted to know more.

I started instant messaging with Jedi Mia, a one-on-one conversation outside of the larger chat room, outside of the context of the game—just one real person to another real person—and through that, I learned about another imaginary world. I learned that simming was short for simulating, and that there were online communities set up to enable it. Dozens if not hundreds of people were playing elaborate simulations set a long time ago in a galaxy far, far away.

Star Wars simming was basically the same as Rhy'Din role-playing, but trade out a wooden tavern for the metal bridge of a star cruiser, and trade out the swords for an X-Wing and a lightsaber.

As soon as I learned about simming, I was hooked.

I still played in Rhy'Din from time to time—to sharpen my game-playing skills or to have something to do—but the Star Wars galaxy was where I was destined to be.

In my offline reading life, while I sometimes consumed elevated works in the literary canon, Star Wars novels were my junk food. And who doesn't like junk food? We eat Cheetos for a reason. Star Wars sourcebooks were full of intrigue for me. I loved learning the intricate details of the Star Wars galaxy, and I jumped at the chance to play a character in the beautiful, expansive canvas George Lucas created. Lucas always said that his galaxy was meant to hold an infinitude of stories. On any planet, there could be a new character, a new race, a new galactic narrative. I wanted to create my own stories within that creative space. I wanted to play in that universe with people like Mia.

Jedi Mia was a kid like me, a teenager who was a little older than me, living in the suburbs of Atlanta. She wasn't hugely popular at her high school, but she found a sense of kinship in online role-playing communities, nerding out with all the other nerds scattered around the country.

As it turns out, there were lots of people like Mia and me—kids who were too smart or too creative, who had grown up too fast or too weird-looking, who were too often bullied for not fitting in. Online, we could all fit in with each other. At the same time, we could create and inhabit characters who were not weird looking, but who were instead tall and handsome, heroic and romantic.

In one way, we were meeting an all-too-real, all-too-human need, creating a peer group in the nooks and crevices of our world. At the same time, we were also engaging in wish fulfillment, presenting ourselves online as something different from what we were, something we could only hope to be, and could only manage to be with our fingers flashing across the keys as our characters conquered a chatroom.

Freud would have had a field day with my first character.

In the Star Wars simming community, as in Rhy'Din, some people created their own intricate characters with elaborate backstories. The more committed players would create a screen name with the name of their character and then use HTML to craft their profiles into extravagant introductions for their fictional personas. Other people played "media" characters from the movies or novels: Luke Skywalker, Princess Leia, Grand Moff Tarkin, Grand Admiral Thrawn.

As in Rhy'Din, those characters could interact in public chatrooms where the game might begin and die out in a few minutes or a few hours. Some of us were galactic travelers in a tavern setting in chat rooms labeled "Mos Eisley Cantina." Some of us careened through space, engaged in intergalactic combat with starfleets or starfighters.

The first character of my own creation was Lekk Starn. Lekk was a Corellian—which is to say, a human being from the planet Corellia. He was tall, around 6'4," with smooth black hair. And he was an X-wing pilot with the Rebel Alliance. He was intergalactically handsome, charming, romantic, and all the rest. Oh, and he had the best training. He had gone to the Academy and joined the Imperial Navy, where he earned his "Corellian bloodstripe," a prestigious military decoration he wore on the right leg of his otherwise jet-black flight suit.

Of course, he defected from the Empire in response to its cruelty. He was a smuggler for a while—not unlike Han Solo, who was also a Corellian who had gone to the Academy, joined the Imperial Navy, earned a Corellian bloodstripe, and so on. My character was basically a taller and more handsome Han Solo with a deeper sense of loyalty to the Rebel Alliance.

And like Han Solo, his parents were dead. Our parents were all dead. In the simming community, it was a kind of perverse joke that everyone's parents were dead. It was part of almost all our backstories. Narratively speaking, our parents' deaths marked the moment when our characters realized there was nothing left for them on their respective home planets. It was the moment when they developed a lifelong vendetta against the group or person that killed said parents. That loss marked the moment when our adventures began.

On the psychological side, I might describe our collective orphanhood as an affirmation that, even in this brave new world that has such people in it, we were still existentially alone. But at least we could be alone together.

I don't know the personal backstories of all the teenagers who made their way to this little community through an online platform in the mid- to-late nineties, but I know that many of them were as disappointed in their parents as I was, as alienated from their peers as I was, and as lonely as I was.

Some of my less nerdy readers will wonder why I spent so much time explaining the dynamics and mechanics of this online world. It's because I want you to see that it really was its own world. This wasn't just high school me hacking away at a computer because it was a fun little diversion. This was me living in an alternate reality, joining with others to create a third space and a new life within it, a life that was better than what I knew in the mundane world.

For me, life in high school wasn't much better than life in middle school. It was a slightly bigger and more interesting world. The books were better, and Trent and the abusers who sat our lunch table were gone. But what were they replaced by? I was still unathletic. I was still weird looking. I was still called "fag" by a lot of my peers who wondered about my sexuality.

I was still smaller than a lot of my peers. Like a lot of kids who were born later in the year, most of my classmates were a few months ahead of me. Everyone else had a head start on physical development—a head start that had exponentially multiplied through the years and become an unsolvable equation by high school.

I was strange and off-putting, and in some ways, I hated that. I wished I could just be a normal person doing normal things. But in other ways, I relished my place as the outsider. With atheism at my side, I could intentionally make myself even more of an outsider. I could engage in the classic strategy of life and social warfare: emphasizing a liability and transforming it into a strength.

You may think of me as strange, I said to the world. But I am unique.

You may think of me as a know-it-all, but I seek and espouse the truth.

You may think of me as an outsider, and in fact, I am the ultimate outsider, the one who will rail against heaven itself because there's something bigger and more real—and I want to tell you about it.

You might push me around in gym class.

You might taunt me and exclude me on the bus.

You might point at me and snicker at me when I read my book while others chat.

But I have at least one thing up on you. I'm a truth-teller. I'm smart. I'm compassionate, as any good humanist ought to be. I'm optimistic, not because a mystical being inspires my optimism, but because I believe in the human spirit.

This defiant attitude was perhaps not the healthiest path toward valuing my emerging authentic self, but it was the best I could do at the time. It was the path that led to the divine aspects of me that compose the image of God within me. Through that path, I would eventually find God herself.

In fact, I wouldn't have said it this way then, but I'll say it now: I was learning to believe in myself, and that's a prerequisite for faith in God. How can I love God with all my heart, soul, mind, and strength, and love my neighbor as myself, if I do not begin by loving the person I'm closest to—if I do not begin by loving the *imago Dei* in me?

At the time, I was painfully aware of my flaws and eccentricities, but I was also wearing them as badges of honor, like a Corellian bloodstripe for my heart and soul. More and more, I was beginning to like the real me.

9

Romantic Affinities

He was the only boy who was brave enough to take a shower.

In the high school locker room, there were ninth grade boys who would dress and undress for the regular, required gym class, and eleventh grade and older boys who would do the same for weightlifting. Weightlifting was an elective class, full of mature kids with well-developed bodies.

Most of us, in either class, were fast and furtive about the things we had to do in that room. We kept our shirts on while we changed our shorts. We kept our shorts on while we changed our shirts. We exposed our underwear for the least amount of time humanly possible. We figuratively held our breath until we could leave the room and wait in the bleachers for the bell to ring and the next period to begin.

Almost none of us took showers in that locker room, except for one boy: Dan. He was the son of a teacher I had when I was younger. Because his dad was a great teacher, I began my admiration of Dan with a fond sense of connection I nursed in my mind and never told him about. That mental connection enhanced the physical admiration, and oh, there was physical admiration.

I had noticed boys before. I knew that I wasn't gay, because I knew that I liked girls, too, but I was beginning to feel the stirrings of other attractions, and those stirrings were confirmed by Dan. Every week, every other day, when I had gym and he had weightlifting, he would walk naked past my locker as he made his way to the showers and back.

There was not a doubt in mind that I was attracted to him, and that I wanted to drink in every ounce of him my eyes could gather. I knew I could not stare at him as openly as I wanted—out of respect for him and fear of others. Still, I looked as much as I could.

Eventually, other boys noticed my looking. If Dan himself noticed, he never said anything. But the other boys made fun of me. They asked if I was gay. Some of them skipped the question and went right to the appellation.

One boy, a notorious bully named Ben Houston, defended me. One time, the usual name-calling escalated to pushing and shoving. Ben put himself in the middle, and with all of his bully's strength and aggression, convinced the other kids to back off. It was brave of him. There was something about Ben's position as an outsider that led him to identify with me—and even to defend me.

Heck, for all I know, maybe he liked me, though he could have never admitted it in our high school social world. For my part, I was just grateful, and glad to be seen as a person worth defending.

In high school, I did not consider it an option to explore my developing romantic affinities. Even with girls, the risk of putting myself out there was too great. The risk of rejection and embarrassment and a deeper isolation was more than I could stand. However, I could safely explore online.

In Rhy'Din, for example, I could enter any number of Red Dragon Inns and meet beautiful elven princesses and dark-skinned hunters who spent their lives in the woods. We could have romantic encounters in the larger chatroom and then, with mutual consent (often involving some "OOC," or out-of-character conversation, achieved in instant messaging windows or ((double parentheses)) in the chat), we could move to a private chat room where our characters could enjoy each other.

In Rhy'Din, I could seek out encounters with men and women and explore them both to my heart's content, and I could do it without the risk of social isolation and ostracism. The transitory nature of this chat room and the world it represented meant I was unlikely to see any of my fellow players again. There were no social consequences to what we were doing and no physical consequences, either. It was just people learning about their bodies, their minds, their likes and dislikes, and their ability to communicate it all with keystrokes in the night.

In Rhy'Din, one of my favorite characters to play was Ariella, an olive-skinned, red-cheeked, dark-haired hunter, skilled with a bow and arrow. She was the embodiment of the kind of woman I most wanted, the image of a woman who existed in what Jung might call my *anima,* and she was a way to have sex with men. As Ariella, men would be struck by my athletic beauty and singular grace, and I would take them to the woods where we could have our way with each other.

In one memorable encounter, the boy I met was so nervous about the whole thing. He was attracted to Ariella and he was interested in what we might do together, but he had never done anything like this before. I spent several minutes talking with him OOC, convincing him to bring his character to the woods. Eventually, I told him not to worry, that I would guide him. Once we got to our private chat room, I typed out a beautiful picture with words that captured the simulated actions of us both. It was a remarkable little romance novella, and we both left feeling excited and fulfilled. He wanted to know when he could see me again. I thought, "That's cute. We're not going to be seeing each other again."

In these encounters, I enjoyed the power I could have over men through Ariella. I enjoyed the power of what I could do to them with my words.

Of course, the boy in the memorable encounter—and any of the other people I met—could have been absolutely anyone on their side of the computer, just as I could have been absolutely anyone on mine. For the attraction to work, I conveyed the illusion that I was a girl "IRL," or In Real Life, and who knows who they were in real life?

Looking back on it, I suppose I was opening myself up to the possibility of predation. But even in our OOC conversations, I never talked to any of these people about meeting IRL. Yes, they could have been anyone and may have been attempting to conjure up some sort of illusion about themselves. But so was I. For a moment, we had a meaningful encounter with each other, as people playing characters who were more or less extensions of ourselves, and that was enough.

Through all this, I began embracing the word "bisexual" as an identity. I found the word through *Chasing Amy* and *Ellen,* the short-lived early-nineties sitcom. I learned more about it through online research, as I strove to make sense of who I was.

I didn't seek out this identity. It found me in the locker room when I was exposed to male bodies in all their splendor and was confirmed by social experiments in my online laboratory. I didn't spend a lot of time questioning whether it was my real identity or not. It was. I knew it. And while I shuddered to name it in the challenging social world of high school, I had no shame about embracing it in my mind.

In retrospect, I am glad I was not part of a church at this time. I am glad I was not a Christian yet. I was able to embrace a sense of who I might love without even a whisper of a notion that it might be wrong to do so. Later, when I became a Christian, I could deal with the retrograde attitudes of people in the church. Later, I could deal with our general fear and prudishness about sexuality. But for now, I'm glad that the kid in this story got to explore who he was without the church getting in the way.

At the same time, in ways I never could have imagined, these high school years set the stage for my religious conversion. They guided me toward the college I eventually attended. They led me to the book that unveiled the possibility of a metaphysical world. Those years were an essential part of my continued emotional journey—my journey through the hard things that lead to something good.

Though my best friends were online, I had a few friends in the mundane world of high school. I found my way to a handful of kids who were smart, funny, and a little nerdy: Sam, Matt, Alex, and Justin, a group that coalesced in Freshman Honors English and stayed together through the next four years.

Like me, these guys were into comedy, and they had seen some of the classics: Mel Brooks and Monty Python and old Saturday Night Lives. We had fun quoting the lines to each other, pretending we were Black Knights who were constantly losing limbs, and demanding more cowbell.

They were one step above me on the high school social ladder. In fact, they all had some measure of athletic and aesthetic prowess—and were sometimes considered to be right on the verge of cool. Thanks to them, I had a socially-average, moderately well-regarded place to sit at lunch.

The alternative would have been the true nerds' table, the absolute reject table, the kids who were even smaller and lonelier than me. Some of them were noticeably very poor. Some of them may have been intellectually disabled or somewhere on the autism spectrum. As an adult looking back, I want to go back there and save them from all the challenges they were facing, including the ravages of the high school social world, but as a kid, I was only concerned about self-preservation—I just wanted to avoid being made fun of.

During my sophomore year, because of the vagaries of the block schedule and class electives, I had a different lunch period than my friends for half of the week. I tried pushing my way into Drew's table, the one I had tried to join in middle school, but it was just as crowded as before. I tried sitting at the so-called losers' table and reading my book, but I was stigmatized, made fun of, and bullied.

When I discovered that some kids skipped lunch and spent that period in the library, I was grateful. I began doing just that—and was glad to escape the madding crowds.

For some brave souls, I suppose this would have been a chance to exercise compassion, to stand up for the kids at the losers' table and use my social capital for their good. But my social capital was limited, and it diminished with each day I sat with them.

Others might have seen this as an opportunity to make new friends, to turn away from the socially ostracized table, sit down somewhere new, and actually start a conversation. Through activities like the school newspaper, our public access TV show, and the Academic Super Bowl, I knew plenty of kids outside of my usual circle. What if I went up to the people I knew and asserted that I had a place at their lunch table?

But this was never me—not in real life, anyway. I was too afraid of rejection, of being turned away or laughed at. This is why I read books during the social moments of high school. My book was a shield that saved me from having to take social risks. My goal was to hide as much as I could, to duck down and avoid attention.

This is one of the many consequences of trauma in my life. My existence was not about thriving, but surviving. The terms of the world were a given truth to be navigated with terror, not a fungible reality to be renegotiated in response to my needs and desires. I was not going to push my way into new friendships. I might be scrutinized. I might be rejected. I could not imagine the horror.

Rather than trying to renegotiate the world and its intricate web of social cliques and hierarchies, it was easier to escape to the library. After all, my real world was online, empowered by all the whistles, tones, and static that remind so many kids of my generation of signing on to America Online. In the online realm, Rhy'Din was for exploration and fun, and I met true friends through Star Wars simming. After high school, I didn't stay in touch with anyone from the mundane world, but I stayed in touch with kids I met through Star Wars.

For example, there was the aforementioned Jedi Mia. My first real romantic relationship.

After meeting each other in the fantasy world of Rhy'Din, we chatted OOC in Instant Messenger, and the connection was electric. It was the kind of feeling I had been longing to feel with another person.

To some observers, I suppose this experience doesn't seem real, because we were missing all the body language and uncertain intensity of an IRL encounter. But in some ways, our online connection was even more real because we were not judging each other physically. In the days before cell phones and selfies, when most people did not have scanners of any quality at home, people had to move heaven and earth to share pictures with one another. My connection with Mia was not a physical one. It was emotional and intellectual. It was built on the firm foundation of our words.

The feelings were real. The emotional intimacy was real. We shared our childhood stories and future aspirations; we shared the joys and travails of navigating our respective high schools. I told her about my dream of becoming a New York City poet; she told me about her love of anime and Japan. The romance was real, and the simulated sex was real, with each of us furiously typing romance novels to each other between the double colons that indicated an action performed in our virtual world.

Mia and I dated, off and on, for a year and a half. Eventually, the romance fizzled and was replaced by a friendship. I was the one who pulled away. I didn't have the language at the time to say that there was an emotional block, that there was only so much intimacy I could handle—that I had to keep stepping away from the relationship—because the closer we got, the more terrifying it was. It was something I both desperately wanted and couldn't bear.

I struggled with some of my classes in high school, particularly math and science. They involved a lot of memorization, and I didn't devote much time to studying equations and formulas. After all, when I grew up, I was going to move to New York City and become a poet. What would I do with chemistry and pre-calculus? But unfortunately, I had to enroll in them. If I wanted to take Honors English, I had to take upper-level math and science courses too, but they weren't my cup of peroxide. I earned Ds and Fs in many of them.

I hate to chalk everything up to trauma, but failing these classes and not asking for help—that was trauma.

Alfred Adler says that, by the age of six, children develop a basic understanding of the world and their place in it. They develop a sense of their own value, basic beliefs about the goodness or harshness of the world, and a sense of the ideal—a sense of what a good life would look like if the goals of their life were achieved. All of this is called a style of life, or lifestyle.

Decades after Adler, we may contend with some of the details of his concept, but the basic idea makes intuitive sense. We learn more by the age of three than we will for the rest of our lives, simply because we are learning language and developing a conceptual map of the world. By the age of six, we learn many of the patterns of relating that will define the rest of our lives, either because they define our relationships with others or because we make an intentional, often arduous, effort to learn new ways of being in the world.

Using different terminology, this arduous work is another way to describe the journey from the false self to authenticity.

For me, part of my false self-conception was that I could not ask for help and expect a loving, meaningful response. Call it my false self, or call it a style of life, but either way this was part of my emotional template.

Some people, in their early experiences, learn to say what's on their mind, to express their thoughts and feelings, to express their desires and needs—and to anticipate a loving response in return. These people are socialized into one crucial aspect of authenticity: community. After all, the authentic self is built for community with others. It is intended to exist in loving harmony with God and with all creation. Some people are raised so that this aspect of authenticity is something they present to the world.

However, for me, my communal instincts were buried. I could be friendly to others. I could even approximate love, but I could not ask them for help. In my mind, no one could or would help, either because they were not able to do so or because they did not care about me.

For any challenge I faced, the solution was to solve it myself, often by withdrawing. So I simply withdrew from these math and science classes. I did not withdraw formally—which would have involved talking to someone and admitting the issue and asking for assistance—but informally, by going through the motions and barely doing the work.

Amidst these failures, I just kept my focus on the places where my intellectual and emotional needs were being met: the books I was reading, the classes I loved, and the online worlds I could create.

When my mom became aware of the academic issues, one of her first responses was to take the internet away. It was a natural response. I spent so much time in the America Online universe. Of course she would reason that it was distracting me from the work most people would have considered more important. But I was a depressed teenager who had found hope and connection in that virtual world. Taking the internet away disrupted the simming at the center of my universe, separated me from my true friends, and was an existential threat to my developing sense of self—and my emerging romantic world.

Fortunately, Jedi Mia would not be deterred by a disruption in the internet. She loved me enough to exchange phone numbers and call me, and the nerdy teenage conversations that captivated us over Instant Messenger transferred to the phone lines, where we experimented with phone sex. That was a whole new level of physical and emotional connection. The intimacy was thrilling and intimidating all at once.

Thankfully, the internet returned soon enough, and Mom tried other means to reach my recalcitrant academic heart. She appealed to my desire to get into a good college, but I didn't need to get into a good college to do what I wanted. For me, any school would do. Don't get me wrong: I was looking forward to college. I saw it as a place where I would thrive as an artist and an intellectual, learn at a higher level, and find a social world that would feel as much like home as America Online. But I knew I could do that at IUPUI (Indiana University-Purdue University Indianapolis) as well as I could at

Sarah Lawrence. My hopes for college weren't pinned to the prestige of my future alma mater.

Mom found tutors for me, and they helped a little, academically, but they weren't able to identify the ache at the center of it all. It would have taken a therapist to do that. The issue was that I just didn't care. I didn't care about external rewards. I wasn't seeking titles like Valedictorian or Most Likely to Succeed. I didn't feel an urgent need to get into a "good" college. I was just trying to survive high school long enough to enable my escape from it all.

And as for Mom, she had enough to deal with, with my sister and her kids and our grandparents and life. I was not the focus of her attention for long.

Could the mundane world of high school have been different for me? Could it have felt more like a home to live in and less like a prison to escape?

There were kids in higher grades who played Dungeons and Dragons, a game I was interested in learning—with people I would have liked to get to know. For all I know, they may have been into Star Wars, as well.

There were kids I met through working on the school paper, one of whom I could have gone to prom with my junior year. We talked about it, but I just never had the courage to ask.

There were alternative kids, who I sometimes hung out with in study hall or in our school's TV production crew, but I lacked courage with them, as well. What would have happened if I had walked up to their clump across from the cafeteria before school? How could I tell them that I liked the same music as them, that I felt like an outsider just like they did, and that I wanted to be an outsider with them? I had visions of them pushing me away before the conversation could even begin.

In one of my gym classes, I hung out with an alternative kid. We were often the last and second-to-last people picked for teams, so we bonded over that. I did try with him. I tried hard to make fun of the class with him, and to make fun of other students. I had some of the same outsider impulses he did, but it wasn't my inclination to be mean-spirited like he was. Still, I hoped I could impress him with my wit. I hoped that if I were smart enough and funny enough, he would become my introduction to the world he inhabited. But our superficial friendship ended when he called me "the most boring person alive" and said he preferred his own company to mine. If crying was something I did at the time, I might have cried.

At the end of the day, I avoided taking risks. I was afraid of rejection. I would rather learn to live with a status quo that was so unbearably lonely, my thoughts had been starting to turn darker, entering the realm of suicide.

Even so, the fear of what could be outweighed the very real pain of what already was.

On the Academic Team, I was the captain of the English, Social Studies, and Interdisciplinary squads. I relished leading our team to state competitions in all three areas, beating private schools like Trent and Gerald's along the way. There was a kid on the Academic Team who was a year younger than me, Subhan. During practices and on bus rides, we loved talking about politics and culture. But did I take a social risk with him? Did we ever arrange to get together outside of school? Of course not.

My friend Justin wanted me to come to his house to play Axis and Allies and listen to Pink Floyd. The only risk I would have needed to take was asking my mom for a ride, but I wasn't willing to do that. I didn't want to be a bother. One day, when Justin invited me over, I said yes, but I stood him up because I wouldn't ask for a ride.

I didn't even get my driver's license until I was in college, even though I learned to drive while I was in high school. I took driver's ed, and Kyle taught me a thing or two in various parking lots and on the road. But getting a driver's license involved a new level of vulnerability: I would have to set up an appointment with the DMV; I would have to get someone, probably my mom, to take me there and wait while I was tested. Ultimately, I just didn't want to ask her to do that. She worked at night and slept during the day, and I didn't think I was important enough to interrupt her sleep. I told myself that it was because I had nowhere to drive. My best friends were online. My hobbies were at home. But really, I just didn't want to ask for help.

Most of all, I didn't want people to notice me. I felt like a piece of crap, like I wasn't worth anyone's time and attention—not as their friend, not as their brother, not as their son. I wasn't worth it. If they knew who I was, they would reject me, but perhaps if I could keep myself hidden enough, they would never see me, and at least then I could last a little longer.

Once, I almost could have thought about dating a girl in the non-virtual world. That person was Sandy Smith, the girl in my sophomore English class, the only other person who didn't raise their hand when our teacher asked us if we considered the Bible a sacred text. She was a beautiful girl with a dyed blonde streak in her smooth brown hair, who wore peasant skirts and wrote poetry, who played the acoustic guitar and styled herself as a singer-songwriter. Throughout the two years I knew her, my heart beat like a drum for her. But I would not allow my aspirations to be raised and then dashed on the rocks. I would rather nurse a secret crush than risk losing even that and even more.

I would not have dared approach her. Instead, she approached me.

The atheistic incident happened toward the end of our sophomore year. She was leaving our school at the end of that year to be homeschooled. She would be self-directing her curriculum, guiding her own education, exploring her own intellectual curiosities. I was intrigued by her academic plan and I was overwhelmed by everything else about her. After the English class incident, she became curious about me. She said she appreciated my courage. She said she'd always noticed me, reading my books and writing my poems. She thought I seemed fascinating. So she gave me her phone number.

But I never called her. As much as I pined for her, I wouldn't take the risk. I stared at that phone number, and thought about what I could say to her, but I never called her.

In later years, I ran into her at church, during the summer between my junior and senior years of college. This was after my conversion and, apparently, after hers. I was home in Fort Wayne and visiting churches around town. One Sunday, I came to the same church she was trying out. She was there with her husband, a nerdy, gangly guy with glasses. Seeing him, I knew I would have had an actual chance with her, but I wondered if we, as high school atheists, would have found our way to God together. For me, the way to Christianity was guided by other people I would meet later, and perhaps her journey needed to be the same.

Still, despite all the missed connections in high school, romantic and otherwise, I was building esteem online. My authentic self was shooting up through the cracks in the pavement, and in many ways, it was thriving online.

Through Star Wars simming, I was friends with Seth, an aspiring poet and future Catholic priest from New Jersey; Dominic (or Dom), a future politician from the suburbs of Atlanta; Elaine, an intellectual from Oregon who was an agnostic when I met her, until she saw a profound sunrise and was overwhelmed with the thought, "the glory of God"; and Julia, who was going to grow up and become a Lutheran pastor, but not before she studied archaeology at the University of Indianapolis. Julia had been advised to get involved in some other pursuit before ministry, and archaeology held second place in her heart. All of these and others were misshaped puzzle pieces in the real world, but in the Star Wars galaxy, we found our place.

We played together in the Star Wars universes we and other simmers created. These universes were organizing schema for the deeper unfolding of narrative arcs for our characters. Dom, Seth, and I were creators of universes who enjoyed providing a platform for ourselves and others. Our thoughts were always less about battles and more about narratives; less about lightsabers, turbolasers, and Force lightning, and more about romance, learning, governing, and building a movement. We were high-minded idealists, an easy thing to be in a world of one's own creation.

Meanwhile, between rounds, we talked on Instant Messenger, not as Lekk Starn or Luke Skywalker or any of the other characters we played, but as ourselves. We talked about politics, religion, sexuality, books—our respective childhoods and emerging identities. With this group, I had a new opportunity to share the story of my early years and process its meaning, another chance to engage in the therapy of storytelling.

We talked about our days—our struggles and our triumphs—and our hopes for college and life thereafter.

I remained friends with Dom for many years after we both stopped playing an imaginary game on a dying online service provider, and I'm still connected with Seth through Facebook. He's not a Catholic priest—more about that later.

There were also romances online. In addition to Mia, I dated Elaine and Julia. As I write this, I'm tempted to put the word "dated" into scare quotes, as though it wasn't a real thing. But I don't want to diminish the emotional quality of these relationships. They were as silly and melodramatic as a teenage relationship anywhere might be. They were just as joyful and inspiring, and just as maddening and heartbreaking.

And for me, they were markers of emotional growth. Perhaps I didn't have the courage to take social risks in the real world, but I was learning to find a voice in this one. Here, I could be honest about what I felt. I could access and name my emotions. I could risk rejection and all the heartaches that come with it, because the risk was worth the potential reward.

I won't say I was perfect at doing any of this. There were feelings that went unspoken and hesitations that dwelled in my heart. There was heartache I caused, when I broke up with these people and pursued someone else, and heartaches I received, when I was not what they were looking for, either. Despite the heartache, these connections endured for years.

When Elaine told me about her divine revelation, I dismissed it, and she went offline soon after our conversation about "the glory of God" in the Oregon sunrise. In that moment, I did not take seriously her experience of God, and in other moments, I had not taken seriously the heart and soul she entrusted to my care. So she withdrew. Still, she would check on me as the years went by, looking me up using the screen name I used in high school, and introducing herself as a random person from Oregon, so I would know it was her. I would pretend we'd never met before and tell her about my life. When she found me again after my own divine revelation, I delighted in telling her about my newfound faith—in letting her know that the God of the Sunrise had finally come for me, as well.

Six years after high school, I think I might have seen Mia in real life. As a young adult, I moved to Atlanta to attend a Presbyterian seminary—high-school-me could barely believe it. One Sunday, I visited a church where I might have met someone who might have been her. Was she the young woman who walked with me as I left the church? She was friendly, but she also advised me to go to another church. She told me that if she were a young adult who was new to the area, she would go elsewhere. I didn't have any inkling of who she might have been, until she got in her car and I saw the bumper stickers: sci-fi and anime and phrases in the Japanese language. Could that have been her? If it was, she had just advised me to stay away from her. She had told me she didn't want to invite me and my capacity for heartbreak back into her life. And so, if it was her, I would respect her wishes.

The rubble of these broken relationships paved the way toward the romance that would help lead me to Jesus Christ. For now, within the life-long journey toward authenticity, this was me grasping imperfectly for the true self emerging from within. At the time, I did not know about either one of these narrative arcs—much less the fact that they were connected all along—but I knew I was somehow growing into the man I would become.

10

What it Takes to See the Light

The first person I told about my divine vision was a person who broke my heart.

There was Julia—the budding archaeologist from Pennsylvania. I was entranced by her intelligence, captivated by her kindness, and fascinated with her beauty. With a Russian father and an Italian mother, she had won the genetic lottery. In some ways, she did not belong with the rest of us mismatched teenagers, cobbling together a social life on the internet because no other options were available. She was a smart person who enjoyed the company of other smart people and wasn't getting enough of that in small-town Pennsylvania.

When I fell for her, I fell hard. It was different from other crushes, online or otherwise.

With Julia, when I finally took a social risk and told her I was head over heels, she suggested we wait, and that I take some time to locate my errant body parts. But eventually, she agreed to date me. I was overjoyed.

We shared our days every day. I wrote her poetry. I planned a future with her. If she was going to the University of Indianapolis to study archeology, I would go to IUPUI to develop my craft as a writer. It would be the beginning of a beautiful life together.

She sent me care packages in the mail—handwritten notes and baked goods and cassette tapes with musicals like *The Scarlet Pimpernel* and *The Phantom of the Opera*. I tried to return these gestures, but my own attempted care packages were clumsier.

Instead, I thought, I would dazzle her with my wit. She told me she enjoyed when I would teach her things, how I was gentle and clear without being overbearing. I took this as license to "teach" her more, so much so that I did become overbearing. I didn't realize it at the time, but too often, I belittled her.

Each day, I looked forward to the moment when her screen name flashed across my monitor. I could not wait to hear what thoughts she was thinking and what things she was doing. When she broke up with me a few months in, it was like a truck slammed into my skeleton and shattered all my bones.

She cared for me. She really did. That's what she said. But she didn't feel good when she was around me. I made her feel small sometimes. And there was the distance to consider. Perhaps, when we could see each other in person, when we lived in the same city, we could try again. In a situation like that, maybe I could be more of my real self and not the arrogant fool I had become with her.

I was heartbroken. But there was also a part of me that was glad to have enough of a heart that it could break. I wasn't as numb as I used to be, and that comforting thought helped me put my skeleton back together. The more you love, the more you are vulnerable to hurt, and that's not the worst thing in the world.

Around this time, I vowed to never again have an online relationship. I would pursue the real thing or nothing at all. But then Seth came along.

Seth was the future priest from New Jersey, a young man who struggled during our high school years. He knew he was attracted to men, and he knew this was wrong in the eyes of his church. He felt certain that his family would not understand. Like many young men before him, he saw the priesthood as a way out of this conundrum, a way for him to live an approved life where desire would not torment him because romance was not an option. I don't mean to say that he wasn't genuinely called to ministry. Only Seth and God know the answer to that. But part of his call was to choose a life of celibacy over a life of sin.

As the open bisexual in our online group, the one who knew enough about himself and his life-options to embrace a queer identity, Seth confided in me. I was glad for his confidence.

Once, he intimated that he was ready to give up his dreams of the priesthood, that he wanted to pursue romance and be with men, or that he at least wanted to give it a try before making a decision about eternity. He wondered if he could experiment with me. He thought he might like to pursue a relationship with me, and I was only too thrilled to say yes. Seth was beautiful, warm, kind, and spiritual. Like me, he wrote poetry and loved Star Wars. What more could I want?

He was interested in sexual experimentation, so we opened a private chat room and simulated a physical connection. Inside the double colons

:: :: that signified an action, we each typed our respective romance novels, though I noticed that mine had distinctly more ardor and detail than his. *Oh, well,* I thought. *He'll learn.*

When we were both satisfied, he dropped the hammer.

He did not want to pursue a deeper connection. He did not even want to experiment again. He wanted to try it once, to get it out of his system, to prepare himself for the priesthood.

Again, I was crushed. My hopes had risen like a wave and been dashed against the rocks.

In the midst of all this heartbreak, the suicidal urges became more real. Despite the wonderful moments of real connection with other lonely teenagers online, the basic reality remained the same. I was lonely. I was hurting. I clung to hope for the future, because all the media I'd ever consumed told me the time for nerds was later in life; the place to thrive was somewhere other than here.

But here felt miserable. Here was a high school I dreaded attending. Here was a fragile online world that could be taken with the snatch of a modem. Here was me being short and ugly, and even in the new social world of college, that wasn't going to change.

And did the people in the online world really know me? If they saw me in person, where I would be a body and not just a mind, would they reject my body? If they knew how awful I really was, how arrogant and insecure, how cruel and miserable, would they ever come anywhere near me?

The safe space of my online world seemed to be collapsing around me. Who knew me better than Julia? She did not like who I was. Seth must not have, either. These rejections confirmed what I knew in my heart, that I was worthless.

For an abused kid, shame can be a better survival mechanism than anger. It is a way to maintain control rather than losing it in a blind, bitter rage, so the sheltered, shame-filled person can protect the present and guard the future. With shame as a driving force, rather than anger, it's easier to live what will be seen as a "productive" life, one that bears the external signs of meaning and thriving, one that looks more like success to the outside world—even as you constantly beat yourself up on the inside.

And that's assuming you survive the shame.

My instrument of death would have been a knife. Wrists slit in the bathtub. Blood flowing into a vessel where it wouldn't be too hard to clean, where it wouldn't cause much fuss. There were a few people that would miss me, but they would be better off without me. Less burdened. More free.

Mom would be at liberty to pursue whatever she wanted, to pursue new degrees and new relationships. My grandparents would carry on. Kyle, with whom I maintained a tenuous hold on a pseudo-parental relationship, would not miss me much.

And what about my sister? When we lived in Hawaii, Nicole had sacrificed so much to ensure my freedom, to ensure that I could make it through with fewer scars than her. But I did not think about Nicole. My pain consumed and blinded me, and it did not cross my mind that my death would mean that all of my sister's sacrifices had been in vain.

At this point, Nicole had a second child: my niece, Tracey. Tracey was an absolute delight from the moment she came into this world. I figured that without me around, there would be more room in the house for Nicole, Latrell, and Tracey.

Nicole's boyfriend Dee had recently run into trouble with the law and wound up in jail, and she and the kids were now living with us. They had been living on their own in a shoddy apartment in an economically wounded neighborhood. This wasn't good for all kinds of reasons, the main one being that their apartment was being broken into all the time. All the unsavory people who had known Dee now also knew that he was gone—and that the apartment was unprotected, so it was being broken into all the time.

It was not a safe environment for Nicole and the kids, so they had to move back in with us. And when they did, I became even more depressed. Their real-life presence infringed on my online one. There were more demands on me in the real world, as I was now called to care for the kids more often, and I could no longer get to my own world without questions, conversation, and scrutiny. The house was no longer a quiet backdrop to the beautiful painting that was my online reality. And the online world wasn't as beautiful as it used to be, anyway—with valued relationships disintegrating, with this new terrain of heartache and desolation.

I should have thought about the kids, about what would happen if they discovered their dead uncle, about what my death might imprint on their nascent hearts and souls, but I wasn't aware of them being conscious enough to be traumatized.

I was thinking only about me—about my despair, my overwhelming sadness, my utter self-hatred, my loneliness. I was thinking about my fierce desire to no longer feel this way.

There was a time in the middle of the night when the deed could be done. Mom was working the night shift at the VA Hospital in Fort Wayne. Nicole and the kids were isolated to their part of the house. There were eight hours each night when I was basically alone. The knives were in the kitchen.

I knew that you had to cut vertically, along the line of the vein, rather than horizontally. A horizontal cut could lead to clotting and a failed attempt.

In the bathtub, in the warm water, I would barely feel it as the blood just drifted away.

But my plan raised a question, one I turned over in my head as I thought about it in the middle of the night: Did I want to succeed? I felt sure that if I tried, it would not be a failed attempt.

I wrote a short story around this time for an English class. In it, a black-clad, misunderstood Beatnik-type fakes suicide and revels in the attention that comes from the attempt.

Writing this story helped me find my answer—which was no. As deeply and seriously as I contemplated it, I never attempted suicide.

I didn't really want to die. I wanted attention. I wanted people to know how much this stupid teenage life was a struggle for me. I wanted them to see how much I was hurting.

All I had was a tiny glimmer of hope in the future, but it was enough. I could stick it out and wait for college, wait for adulthood, wait to see if things would get better.

In the meantime, I was crushed by shame and sadness. My heart was a crumpled ball haphazardly thrown toward the trash can. So, I thought about it. I walked back and forth—thinking about it; knife in hand—thinking about it; more solitary nights than I care to remember—thinking about the end of my life.

But no more than that.

Julia was the first person I turned to when I had a divine vision.

In the midst of quiet suicidal ideation, with a view of the world that saw no eternal future and no eternal consequences, my mom knew something was wrong. She suggested therapy, but I turned it down. After the uneventful experience with a child therapist when I was younger, I was convinced it wouldn't be worth my time. So instead, my mom took me to a bookstore.

Going to bookstores was one of our favorite pastimes. We would go out to dinner, just the two of us. We'd both have a book that we'd read at the table—a mystery novel for her, science fiction or a classic for me. Waiters commented on the oddity of this, a mother and son going out to dinner and reading at the table. We enjoyed being thought of as quirky and worthy of comment. We also liked being able to be with each other without having to talk to each other.

Either before or after dinner, we would go to a bookstore. We both carried books with us everywhere. Like me, my mom often read during those short, in-between times that other people use to connect with each other. At the bookstore, there was never a limit on what I could get. No one policed the content or the price tag, and I was free to follow my curiosities.

One night, during my junior year of high school, when I was especially depressed and my fragile, private happiness was collapsing, I saw a book that piqued my interest. There was an Asian man with a wise, amused smile on the cover, like he knew all the secrets of life and felt utterly delighted by them. I felt oddly drawn to him—and to the promise in the title of the book. The man was His Holiness the Dalai Lama, and the book was *The Art of Happiness*. I put it in my pile.

The book unlocked a whole new world for me. Contained within its deceptively simple chapters was a rudimentary Buddhist spirituality.

The book spoke about gratitude. I remember a passage where the Dalai Lama described the marvels of a modern American grocery store, exploding with bright, beautiful colors, and full of people caring for each other through food. How many of us think of the grocery store as anything more than just another chore to check off our list? For this personification of compassion from Tibet, it was a kaleidoscope of beauty and love. How much happier might we be if we thought of the mundane world as a miracle?

The book spoke about mindfulness, about concentrating on the present and the gifts of the moment, rather than grasping for the ghosts of the past or the future.

The book spoke about meditation, about calming exercises to focus your breathing and bring you back to your body and the moment.

While I was engaging with this book, I had a spiritual experience. It came in a social studies class of all places, during World History, to be more precise. Dan, the boy from the locker room, was sitting near me, and because he was there, I was in a good mood.

We were watching a video about medieval cathedral builders, dedicated men who devoted their lives to constructing beautiful monuments of architectural grandeur. Many of them would not live to see the final revelation of their work in all its splendor. They were motivated by the mission of a creation that would outlive them, an edifice that would touch the heavens to glorify an unseen God, while serving hundreds of years of generations beyond them. They believed in a life beyond this one, a moment in eternity when they would look down from heaven and see the fruits of their labor.

I thought, *How could all this be for nothing? How could so many people work so hard to build so much for what is, in the end, nothing? Could all these people be working on nothing but delusion? Can I be completely sure that their faith is an illusion?*

At that moment, I was transported from the classroom. I entered a space flooded with bright, white light, a light so all-encompassing and beautiful there are no words to do it justice. It was the most beautiful thing I have ever seen. I was outside of myself and yet also inside the holiest and most mysterious space within myself. The light had a physical presence; I could feel it. I was in awe.

I don't know how long this experience lasted. Perhaps it was only a second, perhaps more. When it was over, I was back in the classroom. The video was playing and my classmates were there. There were tears in my eyes, streaming down my face. Through the tears, I could see the book I was reading—*The Art of Happiness*.

I did not tell my mother about this experience, because ours was not a religious household, and I barely knew what to say, anyway. Instead, Julia was the first person I talked to. We weren't even dating anymore, but we were in a post-relationship-friendship-that-could-be-a-future-relationship. She was thrilled when she heard about my vision.

Julia had never tried to evangelize me, but her faith was important to her, and we had talked about that faith at times. I was curious how an intelligent person like her, or Seth for that matter, could find truth in a conception of the world that seemed so untrue to me. She was always honest and kind and patient in her sharing.

She was astounded when she heard about my vision. But she didn't have advice for where I might take it from there. She hadn't evangelized me before and she wasn't going to start now. She was just intrigued to see what God would do with me from here.

So was Seth. So was I.

But ultimately, it was more than I knew what to do with. My vision was proof enough that there *could* be a world beyond this one, that the spiritual experiences described by religious people *might* be more than an illusion, but I couldn't say what was beyond those hypotheticals. I didn't know what I had seen. Part of me wondered if I had really seen anything at all. And part of the problem was that I had no framework with which to interpret this experience. I had no category in which to place it.

I was at least willing to say I was an agnostic and no longer an atheist. I was at least willing to say there might be something to this religion absurdity, after all, that there was a glimmer of a possibility it could be real. But I didn't know what else to do with that glimmer.

Years later, after my conversion, I wondered if Julia's disappearance from my life was part of God's work with me, part of the story of God entering and captivating my heart.

When we had been dating—and even after we broke up, when we still cared for each other and kept talking about our future life in Indianapolis—we imagined meeting and loving each other in the real world.

But she went in a different direction. She enlisted in the Marine reserves. A recruiter found her at her teenage job in the mall. He convinced her that the military could give her a deeper experience of life and better preparation for ministry. She wound up going to college in Pittsburgh.

But if we had met, and if we had reanimated the romance between us, I think the story I'm writing now would have been different. I think it would have taken me longer to admit that God was working in the narrative arc of my life, longer to reach a moment of conversion and to come to Christian faith. After all, Julia hadn't wanted to pressure me. She didn't want to evangelize. But sometimes you need a little pressure to be motivated to keep going. Sometimes you need someone to be firm in their convictions and continue drawing you out. But I'm getting ahead of myself.

Years later, I found Julia on Instant Messenger and we talked about faith. I had converted to Christianity by then, and she had become a Buddhist. I wondered why, but she wouldn't say. She seemed to think that something she could have said might have derailed the journey I was on. I respected her desire to not pursue it, and we lost touch soon after.

As for Seth, he decided not to become a priest. Today, he is a poet living in New York City. These days, with me serving as a pastor in Kansas City, it feels like we switched aspirations, and high school me is a bit jealous of the bohemian life he is living.

After all this, high school me turned away from online romance for good and developed an even deeper love for books. My heart belonged to Allen Ginsberg, Jack Kerouac, and the Beats.

I read *On the Road* again and again, and *The Dharma Bums*. I was led to the poems of Gary Snyder and Lawrence Ferlinghetti. I was drawn to other early-century and mid-century American writers struggling against suburbia, industrialization, and the triumph of commerce at the cost of originality. I found my way back to E.E. Cummings and Truman Capote.

Often, I would take these books to Foster Park, Fort Wayne's Central Park imitation, full of wooded trails and sheltered shade and suspension bridges over muddy rivers. I remember visiting this park with my mom in elementary school. In high school, I went there alone to read poetry, write, and draw from the well of nature. I went there because I had nowhere else to go and I had no friends to go anywhere with. I had no god, and no larger view of the world, to inspire me.

But I had the Beats—their chapters and verses, their parables, their wisdom.

And I had a new kind of heart pounding in my chest. There was a piece of the Dalai Lama in there, a stance of joy and gratitude and love for the absurd and the mundane. There was a bit of Jack Kerouac, open to adventure. There was some nascent Gary Snyder, willing to enter into nature and be swept away by its power. This heart had a little Allen Ginsberg, better able to give itself in love, to shelter itself in brokenness, and to discover that the risk had been worth it all along.

More and more, my authentic self was emerging from the closet. One day, my heart and mind would both blossom like wildflowers, and God would be waiting for them to bloom.

11

I Believe in Something

ANOTHER EARLY- TO MID-TWENTIETH century author with whom I fell in love was Aldous Huxley. Many people know him for the dystopian novel *Brave New World,* but he also wrote a series of essays following up on his dystopian suppositions, *Brave New World Revisited,* and a Buddhism-laced utopian novel, *Island.* Taken together, these books are a fierce meditation on technology, psychology, pharmacology, and politics. By the time I was a junior in high school, I was captivated by them.

I was drawn to *Brave New World* because of its protagonist, Bernard Marx, a man with an A+ mind in a genetically inferior body who never seemed to fit into the world he inhabited. I could relate. I knew first-hand how being a misfit in your world allows you to see that world in ways that others may not.

I was drawn to *Brave New World Revisited* because it is deep and insightful, powerful and prescient. It speaks to the danger of industry and bureaucracy—how complex, large-scale organizations find human individuality problematic. They flatten human difference for organizational convenience.

For its part, *Island* is a utopia that, given the right conditions, may have been possible at one point in history. It takes place on the fictional Pacific island of Pala, where Western science and Eastern religion have come together to create a healthy, happy, and self-supporting society. My *Art of Happiness* inspired brush with Buddhism made me more open to its vision of utopia.

During the summer between my junior and senior year of high school, I decided that I would read these three books every summer for the rest of my life. I believed that I would always see new things in them, and they would be a constant reminder of what was truly important. In many ways, Huxley's trilogy became my Bible. As an adult, I have not followed up on my adolescent resolution to read these three books every summer forever, but my love for Aldous Huxley would eventually lead to a love for Jesus Christ. I'll tell you more when we get to Pala.

In that late high school season, I was enamored with literary figures and with the possibility of college. I did extensive online research. I pored over the rankings in *US News and World Report*, but I especially appreciated *The Princeton Review* and their numbers, which relied on extensive student surveys.

During my junior year, my high school started bringing in a speaker who was selling a gospel—the gospel of private liberal arts colleges. He wanted kids and parents to know that a college like this was within their financial reach. Look past the sticker shock of the per-semester tuition number, he offered. Financial aid at a private school is much more abundant than at a public school. You'll get a better education, he said, and if you are a family of middle income and lower, you may wind up going to a better school for less money out-of-pocket than the local state school.

Mom and I were convinced. She told me she would pay for whatever college I picked, so go ahead and dream big, and don't feel limited by geography. With that charge in mind and the internet at hand, I cast a wide net. From my online perch, I looked at Sarah Lawrence, NYU, Carleton, Amherst, and the New College of Florida. What about Tulane or Chaminade? Perhaps Pepperdine? I came across a Saint Anselm College in Manchester, New Hampshire, where black-robed monks walked the quad between classes.

"No, thank you, Saint Anselm," I said to my computer screen.

I was entranced by the possibility of the future, by the life I could build at a new place with literary and intellectual peers—virtually anywhere other than here.

But my vision wasn't entirely on the future. My thoughts were not entirely escapist. One very earth-bound thing I thought about was politics. The little boy who had once been captivated by US Presidents became a teenager compelled by modern presidential candidates and the issues that inspired them. And why not? They were the modern inheritors of the ambition and compassion that had inhabited my heroes from long ago. While some part of me knew that the age of heroes had passed—that Vietnam, Watergate, Chappaquiddick, and *Monkey Business* had taken the shine off US Presidents and those who would attain to that office—another part of me wanted something to believe in.

It was the year 1999, and the 2000 primaries were heating up, and I was hooked on the political speeches and campaign rallies being broadcast on C-SPAN. At the time, I was easily captivated by political figures, by their personal stories and their ideas. It was easy to be persuaded when politicians and candidates spoke to their own followers outside the context of a debate. When no one was there to articulate an opposing view, it was easy to believe that yes, this person is exactly who the country needs right now.

In late 1999, the Republican presidential primary was more interesting than the Democratic one. Today, while I am solidly in the Democratic camp, there was a time when the Republicans could have drawn me over to their side. After all, I read Aldous Huxley religiously and worried about the impact of large-scale bureaucracy and industry. I was open to a message about small government and grassroots democracy. Little did I know that the Republican Party, even then, was so far from those stated ideals it was laughable. I'm sorry if this is too political for some of you, but Republicans, at least the ones in power, only believe in small government when they can manipulate it to their own ends. Otherwise, they're perfectly happy to sacrifice local control in the name of ideology. In fact, as I write in 2023, their turn toward technocratic gerrymandering, voter suppression, and other means of institutionalizing minority rule are alarming. They have become the party of *1984*-style fascism.

Nonetheless, in 1999, there was a time when Republicans could have spoken to me, and some of them did. I was first drawn to Dan Quayle, a man from northeast Indiana whose intelligence has been unfairly maligned. However, his reputation was too great a hurdle to overcome in that primary. From him, I moved over to John McCain, whose maverick spirit, genial humor, and authenticity were compelling to young people like me.

From there, it was Democrat Bill Bradley. The more I listened to all these figures, the more I understood that progressive politics were in my wheelhouse. I am in favor of using the levers of government to help people. I think it is right to take on debts and deficits in order to invest in individuals and communities, and I believe this move generally pays off in the long run. Most importantly, I think that politics should be about service and compassion, which Bill Bradley spoke about in compelling ways. When I listened to him, the little boy version of me, the one who was captivated by US Presidents and inspired by their ability to change the world, was inspired as well.

I wanted to believe that Bill Bradley could take his walk-the-entire-shoreline-of-New-Jersey spirit into the presidential campaign and overcome—with some combination of spit, gumption, and rhetorical flourish—the institutional juggernaut that was Al Gore. As in my sports fandom, I rooted for the underdog. As in my fascination with the paranormal, I wanted to believe. But alas, it was not to be. Gore won the primary. Bradley lost. And I needed someone else to believe in.

Into this gap came Ralph Nader. Talk about compelling life stories! Here was a son of Lebanese immigrants, a man who took General Motors to court and won, and then used the winning proceeds not to promote himself and his own selfish interests, but to fund public interest groups in Washington, D.C. and around the country. He lived a simple life. He was passionate about his work and didn't need much more than work to fill his life with meaning. His primary indulgence was watching the Baltimore Orioles in black and white on a tiny TV in his ramshackle apartment. It was clear to me that Nader had spent his life putting his money where his mouth is. He had spent his life fighting for common people and living with integrity to his ideals.

As I write about him, I center his personal life because it lends credibility to his ideas. He was a humble man who couldn't (credibly) be accused of grandstanding, a relatively poor man who couldn't (credibly) be accused of greed. Because of that, when he talked about corporate influence in Washington, D.C., you knew that he spoke from experience. He had spent decades lobbying for legislation that helps people—legislation that was deemed "unsafe at any speed" by both parties. When he advocated for campaign finance reform, you could see how passionate he was about creating a system that would truly work for all the people. He wasn't preaching purity with his mouth and accepting corporate donations with his hands, like Al Gore.

For me, Nader felt like everything I believed in and cared about coming together. His running mate was a Native American woman, Winona LaDuke, so his campaign was directly connected to the margins of US history and the voices of the underdogs. His goal was to establish the Green Party as a national presence, and I loved that something grand like this might be done through small-scale, grassroots organizing—so the Aldous Huxley in me was satisfied. I also loved the rebellious, fight-the-system aspect of it all, which fulfilled the Star Wars Rebel Alliance part of me. And I was drawn to the anti-corporate message, which I could engage with alongside the best minds of my generation.

Once I found Nader and the Green Party, I found my true political love. More importantly, I found a sense of hope. I had a basic personal commitment to compassion and imagination, but no real philosophy or worldview with which to make sense of reality. Within that void, Nader and the Green Party gave me a convincing vision of how the world works, what needs to change, and how we can shape the future together. For many other people, these kinds of hopes are metaphysical and religious. For me, they had to be earth-bound and practical. There was no place other than here. No day but today.

For me, this was a religious experience, an experience that inspired faith, hope, and love, an experience that elicited belief in something larger than myself. It prepared the ground for me to eventually believe in a person even more compelling than Ralph Nader, a person whose life also matched his stated ideals, a humble man named Jesus Christ.

Besides all that, the Nader campaign invited me to come even further out of my shell. I don't think Jesus could have reached me unless it had.

I volunteered for the Nader campaign. I felt inspired enough to put my awkward body and my quaking voice on the line for this figure. I became a canvasser. At union events, gay pride events, and apolitical festivals, I joined other volunteers pounding the pavement with a pen and a clipboard, inviting people to sign a petition to get Ralph Nader and Winona LaDuke on the ballot in Indiana.

I knocked on doors. I approached people. I started conversations.

Can you believe it? *Me*. I did that.

I started to discover that the first social risk is always the hardest. But once you have your rhythm down, it becomes easier to knock on doors and say what you have to say. When you canvas, you become less sensitive to rejection and more able to put yourself out there.

I loved working with the people I was meeting. Before the campaign, I had some awareness that there was a crunchy, granola-y, hippie-ish community in Fort Wayne, Indiana, but I didn't know how much they would feel like my tribe. As with high school, I didn't take any social risks to hang out with them outside of campaign events and door-knocking escapades. I didn't use my newfound social skills to build an actual social life. But still, I was a part of something—and that was another part of the religious experience—to be part of a community doing something bigger together.

Of course, we failed to get Ralph Nader on the ballot in Indiana. I say "of course" because Democrats and Republicans make the election rules, and they are always going to make rules that ensure they will continue to be able to make the rules. As a result, getting a third-party candidate on the ballot in Indiana was, and is, a near-impossible feat.

Still, being involved in the campaign was a profound experience for me. One memorable moment came at the Fort Wayne gay pride festival, when I was walking around with my clipboard, attempting to gather signatures for the ballot access cause. I walked past a beautiful gay man who was also holding a clipboard. He held his up and said, "I'll show you mine if you show me yours." We laughed, and some small part of me felt another sense of belonging. I wished I had the courage to talk to someone like him outside the clipboard.

Another neat experience was protesting outside the vice-presidential debate at Centre College in Danville, Kentucky. I got a ride from a guy who went to Valparaiso University, who also sold hemp products out of the trunk of his car. He came to Fort Wayne and picked me up, and then we drove through Indiana, picking up other protesters along the way. We spent the night on a floor at a non-profit in Danville, where we made signs and learned chants as we got ready.

I still remember walking through the streets of that small Kentucky town, each of us with gags in our mouths, protesting the silencing of alternative voices like Winona LaDuke. The politically involved citizens of the town gathered around us, active Republicans and Democrats counter-protesting our protest. I'll never forget locking eyes with a little boy who didn't understand why he was there, who didn't understand why I had a gag in my mouth, who probably would have rather been anywhere else just playing and being a little boy.

I don't know if he knew why he was there, but I know why I was there: because I was abused as a kid, because I viscerally know the experience of pain and oppression—because silence is embedded in my bones, because silence is a way to avoid being hurt—because the people who are getting the worst of life in our society need someone to stand up for them and enable them to speak. I wanted a better society, a better future for me and for the random little boy on the side of the road. I wanted real, compassionate, hope-filled change, and I was young and naïve enough to believe it could happen.

I don't mean that I believed Ralph Nader could become the President of the United States, but I believed we could influence the conversation. I believed our campaign could help make the world a better place.

However, if this experience was about the beginning of the possibility of faith, it was also about learning human limitations. What do we encounter in life that is worthy of faith?

Don't get me wrong. I still follow politics. I'm still captivated by political figures, by their stories and their ideas. As a person of faith, I believe faith compels me to be an active citizen of my society, working through whatever means possible to achieve the greatest good for the greatest number of people. But I don't have faith in politicians or political movements. I recognize their humanity, their natural limits, their failures of hope and imagination.

I recognize that the most idealistic vision of the most egalitarian society we can dream up still falls short of the Kingdom of God.

As a high school senior, I enjoyed learning about and talking about politics. A kind English teacher—the same Mr. Jackson from the earlier story about atheism and the Book of Ruth—suggested I join the speech team so I could talk about politics more. So I did just that.

When I gave my first speech to a room packed full of two judges and two other students, my face turned a shade of red that I never knew existed. I could feel my cheeks burning. I could see my hands shaking. But as the year went on, my face became progressively less red during competitions. Later in life, it is hard to imagine I could have become a teacher—and then a pastor—without first having had this experience. On the speech team, I carved a path through the fear and shame that burned like lava on my cheeks, and I managed to survive the eruption. Thank you, Mr. Jackson.

During my senior year, I competed in a number of state competitions. On the speech team, it was Congress. On the academic team, it was the English, Social Studies, and Interdisciplinary quizzes. In AP Government, our class made a state-level competition—and I had a large hand in that.

Physically, I was also an athlete with a nearly flawless record. Another kind English teacher, Mr. King, recruited me to run cross country, convincing me that it was good for a team to have a lot of people running, even if they weren't fast or talented, and that it would be good for me to learn about perseverance and endurance.

Out of all the races I ran, there was only one where I didn't finish dead last. Like I said, I was *nearly* flawless.

Once, Mr. King was driving me home from a meet, and the subject of religion came up. He didn't understand atheism. He wouldn't know how to go on living if he weren't a person of faith. So he asked me about atheism out of genuine curiosity. What motivates it? What motivates me? Where did I find a sense of purpose and hope?

He didn't know that, less than twelve months earlier, I had thought about killing myself as I pondered those same questions. But at this point, I was thrilled to have this conversation. I clarified that I was agnostic, which is functionally the same as atheism but allows for a little more intellectual humility. I also told him about the things that inspired me—helping people, reading great literature, writing, and changing the world.

He nodded. He didn't think that would be enough for him. But it was enough for me, at least at the time. And I absolutely loved that this adult was treating me like an intellectual equal, like I could meaningfully answer questions of substance about the basic dynamics of life.

That fall, I was taking a mythology class with Mr. King, and I also had a lunchtime study hall. We had a block schedule, where a different set of classes met every other day. So every other day, I would have this lunchtime study hall, and every other day, like clockwork, I would find a reason to ask Mr. King for four passes to leave study hall and go to the school library—two for the two of us who ran cross country, and two for a couple of boys from my slightly-below-average, nerdy-white-guy clique.

During those study halls at the library, we threw caution to the wind. When it came time for our lunch period, we would leave the library, but we wouldn't go to the cafeteria. We'd sneak out to the parking lot, get into Sam's car, grab some fast food, and then drive around.

We felt like such rebels. Nerdy, white, middle-class rebels.

I always had some kind of practice after school, academic team or speech or cross country, so Sam would make sure to get us back by the time school ended. But we all missed study hall and our final class of the day. Someone should have noticed that we were regularly missing class. Someone should have noticed us in the parking lot during school hours. Anyone who saw us in the outside world should have seen a group of truant kids, but no one said a word.

And that's how white privilege works. As long as you act like you have every reason to be where you are, and as long as people see you as the kind of person who probably isn't up to no good, they assume you're doing nothing wrong—even if you are. My little gang of nerdy white rebels was able to get away with things non-white kids wouldn't, because people looked at us—and them—with a bias that was already formed. Many non-white kids are often assumed to be up to no good when that's the furthest thing from the truth. They're often viewed as criminals, and treated like criminals, regardless of anything they've done or not done. When that happens to a person again and again, it wounds their psyche in incalculable ways.

But for us, a group of nerdy white kids who really did deserve to be caught, no one cared. In my current pastoral work, I cite this experience as a clear example of white privilege.

I had another study hall experience. This one would change the course of my life and directly lead to my conversion to religious faith. My friend Justin and I were invited to meet with a recruiter from Wabash College to find out what the school was about and whether we were interested in visiting.

I didn't have to go to this meeting. I could have said I was dreaming about Sarah Lawrence or satisfied with my plan to go to IUPUI, and I didn't need any more information about any other school. But our guidance counselor said Wabash was a special place, and Justin was interested enough to go to the meeting, so I thought, *Why not? It doesn't hurt to sit in a meeting and hear the pitch.*

Wabash sounded relatively interesting. It was a place of academic rigor, with small class sizes. It had a beautiful campus, with a well-manicured quad and classical columns on stately brick architecture; the recruiter made sure to show us lots of pictures and that was a good move on his part.

According to *The Princeton Review,* a publication to which I had been paying attention, it got high marks.

One of its main distinctions is not necessarily its main selling point. It's a college for men, one of only three all-male colleges remaining in the country. As I've often heard from others and said myself, no one chooses Wabash because it's all-male. In fact, until you see it in person, you don't really get the benefits of an all-male environment—such as a strong sense of community, because there's this odd dynamic that bonds us together; or decreased social competition; or increased male intimacy—which a kid who grew up without a father might need on a level he could never really name.

When you see it in person, you learn about the trust Wabash places in its students. You learn about opportunities for leadership, responsibility, and personal growth. You learn that there's one rule at Wabash: "A Wabash Man shall conduct himself as a gentleman and a responsible citizen at all times, both on- and off-campus." That's it. We trust you. We hold you to a high standard and we expect you to meet it.

I was intrigued enough to accept the invitation to visit. And so, one weekday, Justin drove us both down to Crawfordsville, Indiana. We met with professors and observed classes. I liked how I felt there. Justin wasn't all that interested, but I was willing to consider it.

At least for a time. But then I decided IUPUI would work for me. And my mom exploded over that.

Don't get me wrong, I thought Wabash was a fine school. I liked the aesthetics of it. But even with scholarships, it was going to be a lot more expensive than a state school, and would all that extra money be worth the cost to a long-haired urban poet (yes, I had long hair back then) with New York City skyscrapers in his eyes? What could Wabash deliver for my intended future that a public school in the city couldn't?

I came to the same conclusions about all those schools I had looked at online. Sarah Lawrence, New College, Reed—all of them. For each of these schools, I found some reason to put them aside. I would go to school in Indianapolis. I would rekindle my romance with Julia. And I wouldn't worry about getting the most prestigious degree from the fanciest institution. I had read that, for a writer, you probably needed a bachelor's degree from somewhere, but it didn't really matter from where. Getting into an MFA program, getting published, doing anything with this crazy dream—it all depended on the quality of the writing. You could go to school in a rowboat in the middle of a lake so long as the writing was good.

But Mom had her heart set on Wabash. We attended a local admission gathering at a country club, and she was very impressed. She liked what she heard about the student experience and the alumni network. She sensed that I needed a place like this—that I needed the close attention of a private college with small classes, where I couldn't just fade into the back of a lecture hall and slide below the radar. Academically, I needed people who would hold me accountable. Socially, I needed a community of people who cared.

Mom tried to explain all this to me, but I didn't get it. I insisted that I was just looking for a degree that would enable my chosen path. I just wanted a place where I could write and study poetry and be a Beat.

Mom told me about her own experience—when her small-town doctor had offered to send her to undergrad at DePauw University (Wabash's rival) and to medical school at Indiana University if she would take over his practice when he retired. But she had turned this opportunity down. After a couple of years of wandering, she waitressed her way through a nursing degree at a regional campus of Purdue. And now, would I have the same kind of college experience as her? Would I turn down a great opportunity to go to a wonderful school and instead muddle my way through anonymous lecture halls and a faceless student experience?

What had she been working for all these years? What would become of me? She was irate.

Mom told me I could go to IUPUI. After all, I was an adult and it was my decision. But I would have to figure it out by myself. She wouldn't help pay for it. She wouldn't help with the FAFSA. She wouldn't guide me through the vagaries of enrollment.

I felt capable enough to do these things on my own, but I couldn't bear the idea of that much conflict between my mother and me. The threat of a personal rift was more compelling than the threat of having to stand on my own two feet, and for that reason, my eyes turned back toward Wabash.

You may think of this as an odd amount of detail to go into about a college-enrollment decision, but Wabash is the place where I became a Christian. It was in the basement of their library. It was due to the influence of many of the people I met there or through there. The story of how I got to Wabash is significant because I believe God was orchestrating it every step of the way.

When I applied to the school as an early-admission applicant in December, my application included a middling high school GPA—bolstered by good grades in English and social studies and marred by poor grades in math and science—and good but not great scores on the SAT, 630 verbal and 560 math, 1190 overall. At first, I was put on the waiting list.

I considered other schools. I thought about the University of Indianapolis. I never visited the place, but I started an application and talked to an admissions rep. He thought we would be a good fit, and that I would be a shoo-in for the alumni scholarship, and he was willing to sponsor me. I started an application there, but I never finished it. I thought about Earlham, Antioch, and Oberlin, places where granola reigned supreme. But I liked the intellectual diversity of Wabash. I liked that many of my fellow students would be different from me. I even liked the oddity of its all-male status as a historical curiosity. I've always had a thing for people and places that are different.

In January, I took the SAT again and reported the scores to Wabash. I scored 790 on the Verbal. A few days later, they sent me a letter congratulating me on my acceptance. At that time, I was offered a modest Presidential Scholarship. I went on to earn a Fine Arts Fellowship for my poetry and short fiction. But my primary scholarship support was the Honors Scholarship I earned on Honors Scholar Weekend.

Oh, Honors Scholar weekend!—a springtime Wabash tradition where most of next fall's incoming class descends on campus like a Biblical plague of locusts, where a campus of nine-hundred students somehow finds room to house another four-hundred prospective students, about half of whom will matriculate to Wabash. For prospective students, the weekend features two main events: a battery of tests that can earn the highest scorers an Honors Scholarship, and the beginning of fraternity rush.

At Wabash, around 70% of the young men live in one of ten national fraternities planted around campus. The college depends on this fraternity housing—there wouldn't be enough space to house everyone without it. On most college campuses, dorms are the norm and Greek life is the exception, so fraternity living gets a special moniker like "Greek life" or the dreaded "frat boys." But at Wabash, the opposite is true. Most of the students are in fraternities. Young men who live in the dorms get a special name: "independents."

Given the need for housing and the culture of the campus, fraternity rush begins the spring before you get there. It continues through the summer, with fraternities keeping in touch with potential members and holding regional rush events. And then it finalizes in one big push the week before classes begin in the fall, when everyone gets settled into place before the academic term begins. As you might imagine, it's a big deal.

During March of my senior year, when I came for Honors Scholar weekend, it was not my desire to stay in a fraternity. When I was filling out my RSVP to Honors Scholar Weekend, I checked the box for independent living, for staying in a dorm room and getting to know the other independents as I experienced my first taste of college life. There was no way I was going to join a fraternity. After all, I was a long-haired poet. I was born to live free.

But they placed me in a fraternity anyway. There just wasn't enough room in the dorms. That was fine, but I wasn't going to pay a whole lot of attention to the frat house's sales pitch, and I figured they wouldn't be terribly interested in me either.

But God had other plans for me. I was put in the exact right place.

The fraternity I stayed with was Tau Kappa Epsilon. Before I go further, I need to say a word to readers who may have gone to big, state universities with Tau Kappa Epsilon chapters: Your TKEs (pronounced "Tekes") are probably very different from my TKEs. At a big, state university, where only a small percentage of students participate in Greek life, and where Greek life is a problematic afterthought to the overall student experience, TKEs are often more gifted athletically and aesthetically than academically.

It was not so at Wabash. At Wabash, almost every student was a nerd on some level, but the TKEs were especially so. They had a Dungeons and Dragons flavor, as many of the young men enjoyed a good tabletop fantasy game. They also had an international flavor. They had so many Hispanic students that they referred to their main dining hall, the Apollo Room, as the "a *pollo* room." You know, the Spanish word for "chicken?" These TKEs, who would eventually become my TKEs, were smart and funny and diverse, and I found that I didn't mind hanging out with them.

I started to warm to the idea that it might be a good thing for me to be in a frat—that for me, as a shy kid who often had trouble standing up and speaking out, a fraternity would mean an automatic set of friends. There would be parties and social events that someone else would organize but that I could still attend. I could have a social life—a real-life one. I could make the most of my college experience. At the very least, I would experience some things worth writing about.

I visited a few other houses around campus and took part in their rush events, but I was too shy to make any real connections. And I could tell from looking around that I wasn't in the same tribe as guys in the bigger, more popular houses. I fit in just fine at TKE, and they offered me a bid. Most people who stay in the TKE house are offered a bid. Most people who hang out for a while during rush events are offered a bid. They're not picky. Or, to put it in a more positive way, they have an inclusive spirit.

But I held my bid through the summer and didn't make a decision right away. Part of me wasn't sure I needed the social crutch of a fraternity. After all, through speech and the Nader campaign and other high school activities, I was becoming less shy and more willing to speak my mind. I still shrank like a violet when I visited other houses on Honors Scholar weekend, and I did not run to talk to other kids as part of my work on the school newspaper or yearbook, but like a baby deer standing on its shaking legs, I could kinda, sorta, maybe navigate my way through a social opportunity! Did I really need a fraternity?

What I needed were some assurances. What was it like to be "a pledge?" And what was it like to be queer in a fraternity? The rush chair assured me that other guys in the house were gay or bisexual. I should have expected nothing less of the nerdy, inclusive house I was joining. And I knew a little social help never hurt anyone—and I knew that I needed it more than most. So I accepted my bid.

During my senior year in high school, you could have knocked me over with a feather if you had told me that joining an LGBT-accepting frat would lead me to Jesus.

12

Spiritual but Not Religious

My mother was sold on me going to Wabash, but living in a fraternity? She had her doubts. In the fall, when I moved into Tau Kappa Epsilon, Mom interrogated one of the active members:

"Why those particular Greek letters?"

"What's with all the Apollo stuff?"

"Why the triangles?"

The active member put the best possible face on TKE's past and present. He said that TKE had been founded by working-class men who couldn't get into traditional fraternities, that our chapter had been founded by Jewish students excluded from other brotherhoods, and that our chapter had been the first on campus to induct an African American man in the 1960s. And we continued to recruit diverse pledge classes. We continued to live into the historical spirit of inclusion.

Why the triangles? In an equilateral triangle, he said, the strength of each side reinforces each of the others. Why Apollo? In Apollo, we have a symbol of wisdom, truth, youth, and virility. Why Tau Kappa Epsilon? He didn't know that one. There's probably someone, somewhere, who knows.

"What's with the skull?" Mom asked, pointing to the red and white paint splashed against cement blocks, the image of a skull-and-crossbones that was taller than either of us.

"To remind us that life is short," he said. "So each day is a gift, and it's our job to make the most of it."

I'm sure that was the reason, and not because it looked cool or anything.

I could tell Mom was still a little skeptical, but she was convinced enough, and I began my year at Wabash as a Tau Kappa Epsilon pledge.

I imagined my new life in the fraternity as an opportunity to start again. No one here knew who I was in high school. No one here knew I was cripplingly shy. In my new life, I would take social risks. I would put myself out there. And if I fell flat on my face, I would just leave the house and move into the dorms—or leave the school and go somewhere else. If I completely failed and embarrassed myself beyond repair, I would just leave and start over again—again.

I can always leave and start again. It's been my modus operandi. "I'm going to leave you before you have a chance to leave me. You aren't going to have a chance to hurt me because I'm already long gone." In the great dance of life: Maybe I don't take the chance of approaching you in the first place. Or maybe I do dance with you, but I'm emotionally disengaged and won't let myself fall in love. Maybe we dance and you say you want to see me again, but l turn down your invitation into deeper relationship, or I maneuver the conversation to avoid an invitation to the next thing. I don't want you to feel obligated to invite me to the next thing. If you do, I'll feel sure you don't really want me there, in whatever space in your life you've opened up for me, or that you wouldn't want me there if you knew who I really was.

But no one in the fraternity knew me that way, not yet anyway. Here, I could pretend I was not inhibited like that. I could invent a new reality and pretend it was me all along. And if it didn't work, I still had an out. There was a lovely exit stage right.

So I told the guys I was an international student, a Canadian, and they believed me. I told them I smoked pot every once in a while, and because of my long hair, they believed me. I told them I was a Communist. I had, in fact, read Marx, Nader, Bakunin, and anthologies about temporary autonomous zones and anarcho-collectivism. I could credibly talk about Communism—and I loved the notoriety of the label. I wasn't entirely sure if I believed it, but those initial weeks were all about trying on a new set of clothes, and I was glad to wear the red star.

In fact, the summer before college, I had been dabbling in leftist politics. I went to the Campus Green Party national conference in Chicago, as the lone representative of a new chapter I had yet to start at Wabash College. I took a Greyhound bus to Chicago, traveling by myself for the first time in my life. With other young activists, I slept on the floor of a radical church near the campus of UIC. I visited Hull House on my own, just because I was curious to see it. I sat in a crowded theater with other kids from the conference and heard Cornel West rock the place with his speech.

But I didn't talk to anyone. No one from Wabash was there, and I didn't know a soul, and I must have erected a strong enough social shield to prevent others from attempting to talk to me. It was weird. I expected someone else to at least be mildly curious about me, to at least reach out and start a small conversation, but almost no one did. In some ways, that was exactly how I wanted it. I didn't want to have the pressure to muster up words for conversation. But in other ways, I was longing for human connection. At this conference, I was hoping to meet someone who shared my passions, ideals, and creativity. Instead, I felt invisible, like no one else was able to see me, like I was a ghost passing through the walls of the radical church and the staid convention hall.

I did have one good conversation. Another kid from some other college wanted to gather all the queer kids into a lavender caucus. There were caucuses for environmental issues, labor issues, and gender equity. We needed one for LGBT inclusion, as well. When I talked to the kid who was organizing the lavender caucus, that was my one moment of human connection during those three days. And that moment was beautiful, but the rest of the conference was disheartening.

I was determined that college wasn't going to be like that. The actual experience of college was not going to be that same kind of self-loathing, self-isolating, grateful-to-enjoy-what-I-can-of-the-gifts-of-life-even-while-I-look-with-longing-toward-others-who-instinctively-know-how-to-make-friends-when-I-don't kind of experience. That's one of the reasons I joined a fraternity in the first place.

So I dove into this new social world, this protected space where I had automatic relationships and a reason to start conversations—this whole new world where I was going to try to be a new man.

I got to know my pledge brothers, the other incoming freshmen. There was Tim Tamberlaine, the pudgy kid from a small town in Indiana who was creative, witty, and an accomplished author of short stories—a true peer for me. There was Ric Morales, the Hispanic kid from San Antonio who dressed in black, loved Pearl Jam, sported great eyelashes, and had a car and a gas card. His parents encouraged him to use both to make friends. There was Nathan Mutanguha, a Rwandan freshman who I had recruited to the fraternity. We were part of the same orientation cohort. When I found out he was looking for a place to live, I told him about Tau Kappa Epsilon.

All told, there wound up being ten of us, including two international students, a swimmer from Oregon, and an anime-loving genius who could never seem to apply his genius to his schoolwork. There was John McDonnell, a spirited Christian with a plucky attitude and a love of soccer. There was Francisco Rodriguez, the gay kid from Brownsburg, TX who could finally be himself in this new place.

The more I got to know these new pledges, and the active members as well, the less of a front I needed to put up, and the more I could have faith in who I really was. I found that I could connect with these people as a geeky creative writer who loved literature, politics, and a good joke.

I didn't have to be Canadian, so I dropped that pretense in a matter of days. I didn't have to be a drug user, so I let that one go, as well. I told them that "Communist" was an exaggeration, but that I was certainly a progressive. Nonetheless, my official fraternity nickname became "Commie Steve."

When we ate our meals in the Apollo Room, there was a lot of wit around the table. Sure, some of the jokes were crude, not unlike the humor that got me kicked out of restaurants when I was a kid, but some of it was genuinely witty. These were smart kids, young men who excelled and stood out in the places where they were from, and now we were all together in the same room, living under the same roof. It wasn't exactly what I dreamed college would be. It was better.

Freshman year was a roller coaster ride. I got to take a class on Beat Poetry!—and other literature courses that blew my mind. I joined the editorial boards of a national undergraduate literary magazine, a humanities journal, and the school newspaper. I wrote an opinion column for the newspaper, and I quickly ascended to Opinion Editor because no one else wanted the job.

9/11 happened. The first plane crashed when I and others were in a class on early American literature. As we came back from class, we heard the rumors of the news. We gathered to watch TV in shock and horror. We saw the second tower go down together. Some guys called home, or their mothers and fathers called them. I hadn't even set up my student phone account yet, and my mom wasn't trying to call me anyway. She assumed I was fine unless she heard otherwise.

In response to the tragedy and the war that followed, I wrote incendiary columns for the school newspaper. I was inspired by Noam Chomsky, Walden Bello, and other radical authors I read in high school. I wrote about tragedies perpetrated by the United States all around the world, about antidemocratic actions and the deep pain we had caused. I wrote about the new tragedies that were going to be committed in our names through the war of revenge that was surely coming. Was it any wonder, I asked, that the world had visited on us what we had been visiting upon the world?

I wrote passionate columns in college. I wrote passionate poetry, both for class and for myself. I discovered alcohol. Really. No one even knew about it before me.

And praise God—I was a happy drunk. Alcohol lowered my inhibitions, and it did not reveal a lonely, scarred, bitter narcissist. Or an acidic insult comic. Or even a Canadian communist. Instead, it revealed a fun-loving poet, a hopeless romantic who appreciated life and had a piece of the Dalai Lama in his heart. That was the person I wanted to be. That was the person who could be found beneath my false personas and incongruous inhibitions.

One night freshman year, I flirted with a girl who was older than me. I told her I was a poet and I would write her poetry as beautiful as she was. At some point, I drank beyond the point of memory. I'm told that the older guys who were interested in the same woman put me in an empty trashcan and rolled me around the Apollo Room.

Later, she read my poetry and said it was pretty good. "I didn't believe you," she said, "when you said you were a poet, but these are impressive." She felt she lived too far away to date any of us, which was a nice way to let me down. I don't know what I would have done, anyway, if someone had agreed to date me. I didn't even have a driver's license.

But I didn't need a driver's license to have my first in-person sexual experience. One night, my fraternity brother Francisco was plying me with alcohol. I'm not sure why. I would have been perfectly happy to drink without any encouragement. But it seems he had plans for me that night.

He invited me to his bed. He told me he had to take care of me—because I was so drunk and all. And that I needed to remove my clothes—because I was so drunk and all. I wasn't all that drunk, and I didn't need to be to have this experience with him, but the alcohol helped me act with more confidence. Soon, we found ourselves under the covers. We took turns pleasing each other. My online experiences were worth something after all. They gave me a sense of what to do with him.

I remember him whispering, "I never imagined my first time would be like this. Did you?" That night, I was feigning confidence. In the moment, I pretended to be worldly and experienced, like this little thing was nothing compared to everything else I had done. I suppose, even with alcohol, there was some room for a false persona, but I didn't mind this one. He and I both needed me to be confident. We needed to believe that one of us knew what he was doing.

Francisco and I came together for just one night. He wanted to have his first sexual experience with me, but nothing more, just like Seth before him. I was mostly okay with that. He was furtive and nervous, in bed and otherwise, and it's not like we had a super-great friendship to build on—just a regular one. Still, I wouldn't have minded if he had wanted to pursue something more. I would have tried, and I would have pretended I knew what I was doing.

Alas, college life kept barreling on.

I was thriving academically. I began to think of myself as an English professor in the making, a person who could write poetry and teach it at a small, liberal arts college. I was finding my place at Wabash and wondering if I could just stay there forever.

Socially, in my ongoing quest to release my inhibitions, I tried pot for the first time. Tim scored some in his hometown and brought it back for me and other close friends. We smoked some before going to see our college's production of *The Complete Works of William Shakespeare (Abridged)*. Apparently, I had just enough to not be paranoid about getting caught, while still enjoying an enhanced comedy experience. I wrote a one-act play about the evening for a playwriting class. Some of the abridged Shakespearean actors were there as it was read and they were highly amused.

I discovered another addictive drug that year: Steak 'n Shake. At three in the morning, after a night of drunken conquests or a night of writing papers, a group of us would pile into Ric's car, drive half-an-hour on dark rural highways to Lebanon, Indiana, and talk about life, love, and everything in between. I enjoyed the Frisco Melt and a chocolate-banana shake. But I enjoyed the brotherhood even more.

Another important aspect of freshman year was the ups and downs of pledgeship. My fellow freshmen and I cleaned the house after weekends of debauchery. We experienced campus-wide rituals, like Chapel Sing and the Monon Bell Classic. We also experienced fraternity rituals, some of which were meaningful and contributed to personal growth, and some of which can't be classified as anything other than "hazing." I know that all of them were watered down from what they had been in previous years. I know our fraternity had the shortest pledgeship on campus and the smallest number of depledges, so we must have been doing something right. I think we were at least encouraging enough during the most absurd parts to keep our little crew together. But man, it was still absurd.

One of the more ridiculous rituals was the old "Oh, I'm sorry, just when you were on the cusp of joining, you failed some silly test and we're throwing you out" gag. In our fraternity, this was meant to inspire fear, desperation, and longing. But it didn't work on me. I was ready to go if they tried that crap on me.

Don't get me wrong: I liked it there. I'd made friends. But I was ready to cut them off if they rejected me. I was not someone who clinged. I had learned the futility of that long ago. I wasn't going to let myself be hurt again.

During that final ritual, the details of which are locked in a vault of fraternal secrets, the pledges were separated from each other. We were each in an individual room without cell phones or computers. Technology and connection might have shattered the illusion. Individually, we were all told we failed the final challenge and asked to write a letter to the active members, explaining why they should make an exception and let us join.

I knew this was supposed to rend us into spasms of heartbreak and regret. We were supposed to write a contrite, despairing letter to the active members, explaining how sorry we were and how desperate we were to join.

I did end up writing a little essay, because all things considered, I would rather join and keep these friends and not have wasted my time cleaning grout with a toothbrush. I didn't *want* to be cast into the outer darkness. But if I was going to be, then fine. Honestly, guys, no big deal.

Even as I went through the motions of wanting to belong by writing that letter, I still told myself I didn't care; I was still prepared to leave them before they left me. The defense I chose was angry, preparatory isolation. I fortified my emotional walls and told myself I didn't need that stupid fraternity. Cast me aside if you want. I'll wander. I'll find a new home. I'll survive. And I'll learn to make the best of it. As I always do.

In the end, it was all a big joke and we were all accepted into the fraternity. When the older guys revealed the gag, I laughed. Others were relieved. Some threatened the active members with humorous acts of violence. They were all far more passionate than me. I had already numbed myself in preparation of rejection, so the only emotion I could muster was an ironic, distanced laugh.

If this had been real, and I hadn't been allowed to join, I think the emotions would have come eventually—the shame, the embarrassment, the grief, the loss. But the feelings would probably still have been muted. I wanted to be there, I wanted to belong, but I also needed my thick emotional walls, with menacing skull and crossbones painted across the plaster, to express the push and pull between connection and isolation.

Before I could let God into my heart—before I could acknowledge the one who was standing there, knocking at the door—I had a lot of growing to do. I had a lot to learn. And I needed to find my way to deeper feelings.

That first spring, an opportunity for emotional growth was offered by a delightfully nerdy fraternity brother, Jake Williams, who said one simple thing that changed my life forever.

Jake was in the class above me, and I admired him. His glasses were the height of nerdom, his skin was pasty white, and his brilliance was unparalleled. I'm sure he would have bested us all in an I.Q. test. After graduating from Wabash, he would go on to doctoral work in Chemistry at a prestigious research university, where he would win the highest award available to a doctoral student of any discipline. That's the kind of smart he was, and we got to bask in his brilliance for a few years.

Jake was witty and liked puns. He liked to memorize the latest rap song and delight us all with nerdy, impromptu rap sessions. His humor was always positive, but mine was not. During the spring semester, I was trying on a new persona as an acidic insult comic. I was cutting and crude, and I delighted in deflecting attention from my flaws by highlighting someone else's. I relished the attention I received from comments that hit their intended mark. I began practicing this form of comedy while defending others, verbally stepping up and fighting back when other people were being cut down. But the more attention I received, the bigger my head got. Soon enough, I was the aggressor. This was not the way of Jake Williams.

Jake would go out of his way to help people. I once saw him break up a fight between two of our fraternity brothers, jumping in without a moment's hesitation. He pulled them apart, yelling at them both until they were jarred back into their senses. Usually, when he went out of his way to help, it was tutoring us in math and science, but sometimes it was through acts of physical bravery like that one.

Jake was an atheist. I mention that because I don't want you thinking he offered me a shining example of Christian morality. He would no doubt be amused to know he had some role to play in me becoming a Christian. But Christians don't have a monopoly on virtue.

Anyway, we were sitting around the suite of rooms occupied by Tim and me and a couple of others. We were making fun of someone. I don't remember who or why. I said something mean. I don't remember what. What I remember is that Jake turned to me and said, "Man, Steve. If you weren't already my friend, I wouldn't like you at all."

Simple words, like I said, but coming from a person like him, they were jarring. I felt them in my gut before my brain had a chance to analyze them, and I got quiet. Later, I reflected on the course of my life and that unfolding freshman year. How did I get from an abused kid to a nascent adult who verbally abused other people?

When I first came to school, I was a long-haired Beat poet, a gentle-hearted Green Party activist with Buddhist inflections. I was full of idealistic visions for world peace and social justice. I was going to change the world with poetry and protest. As a child of abuse, I wanted to use the outsider feeling I had felt my whole life to motivate compassion for other marginalized people. I wanted to stand beside them and inspire others to do the same. But to gain the approval of others, I had gone on a rampage. I had tried on the identity of a verbal swashbuckler with a razor-sharp wit. And I realized I didn't like it. I barely liked myself on a good day. But I really didn't like who I was becoming.

It was time to make a change, and I knew of a book that might help. I had bought Aldous Huxley's *The Perennial Philosophy* back in high school and brought it to college with me, but I hadn't opened it yet. In retrospect, maybe God was behind this, guiding me to wait until the right moment to explore its pages.

I already respected and admired Huxley as a writer. I was already primed to hear what he had to say with a bias toward affirming his perspective. Maybe he would offer some timeless wisdom that could help me be more like the person I wanted to be.

In *The Perennial Philosophy*, Huxley presents himself as an editor and the book as an anthology. He styles himself as a curator of ancient wisdom from the mystical traditions of the world's great religions, but the connecting words he writes between quotes from great mystics go beyond simple editing. If he is indeed an editor, then he is an editor with a clear agenda. His contention is that there is an Ultimate Reality, a spiritual force that grounds all things and guides all things, a divine something that is beyond explanation and description. This divine force is bigger than every religion, and all the world's great mystics, from every religion, have seen and interacted with it. You can see the outlines of it when you read their writings. When the mystics describe their visions, despite the different traditions they represent, the visions are the same—a bright white light that overcomes reality, an awareness of some presence beyond the grasp of human words. And when you look at their moral teachings, they're essentially the same: do unto others as you would have others do unto you, a golden rule that repeats itself in variations throughout the world's great religious traditions. Virtues like compassion, community, humility, and gratitude—all these are connecting points from one mystic to the next. When you look at their spiritual disciplines, Huxley says, they're all doing the same things: contemplation, meditation, mindfulness.

One of the first things that struck me about this work is that it neatly answered my childhood objections against faith. As a fourth grade atheist, I had argued that religion was unjust, that it was unfair to think of one religion as true while the others were false, and cruel to reward one group over another because of the accident of birthplace. In response to this incongruity, my childhood self concluded that no religion could be true. However, Huxley seemed to use the same propositions to reach a different conclusion. For him, it was also absurd to think of one religion as truer than any other, and his conclusion was that all of them were true—that all faiths contained seeds of holy truth that point to the Perennial Philosophy above them all.

Now, speaking as my contemporary self, it's worth saying that Huxley was not exactly the neutral, religious arbiter he presented himself to be. He was, at heart, a Buddhist, even if his spiritual and intellectual system was bigger than Buddhism alone. His interpretation of the teachings of mystics from other traditions tended to make them look a lot like Buddhists.

It's also worth saying that today, as a Christian, I evaluate *The Perennial Philosophy* differently. I would say the Perennial Philosophy he was describing is most fully and most truthfully described, not in a weighted anthology of quotes from various mystical writers, but in the life of Jesus Christ—and in the Bible that stands as a witness to that life and to other ancient acts of God. Today, I would say that Huxley found all the remarkable similarities he noted across traditions by reading Buddhism into everything, by not respecting the unique singularities of these writers and their paths. He was seeing in their works what he wanted to see rather than what was there. I would say there are real similarities to highlight in these writings, but Huxley may have oversimplified them, and I believe the similarities that are there are more fruitfully viewed through a Christian lens.

But I wasn't a Christian back then. Back then, I was a Buddhist-inspired agnostic who had a spiritual experience while reading *The Art of Happiness* two years prior, and I still didn't know what to do with that experience. I still didn't know what it meant or how to interpret it.

But with this book, my eyes were opened. I finally had a framework for my strange vision—a vision of a profound, overwhelming white light that overshadowed reality, left me in awe of its beauty, and made me wonder if it even really happened. With this book, I could affirm that what I had learned back then was an introduction to the Perennial Philosophy. Reading *The Art of Happiness*, I had been introduced to a rudimentary Buddhist spirituality, not as rigorous as the spiritual practices of the mystics, but not wholly unlike the meditation, mindfulness, and prayers of gratitude that captivated their spirits.

And I had been blessed by a vision of the ultimate divine reality. It had come to me not because I was a worthy sage who had been laboring for years, hoping for a vision of a world beyond my own. It had come to me because I was desperate, because I was unhappy to the point of despair, because I was almost ready to end my life. In religious terms, I was humble. I was broken. I was empty. When you are completely devoid of all pretenses, and when all your defenses have been overcome, the divine reality may just come and fill the empty vessel that is you.

Now, with this frame of interpretation, I had some grasp on what had happened to me. But of course, I hadn't known what to do with it then. Interestingly, the great mystics often expressed perplexity in response to their visions. *What is this?* they often thought. *What do I do with it? How do I tell other people when I can barely describe it to myself? Did it even really happen?* These were all questions they, and I, had asked—in a moment that already felt like a dream to me, in a moment that was shrouded in distance and memory.

Given all this, I felt I had little choice. Under the guidance of Aldous Huxley, I gave up the agnostic label, and, like so many of my generation, I became "spiritual, but not religious."

It was unclear what this change in label would really change in me, if anything would happen on the outside to make this more than an intellectual shift. Would I meditate? Was there a Buddhist community I could join? Would I begin thinking of Christianity as my culture's expression of the Perennial Philosophy? Would I start going to church? Could I adopt some filtered, edited version of that faith? At the very least, I would try to be a better person, try to live by the moral code of the great mystics. I would strive for compassion, try to be humble, and try to forgive others.

At the end of the day, this humble moral striving was the path I chose. I didn't join a spiritual community or take on any spiritual practices. But I did try to become a better person. And intellectually, an important shift had taken place. I was no longer simply open to the possibility that there might be a metaphysical reality in the world. I now believed in one. And I was no longer beholden to intellectual ways of knowing alone. Huxley had shown me an intellectual framework for emotional and spiritual knowing, a way of seeking and sharing truth that was more than reasoning from a supposedly objective set of propositions.

Because Huxley expressed these views, and because my experience confirmed them, I could believe them. Because my earlier reading and experience led to this, I could believe it.

Beyond belief, there is action. Beyond knowing, there is doing. The moral prescriptions presented in Huxley's book painted a picture of the person I wanted to be, a person I was not at the moment, but a person I had seen flickers of over the years—a challenge I could grow into.

At the time, I did not know that this ideal, compassionate self was very much like the whole and holy person of Christianity, the person who emerges when you die to your false self and your true self emerges from the depths of your heart, gaining expression in a new life dancing in the heart of the world.

At the time, I would not have seen a place for myself as a religious believer, as a devotee of any one religion. I still had some of the same religious antipathy I held through middle school and high school, the same sense of scorn for mythology, the same conviction that religion had done incalculable harm in the world, though I was beginning to be open to the possibility that the good might outweigh the bad.

Still, I was glad to be "spiritual, but not religious," with an emphasis on both parts of the term—because I was certainly spiritual and definitely *not* religious.

13

All My Heart

DURING MY FRESHMAN YEAR of college, my emotional awakening continued to unfold, and I began the relationships that led me to God.

There were fraternal relationships. There was my pledge brother, John, a committed person of Christian faith. I could see his kindness, his intelligence, and how religion was an animating spirit for him. As I got to know him, I asked him about his faith and what it meant to him. He never convinced me to change my mind, but like my earlier friends Seth and Julia, he helped change my outlook on faith. He showed me that you could be an intelligent person and still believe, and that belief could be a powerful thing that energized and vivified your soul.

There were academic relationships. To check off the religion box on my liberal arts checklist, I took Religions of China and Japan. The professor was a kind man who had graduated from Wabash, gone on to divinity school, and become fascinated with Eastern religions. Getting to know him and experiencing his soulful, meditative teaching, my heart was further softened toward religion.

Outside of class, through the school newspaper, I interviewed Dr. Bill Placher, also a graduate of Wabash. He had been on campus thirty-one years prior to us, when the Kent State shootings led to a series of sit-ins and teach-ins. Given the state of the world in 2002, in the wake of a massive terrorist attack on US soil and foreign wars on the horizon, we were curious about how previous generations of Wabash Men had responded to times of turmoil. In our interview, I found Dr. Placher to be warm, good-humored, and insightful. Here was yet another figure, a decidedly Christian theologian, softening my heart toward faith.

But I can't tell you the story of my conversion without telling you about Dani, who was my first in-person kiss and my first in-person love, and I can't tell you about Dani without Gabriela. And I wouldn't have met anyone remotely like them if not for Ric. He was my social connection—and almost as importantly, he was the one who had the car.

Through Ric, we made a connection with the young women who lived on the fourth floor of Mason Hall at DePauw (the same DePauw my mom could have attended as an undergrad if she had accepted the town doctor's offer). Ric was nice enough to take his pledge brothers with him on the half-hour drive to our rival campus. We partially went because we needed some "feminine energy" in our lives. And yes, those were the words we used. We weren't being crude; we just didn't want to spend all our time in a hyper-masculine space. The young women we met were freshmen, just like us—first-years, as they were called at DePauw, because DePauw was more socially aware than Wabash.

When the guys and I visited DePauw, I wondered if I might impress some young woman with my poetry. I would have been glad to impress a young man with my verses, as well, but there were plenty of men at Wabash. I didn't need to travel for them. We visited Mason Hall because of the women—and not simply because we wanted to date them, but because it was nice to be in well-decorated spaces that smelled good. It was nice to be with people who were softer around the edges.

So I was glad to join Ric, Tim, John, and whoever else came on our frequent sojourns to Mason Hall. And on one of those trips, I met Gabriela. I fell for her the moment I saw her. She had a strange accent that was hard to place at first. I soon found out that she was born in Guatemala and raised in Chicago, and her voice was a mélange of these and other influences. She had done some modeling. And she was clearly beautiful. But it was more than that. There was just something about her, something you could see in her eyes if you took the time to look.

Gabriela had found her way to DePauw through a special program for promising kids in the inner city. Part of the reason she stood out from the other girls in Mason Hall is that she never really belonged there. She was from another place. She was going somewhere else. A sense of difference emanated from her body and soul. Gabriela was tall for a woman, a little taller than me. She had fair skin, long and lustrous black hair, and eyes that had seen too much of the world. They were kind eyes, deep and perceptive, but there was a barrier in them. She was slender, with graceful legs, and it was easy to believe her when she told us she had done some modeling. She said that she had modeled for an art student who needed a nude figure for a painting. I asked if she might consider posing nude for a poem. She laughed and declined.

The citizens of the fourth floor of Mason Hall were curious about the world and curious about us, and we were curious about them. At first, we came to visit John's girlfriend Alexandria and her roommate, Kylie, but it didn't take long for other young women to emerge from their cocoons and spread their curious wings in our direction.

Just as I was falling for Gabriela, another girl was also capturing my attention. Her name was Dani, and that's an American name if you couldn't tell, short for Danielle. Dani was fluent in Spanish—but she was also studying Spanish literature, with a double major of Spanish and creative writing. She was conversant in the language of poetry and had written promising poetry of her own.

She had a joyful spirit and a laugh I longed to hear again. One night, when our group was about to leave, she grabbed my wrist and told me I couldn't go. I ran up and down the hallway, with her running behind me, holding my wrist, both of us laughing like the long-lost kid in my soul.

Dani was a person of faith, an evangelical Christian. If I had met her in high school, I may not have even thought of liking her, but now, my heart was softened toward faith. Now, I was spiritual, but not religious, and I didn't mind if the person I was next to was on a different spiritual path.

Unbeknownst to me, she had been praying about me that spring, asking God if it would be okay to date me. She had never really dated anyone in-person, either. She had never even dated online, as I had.

But I needed to get Gabriela out of my system first.

One night, I was chatting with Gabriela on Instant Messenger. This wasn't uncommon for me. I didn't have my own computer at school, so I would go to one of the computer labs on campus or borrow one from a guy in the fraternity. I often chatted with people I'd known online for years—people like Dominic and Seth, who were beginning their own college adventures. But I was also chatting with these new friends from Mason Hall, with Dani and Gabriela especially.

One night, around ten o'clock, Gabriela told me she was bored. It was spring break. Most of the kids on both of our campuses were home or in Florida. I didn't mind the quiet, and I looked forward to all the uninterrupted reading I could do, but Gabriela felt differently.

I wrote, "Let's play freeze tag."

She wrote, "You're on."

I asked Tim if he was up for a drive and he said he was. I told her we'd be there in half an hour.

That night, Gabriela and I organized a giant game of freeze-tag. There were girls from Mason Hall, other friends of hers from around campus, and Tim and me, running through the various quads of DePauw University, disturbing the peace of the arboretum.

Eventually, the game broke up. Gabriela and I sat on the grass, talking, outside of Asbury Hall. Tim, ever the gentleman, found something else to do, so we could say the things we needed to say. That night, we told each other our life stories.

Gabriela had a rough childhood. She said she was never really loved and never really accepted by the people who adopted her in Chicago. She felt like the city was her home, but she didn't have a home within that home.

I told her a version of my own childhood story, some version of what you've read here—only much shorter, thank goodness. I told her about living in Hawaii, experiencing abuse there, being relegated to foster care, and how life was never the same after that.

I told her about a dream I'd been having. I am locked away in a white tower, with reams of paper scrawled with words no eye would ever read. Through a crack in the cobbled stone, I can catch an occasional glimpse of the outside world. All of a sudden, a woman rides up on a white horse. The horse rears up, kicks out its front hooves, and knocks down the castle walls. I leap from the tower onto the back of the horse and we ride away together.

Gabriela nodded as I told the story. She smiled and said she could offer an interpretation. "The white horse is an archetype," she said. "A common mythological symbol. It's the hero's horse. You've been locked away in an ivory tower, an academic one. The woman is coming to rescue you."

This resonated with me. Although I hadn't had an adult therapy session at that point, I knew enough to know that I had survived the past by erecting intellectual walls and emotional fortifications, and that the way to freedom was to knock them down and live.

We kept talking, discussing visions of the future, whether she really fit at DePauw, asparagus, and what life was all about. "Asparagus," you ask? Yes, I think we were talking about our favorite and least favorite foods, and I expressed antipathy toward asparagus. She explained to me that Americans ruin asparagus and most other vegetables. When you boil them, they become tasteless blobs of what they might have been. In Guatemala, they know how to make vegetables. You grill asparagus. Then it's wonderful.

When we began to see the first hints of the sun, we knew the evening had come to an end. We found Tim sleeping on a comfy chair in the lobby of Mason Hall. Tim was a trooper. He'd hung out for a while with some people he knew, found a book to read in the lobby of Mason, and then fell asleep in the lobby. Gabriela and I hugged goodbye. I woke up my pledge brother and we went out in search of breakfast.

After that night, I was officially madly in love with Gabriela. If I knew more about the world at that time, I would have found some excuse to get closer to her during that conversation. When she was sharing her struggles, I might have found a way to reach out with some comforting touch. At a moment of high humor, I could have leaned in and attempted a kiss. But I didn't know how to do all that.

And if you're me, you have to know how to do a thing. You find your way through uncertain terrain because you have an intellectual map. In this situation with Gabriela, I was learning to be bolder, but I didn't have a map. I didn't have a way of studying before acting.

On our next trip to the fourth floor of Mason Hall, I told Gabriela how I felt about her. How amazing she was. How she was the embodiment of everything I hoped for in a girlfriend. And if she felt even a smidgeon of something for me, could we go on a date?

She was flattered. Her body language was positive. She didn't reject me out of hand, but she told me she would think about it. She asked that I give her some space, and that I not come back to campus while she considered it.

For the next seven days, she was all I thought about. Sometimes, I would see her online. I would engage her in conversation, ask about her day, being careful not to mention the elephant in the virtual room.

I listened to moody, romantic music. I wrote bad poetry about asparagus. I dreamed about her. I fantasized about her. I yearned for her.

Eventually, I found myself chatting with her on a borrowed computer in the frat house, and she gave me her answer. It was no. She said it might have been yes under other circumstances, but I had come on so forcefully, emitted so much pressure. I was too much. I... Tears flooded out of my eyes. I didn't think about them. I couldn't control them. They just came.

I ran down to the basement, looking for some quiet corner of the house where I could be alone and just weep. I had never sobbed like this. The last time I cried, it was my junior year of high school, and I had just seen a vision of the most holy and beautiful thing I'd ever seen or ever will. Even then, the tears had been quiet. My eyes welled up. One or two teardrops quietly strayed down my cheek. It was not like this. Before high school, I hadn't cried since fourth grade, when someone tossed a flat, wet basketball as high as they could into the air, and it just happened—and I believe this was thoroughly an accident—to come down like a slap against my cheek. I cried then, but not like this.

These were ugly, unmanageable, snotty tears, because I was crying not just for Gabriela, but for everything. For all the chances I'd never taken. For all the life I'd missed out on. For all the moments that could have been different. For all the pain I'd suffered and tried to hold at a distance.

Intellectually, I knew there would be other people to love. I knew I could learn from this and come on less strong next time. But at the time, none of that mattered. In that moment, she was my hope for the future. She embodied the concept that all the suffering had been for something, that my absurd childhood had made me a sensitive, creative creature to prepare me for her, that it had given me stories to tell so I would have something to share with her, that I had failed to live life with other people in other ways because the whole journey had been leading to her. On that day, a whole damn lifetime of hurt was streaming down my face.

But in the midst of the sobbing, there was this: I felt something. I didn't know I could feel that much, express that much. I didn't know I had all those feelings within me waiting to burst out like the water swelling behind a dam. In order to truly grow as a person, I would need to experience these feelings again and again. But this was a turning point. This was not the final mountain of complete emotional growth, but it was a tall hill to climb along the way. I don't know if my heart would have been as open to Dani—or to God—without it.

Meanwhile, life carried on. Classes were taken. Papers were written. I practiced being a better person in the dining hall and Steak 'n' Shake and all those places where I had been a jerk throughout the year. At the same time, I kept talking to Dani, and I was amazed by our conversational chemistry. We laughed through language, literature, and life. We shared our stories. We discussed all the things young people talk about during that initial phase of a relationship—when you exaggerate similarities, dismiss differences, and think you have never had and never will have as much in common with any other human being.

As the end of the semester approached, I considered asking her out, but I knew we weren't going to see each other over the summer. She was going to be at home in Indianapolis, and I would be in Fort Wayne.

I was considering some travel. I had money saved up from previous summer jobs, and I wondered about visiting some of the people from my online world. I wondered about jumping on a Greyhound and seeing America, a la Jack Kerouac. But my online friendships were fading. Julia wasn't talking to me much anymore. Neither was Mia. And Dom wasn't sure his mother would approve of some random guy from the internet coming over.

Gabriela thought I could come to Chicago. She wanted to show me the Taste of Chicago Festival. I was excited for that. And Ric invited me to come to San Antonio and hang out with him. But as for Dani, it's not like I had a car or a driver's license. I couldn't just show up with a bouquet of flowers in Indianapolis and take my romantic chances. I could travel to see people who knew me, people who didn't have particular expectations of me, people who could put me up for the night. Dani wasn't in that category.

Still, toward the end of the semester, she mentioned in an online conversation that she'd never been on a date. She wondered if she ever would be. I told her that when we came back in the fall, I would ask her out.

"I don't want a pity date," she wrote.

"It's not a pity date," I responded. "I like you. I love talking to you. I'd like to get to know you better."

"Okay," she said. "I'll think about it."

What she would do, of course, was pray about it. What did God think of the idea of her dating a non-Christian?

That summer, we kept talking, and soon the floodgates exploded. We knew we liked each other, and we didn't want to wait until the fall. She drove up to Fort Wayne on a Saturday, and I planned a whole day for us: a movie at the indie theater, the art museum in downtown Fort Wayne, lunch, and ice cream. We held hands. We hugged. We didn't kiss. We were both too nervous and unstudied for that. But at the end of the day, we knew who we were to each other. We were dating. For both of us, there was no one else.

As the summer unfolded, I went to Chicago for the Taste of Chicago and, more importantly, to see Gabriela. She was glad to hear about me and Dani, and I was glad to let my former crush go on her way.

As Gabriela and I sat on a grassy hillside, enjoying our various tastes of Chicago, a palm reader approached us. Would we like our palms read? Gabriela said yes, and I said no. The woman took her fair-skinned, Guatemalan hand.

Gabriela was seeing someone at the time, a Chicago-based boyfriend I met when we toured her neighborhood. The palm reader sensed there was trouble in the relationship, some kind of fracture between her and her lover. When the palm reader left, Gabriela explained that the palm reader assumed that she and I were dating. Since she had said yes to the reading and I had said no, the reader assumed there was some kind of blood in the water. I laughed. "How clever," I said.

During this visit, I learned that Gabriela would not be returning to DePauw. She was a wild spirit and a rolling stone. She loved adventure too much to be contained by Greencastle, Indiana—not unlike my mother before her.

Meanwhile, I was the one delving into a relationship with an inherent tension, an oppositional force that any palm reader worth their salt could have seen. Dani was an evangelical, churchgoing Christian, and she believed

I was not saved. I was open to her being who she was, to her faith being what it was, and to it all being part of the beautiful package of her, despite all the prejudices I had formed about religion in the past. But she was less open to me. She liked me. She was willing to take a chance on me. She had been praying about me and she believed she had been given the green light from God. But to what end?

That summer, through the magic of Greyhound, I visited her in Indianapolis. It was a complicated arrangement. Dani's parents were divorced, and Dani lived with her dad and younger brother. Her mom had an apartment nearby, and that was where I would spend the night. During this trip, I learned about her mom's schizophrenia. She heard the voices of angels. At times, they would leave her in ecstasy. But at other times, many other times, it was agony. She had to keep the voices at bay by being consistent with her medication. She also had to avoid stimulation. She kept the apartment lights dim. She did everything she could not to leave the apartment. She couldn't give the voices even a moment of real estate in her mind.

I was sorry for her mother, and for all the ways schizophrenia limited life for her and those closest to her, but it somehow comforted me to know that Dani's family was odd, that Dani had suffered during her mother's descent into madness. Obviously, I wished it were not so, but the fact of childhood pain is such a formative part of me, and I didn't know that anyone could fully get me if they didn't have some kind of tragic story of their own.

Later in life, I would learn how frighteningly common it is to have a tragic story, how we all have something hidden away in the deep recesses of our mind, something we hope we never have to talk about, whether it's a tragic event or simply our own perceived depravity. We all have those hidden things that Jung came to label our "shadow self." We all know what it's like to be tortured—or, at the very least, to torture ourselves.

That weekend, I met Dani's father, who immediately made it clear he disapproved of me. How would I support his daughter? I would be a writer, and perhaps a teacher. Had I ever done a day's hard work in my life? I had a newspaper route. I worked in a grocery store. That was nothing. He respected people who produced things. He was a person who contributed something tangible to the world.

I couldn't help but think: If I grew up to marry her and we somehow wound up moving in with him, it would be *All in the Family*, and I already had the hair to play Michael Stivic. Not the mustache, but the hair.

Speaking of hair, and how mine was long and a bit feminine, you may be wondering whether my bisexuality was an obstacle to my budding relationship with an evangelical Christian. It was something we talked about, for sure, and she decided she was okay with it. She was the person I was dating, and I wasn't going to be dating anyone else of any gender, so it was fine. If I were to convert to Christianity, she would expect me to not claim that part of who I am. But for the time being, I was bound for hell anyway, so what was one more sin?

But it wasn't something her parents needed to know about, and that was fine by me.

Throughout our relationship, Dani had various thoughts about bisexuality and the impact it had on us. Sometimes, she referred to me as her long-haired David, an aesthetic work of art who could stand in as a neo-classical model of biblical heroism. She also appreciated my sensitivity, my warmth, my affinity for art and poetry. There were parts of me having a touch of femininity that she liked. But at other times, she was disturbed by me. She wondered if I was masculine enough to be the commanding head of the household that her version of the Bible demanded. She wondered, even if I became a Christian, if I could be the love of her life.

That summer, we took in the Children's Museum in Indianapolis, the Art Museum, and the river walk. On Sunday morning, we went to her home church, a Methodist church in her neighborhood, right next to the campus of the University of Indianapolis. "What a small world," I thought. "In some alternate storyline, could I have gone to the University of Indianapolis and wound up meeting her all the same—on campus, in the neighborhood, maybe even at this very church?"

That summer, we kept talking. Our relationship was mostly on Instant Messenger and the phone, and that worked for me. Those were the only formats where I knew how to be a boyfriend. And that worked for her, too, since she was even less experienced in the world than me.

As we kept talking, three distinct things came into focus: First, we were falling for each other. We looked forward to seeing each other's screen names pop up on Instant Messenger. We loved pouring our hearts out over the phone. It was a joy to have someone to share the day with, someone to know even as I was known.

The second thing was that all of this was on a timer. She told me she could date a non-Christian, but not marry one. Yes, there was some Scripture about a non-believing spouse being saved by his believing spouse, but in those instances, neither partner was a believer in the beginning of the marriage. She did not wish to be unequally yoked with a life-long partner.

But the third thing was more hopeful: The fall was coming. At the end of the summer, I was in San Antonio with Ric. I had taken several Greyhound buses to get there, and we had several adventures, which would culminate in me sitting in the passenger's seat of his legendary car as he drove us from Texas back to Indiana. It didn't matter to him that I couldn't share in the driving. He wasn't going to let anyone else touch his steering wheel, anyway. Meanwhile, Dani was wrapping up the summer in Indianapolis and preparing to head back to DePauw. She and I started making plans.

She didn't want to come and visit me at Wabash. She could maybe come for a day, but she didn't want to spend the night in a fraternity. Still, she knew some people at the geeky fraternity at DePauw; I could spend the night there on weekends when I visited her. At the beginning of the weekend, I would arrange with Ric or Tim or whoever else to take me down on Friday and pick me up on Sunday. We wouldn't necessarily have to spend the whole weekend together. We both had homework. We both had books to read and poems to write. But we could cram a relationship into two or three concentrated days every week. Why not?

That first week in the fall, I convinced her to come up to Wabash just for a day, to support our house as we tried to recruit young men to join us. As you might imagine, on an all-male campus, it helped to have women hanging out during rush events. You wanted to show the young men that, if they joined your house, they would not have to lead a celibate life.

Dani had an infectious spirit. She was an atmosphere of joy. She played card games with the guys. She got to know them. I was glad she came. That day, we had our first kiss, and it was terrible. Neither of us knew what we were doing. We were both just pressing our lips against the other person's, not understanding how to lock them together, how to make it into something magical and real. We burst into laughter.

Fortunately, during my weekends at DePauw, we kept practicing and we figured it out. In fact, once we did, a hunger was sparked in both of us, and we made out all over campus. I discovered that it drove her crazy when I kissed her neck and ears, and I loved eliciting that reaction out of her. My hands were sometimes in the wrong place, and honestly, that was accidental. I was just glad to kiss, glad to have this connection with another human being offline. I didn't want to violate her boundaries. And even for the part of me that did, I didn't know how.

During the spring semester of her freshman year, Dani joined a sorority. DePauw has its fraternity and sorority rush during the spring of the students' first year. That way, people have a chance to get to know the houses, and the sisters have a chance to get to know new recruits, before they commit to each other. Dani wound up at Delta Zeta. As we were sophomores in a nascent relationship, much of our dating life took place at DZ.

We were in the sunroom of the sorority house when she tearfully told me that we needed to break up. The kissing was too much, especially on the neck and ears. It was too much pleasure, too much temptation. It was impeding her spiritual progress and distracting her from the God who should have been at the center of her life. I was taken aback. I could see, from her perspective, how she came to those conclusions. But I was in love with her. I didn't want to let her go. And she didn't want to let me go, either. She felt like she had to. She admired and appreciated me and wanted me to be close to her—but she wanted it too much for comfort.

In response, I comforted her. I told her we would remain friends. I told her it was okay. I backed off, but we kept talking, and it wasn't long before we were dating again. We set new physical boundaries for the relationship. The neck and ears were out of bounds. But the heart was not. For me, I continued to long for her in all the ways that her version of the Bible forbids, but I was content to hold back for the sake of an emotional connection—an emotional intimacy from which I had always fled but was beginning to embrace, with a heart that was being resurrected.

14

With Me All Along

Before meeting Dani, I didn't know it was possible to spend that much time with a person and still like them—or that they would still like me. I had never conceived of a concentrated relationship like this, manifesting itself each weekend at DePauw. We shared meals and study sessions, and then each night she dropped me off at Sigma Nu, and then I would see her again the next morning.

One evening, we were hanging out at Sigma Nu, and we didn't want to leave each other's company. She was tired. It was a long walk back to her place. It just made sense for her to spend the night with me, for us to cuddle on a twin bed and fall asleep in each other's arms. We wanted to make the most of every second of those magical weekends, so we started to spend the nights together, as well.

And all of that raised the question: What do we do about Sunday morning? Dani was always very clear that I didn't have to go to church with her. I was certainly invited and welcome, but she wasn't going to mandate that I come to church. If I came, it was my choice.

I was open to learning more about her faith—and not just because of hormones. Dani's faith was the most important thing to the person who had become the most important person in my life, and I wanted to experience it for the sake of getting to know her more. But I was also curious about faith on its own terms. I wanted to experience the feeling of worship and community. I wanted to know if there was something there for me—if church could be a place where I worshipped the Ultimate Reality of the Perennial Philosophy, in the form it had taken through the dominant religion of my culture.

Aside from this, I was also curious about my family's Christian heritage. When I was a teenager, my mom had become interested in genealogy.

It started when we explored the Indiana Highland Games, an annual Scottish heritage festival that took place each year in the bright metropolis of Fort Wayne. At the games, we enjoyed the music, the dancing, the contests, the food. Well, not the food. No one "enjoys" the food. You tolerate the food. But, aye, lassie, we tolerated the food!

From the Highland Games, Mom began to research our own family tree, and she discovered a distinct Scottish heritage in our bloodline. We were descended from three Scottish brothers who came to the American colonies in the 1740s to practice their Presbyterian faith more freely. Each of the brothers fought in the American Revolution, which was derisively called "the Presbyterian War" by some of the wits in King George's court. Some of the sons and grandsons of these three ancestors were educated at Yale and became Presbyterian ministers.

Indeed, looking back further, we could claim in our line Alexander Henderson, one of the Scottish divines who helped compose the Westminster Confession. I didn't know much about what that was, but I knew it was important, and that Christianity was somehow in my blood.

Dani's non-denominational, evangelical church was not Presbyterian, but going still felt like a connection with my ancestors, like a connection with those religious figures of the past. Dani offered that we could go to a Presbyterian church one day, and I was intrigued by the offer, but for the time being, I was happy to go to her church. I wanted to learn about what was important to her. I wanted her to have the weekly experience that was vital to her lifeblood.

And so, we went to church, and it was not horrible all the time. But it was horrible some of the time. In the eyes of the charismatic, middle-aged preacher and the PowerPoint that accompanied his sermons, you could not vote for a Democrat and follow God. Nor could you believe that femininity had any connection to the divine. He once devoted a long, rambling portion of his sermon to explaining that the Holy Spirit is a "he" and not a "she," as though this was the most important theological question the church had ever faced.

But sometimes, when he preached, I did feel uplifted. Sometimes, there were emotions stirring in my soul, and I felt connected to an Ultimate Reality that usually existed only in my mind. At that church, the Ultimate Reality could sometimes be more than a bloodless idea. Sometimes, I felt emotions stirring when we sang together. As in my middle-school encounter with a non-denominational, evangelical church, I loved some of the songs. I loved the experience of singing with a group of people. And despite the occasional terrible sermon, I often found the sermons to be edifying and uplifting.

But there were moments that felt jarring, too. Moments of exclusion. Moments of defining who we are by excluding those who we are not. Moments when the gathered body felt less like a warm and inviting hug, and more like an army on the march. When they sang, "Our God is an Awesome God," I imagined them clad in armor, marching in lockstep against the infidels. Marching in lockstep against me.

And this feeling was not entirely in my imagination. One Sunday, Dani was having lunch with her sisters at Delta Zeta. I was in the sitting room, reading; waiting for her so we could continue our afternoon together. But I heard some of her sisters talking about me. Why was I coming to church with them? What place did a non-believer have in their ranks? According to them, my presence was a blemish on the Body of Christ.

That morning, I had taken Communion because I was curious about it. I felt good about the service that morning, and I was inspired to try this sacrament. For some of the sisters of DZ, this was an especially egregious sin, a brazen sign of my base unworthiness. Only those whose sins are forgiven can drink the cup and eat the wafer. Dani stood up for me, asserting that all are welcome, and that this is what evangelism can look like—to expose someone to faith and arouse their curiosity. She was on my side, but nevertheless, they persisted.

In the churches I have pastored, I have always articulated the openness of the Communion table. The table belongs to Jesus and not to us. He invites everyone and excludes no one. You do not have to be "worthy" to sit at Christ's table. You are welcome because you are a child of God, made in the image of God, and you do not have to do anything or be anything to earn a place. Besides, the sacrament of Communion can transform you. It can help you become someone who bears the image of God with more grace. Like the baptism I received for all the wrong reasons during foster care, the sacrament doesn't depend on you and your state of mind. It's about God. It's about the good work God is doing. You are invited to come along for the ride.

I'm glad I received Communion before I was a believer. Today, as a pastor, I'm glad to offer it to anyone who wants it without a litmus test. But back in college, as a non-believer, I was furious at those women for talking about me like a theological circus freak. Embarrassed and angry, I had no interest in becoming a Christian if it meant becoming anything like them.

Still, despite all the dynamics that stood in the way, there were other moments when faith did not seem impossible. Dani was slowly and surely evangelizing me.

In fact, for the most part, I liked going to church. I was even starting to feel stirrings of faith. When the pastor talked about "a personal relationship with Jesus Christ" and knowing Jesus intimately, I could see that he was more closely connected to his personal image of God than I was to my abstract Ultimate Reality. I could see in Dani and in others how much faith meant to them, how it inspired them in ways my spirituality did not, how it animated their lives and, aside from a few notable exceptions, filled them with compassion.

The next week, the preacher went on his rant about the Holy Spirit being male, about how masculinity and divinity are inextricably entwined.

At lunch, I argued with Dani. Why go on a rant like that? What's the point?

"Because it's true," she argued. "It's important for us to assert what's asserted in Scripture. We have to hold to what the Bible tells us."

"But what about when revelation contradicts the Bible?" I asked. I reminded her of my vision from all those years ago; The bright white light that appeared to me back then did not appear to have a gender. For her part, she accepted my vision as a valid and holy experience, but she discounted my understanding of it because my mindset wasn't Christian enough. My ability to think theologically was not formed enough. If I really had experienced the Holy Spirit, Dani said, it's not like I saw the spirit's gender in my mind. It wasn't possible for a true revelation to contradict Scripture. That's how you test the spirits, how you discern if they are true or not. Scripture always wins.

We went back and forth for some time, me arguing that true divinity encompasses all genders and is beyond them at the same time, and her contending that Scripture is the bedrock upon which the house of faith is built, and that it can't be altered even a little.

It was infuriating. I got so frustrated with her I wanted to hit something, but there was nothing to hit. I didn't know what to do with my feeling of anger, so I threw a potato chip on the table. A single potato chip. It cracked open and bounced across the table. She laughed, and then so did I. Through her joy, the tension, like the potato chip, was broken.

As our sophomore year progressed, I started reading the Gospel of John. You see, Dani had given me a Bible. Like my friend David's sister in the fourth grade, she felt sure that if I were simply exposed to Scripture, I would understand its truth and feel its power. Out of respect for her, out of the curiosity that had been provoked by her church and other people—and out of an intellectual desire to better know the religion that stood at the foundation of my culture—I started reading.

I had heard somewhere, perhaps from a pastor or a friend, I don't remember who, that John was a good book for a beginning Christian or a curious non-Christian. I wondered if it would bear some imprint of the Perennial Philosophy—and if I might connect with it on that level.

I didn't think it would lead me to faith, though. No matter what I read in the Bible, it couldn't possibly answer my objections. The Bible could give its own testimony about itself, but it couldn't step outside itself to argue for its own validity. It couldn't speak to the other religions of the world, those other faiths whose claims were just as exclusive and just as irrational as Christianity's. It couldn't speak to the exclusive claims of salvation or the undeserved limits on the supposed compassion of God.

It couldn't speak to the reality that most Christians did not live up to their own faith, Dani notwithstanding. In my view, most Christians were self-righteous more than righteous. And a lot of the world's best people were people of other faiths or no faith at all. And the same could be said for intellect. I had met some intelligent Christians, but I hadn't seen in them a rational basis for Christianity. No one I had encountered could make a systematic argument for it, not like Aldous Huxley did for his Perennial Philosophy.

Even though I was interested in and open to learning from this Christ figure, I wondered if I might catch him in a contradiction, if I might see that Christianity was not consistent even in its own holy text. I also wondered if I might see evidence of a culturally biased and religiously exclusive force that could not cohere with an open, accepting Ultimate Reality.

Still, part of me wondered if I could believe. Part of me wanted to believe. If I were convinced of Christian faith, it would resolve a significant tension in a relationship that was becoming increasingly important to me. And I might find some of the animating spirit that inhabited the Christians I knew.

The Gospel of John was interesting. It was perplexing. It was spirit-centered. It was maddening. I loved seeing Jesus turn over the tables in the Temple and stand up for the downtrodden and excluded, but I hated seeing him on the attack, condemning people and preaching about hell. I hated the constant repetition of "the Jews" and all the invectives aimed against them. I didn't necessarily catch Jesus in a contradiction, but I didn't see the universal love I was hoping to see, either. In its exclusivity, in its moments of hubris, in its intolerance for others—even in the midst of a story where the protagonist is a victim of intolerance—it was not something I could claim as my own.

I could see something holy in Christianity. I could see it as a valid, virtuous, and valuable path for some. But it wasn't for me. I could never believe it.

That is, until the weekend Dani visited me at Wabash. That weekend, something strange and powerful happened.

For the most part, our relationship had been happening on those intense weekends when I visited DePauw, but one weekend, she was willing to come to Wabash and see me. She made it clear that she was not going to spend the night. For her, there was a line between our sleeping next to each other in a space that belonged to Sigma Nu and sleeping next to each other in a space that was mine. The power of temptation demanded that a line be drawn.

There was a Saturday night party at another frat house at Wabash, and some of her sisters wanted to go, and she would be their designated driver. The plan was that I would wait for her outside of the other house and intercept her before her group entered the building. I would take her back to my place and we would spend the evening together. When her group was ready, they would call her and she would take them home.

I walked across campus, determined to arrive in time to intercept Dani. I had planned a whole evening for us. But as I walked, I became at first slowly and then intensely aware of a pain in my right leg. At first, it felt like a tingling, and then it felt sharp and painful, like electric shocks. It felt like the nerves along my leg were waking up after years without sensation, like a much more intense version of a limb having "fallen asleep" and now waking up again.

I didn't know what it was, and I was limping from the pain. I just wanted to go back home, to deal with it somehow, to rest or see a doctor, or I didn't know what. I was feeling nervous that evening—about the prospect of skulking around outside of some other fraternity house. What if they saw me? What if they made fun of me? It would be weird to just stand there outside of a party. I had worked so hard to not be some random, shy weirdo on this campus, and there I was walking into a situation that reminded me of the worst of middle school and high school.

As an adult looking back, I wonder if the mystery pain was psychosomatic. That year, I was growing more and more into my emotions. Feelings were bursting through the floodgate that had been opened by my tears the previous spring—when Gabriela broke my heart. But I was also still suppressing emotions, because growth is a long process, and we human beings are never entirely one thing or another. We are dynamic creatures who are perpetually in process.

Perhaps the situation that night, which reminded me of so many past situations where I'd swallowed emotions and buried them deep within—but experienced at a time when I was newly open to feeling feelings—became the focal point for all those other moments of shame and embarrassment.

All those feelings of horror and humiliation. And my body expressed it through a pain in my leg—a pain that I couldn't deny, couldn't intellectualize, couldn't distance myself from. It hurt. I had to deal with it. I thought about turning back so I could deal with it.

But I didn't. Instead, I kept going. Near the other fraternity house, I found a spot to stand that seemed anonymous enough, close enough to see people going in and far enough away that I wouldn't look like a creepy weirdo stalker.

Unfortunately, a group of guys wound up noticing me. Across the street, there was another, rival fraternity, and boys from that house were hanging out of the windows, shouting into bullhorns. They were making fun of the fraternity throwing the party. They were trying to convince girls heading to the party that they should come over to their house, instead.

Some of them saw me and decided I was a perfect target. They recognized me as a columnist for the school newspaper and went after me for things I'd written. They shouted insults. They recognized the weirdness of me standing where I was and wondered what I was doing. They called me a "fag." They called me a "weird fucking jackass." They were ruthless. It was an embodiment of my worst fears about this whole stupid situation.

Between them and the damn pain in my leg, I decided to leave. It was all too much. But as I walked back to my own house, I questioned what I was doing. Dani was counting on me. Was there any way I could get in touch with her once she went inside that other house? Would I have to go to the party to find her? Would they even let me into their party? And what the hell was going on with this with this fucking leg thing? Goddamn, it hurt.

I thought that if I could just think clearly, I could figure it out. I tried to affirm the pain away. I told myself I had created the pain out of thin air; I had manifested it with my anxiety. If I could just convince myself that I was making it up, it would go away. But it didn't go away.

I tried praying to the abstract god I believed in—the god of inexpressible light I found in the Perennial Philosophy. But no help came.

In a last-ditch effort, I tried praying to the "paternal, Judeo-Christian God who I don't believe in." Those were the words I used in my head. The image of God that subsequently formed in my mind was of an old white man residing in the clouds. He had a beard and glowing eyes. He was a combination of Zeus and the cartoon God of Monty Python. It was a ridiculous image, and I didn't believe in it, but I prayed to it nonetheless.

The pain went away. My anxiety calmed. My mind cleared.

Once I was able to think again, I returned to the house with the party and found a new place to stand, out of sight of the guys with the bullhorns and in sight of the entryway. I saw Dani and she came home with me.

That night, there was a series of miscommunications, and Dani's friends wound up going back to Greencastle without her. They were probably drunk, and it probably wasn't safe for them to drive, but they made it back okay this time. Dani knew these girls well, and she thought this might happen, so she brought a toothbrush in her purse just in case.

On Sunday morning, we had breakfast. She wasn't sure about going to church, since her usual place in Greencastle was not an option for us, but I wanted to visit the Presbyterian church just up the road from Wabash. I wanted to experience worship that came from the tradition of my ancestors. I wanted to explore the part of this tradition that pulsed in my blood. Most of all, after what I had experienced the night before, I was curious to explore other perspectives on this paternal, Judeo-Christian God I didn't believe in.

That morning, we walked to Wabash Avenue Presbyterian Church, and it was incredible. It was so different from the non-denominational, evangelical congregation I had been attending with Dani. The focus was not entirely on the pastor. Other people spoke from the stage up front. There was congregational participation in the service, times when anyone there could raise their voice and be heard. With the sanctuary's amphitheater-style seating, there were places people could sit that were above the pastor, symbolizing that he was not the primary focus of the experience.

I loved the architecture. The entire building was traditional, stately, and dignified. There was a sense of holiness about the place.

I loved the music. This was not the snare-drummed, militaristic assertion of "Our God is an Awesome God," but the plaintive cry of "For Everyone Born, A Place at the Table."

I loved the sermon. The pastor was engaging, funny, and self-deprecating.

Most importantly, I felt comfortable the entire time. I can't emphasize enough how delightful and jarring that was. After all those Sunday mornings where I felt tossed back and forth in the other church—from warm, welcome, and spiritually connected to vilified, horrified, and cold—at this place, I felt comfortable the entire time. At this place, I felt connected to the divine.

At the pastor's invitation, I picked up the welcome pad in our pew and checked a box requesting a call from the pastor. When he called, I figured we would have an intellectual conversation about faith. I would tell him all the reasons why I couldn't believe. He would give me his responses. We would debate the question, and I would come away a bit closer to faith, perhaps, but still a non-believer.

During the week after that fateful weekend, I couldn't stop thinking about the whole string of events, all the strange circumstances and coincidences of the weekend.

In many ways, life went on as normal. I attended classes. I wrote papers. I did fraternity things and newspaper things. I studied.

For the year and a half that I had been at Wabash, when I had some serious studying to do, I would go down to the basement of the college library. I had a favorite spot in a back corner of a little-used section, where there was a large table with four straight-backed wooden chairs. I could spread out all my papers and books on that big, sprawling table. And aside from an occasional, random student looking for a book, I could count on being alone.

One night that fateful week, I had some work to do, so I headed to my favorite spot in the library, spread out my books and notebooks, and settled in for the evening. And then I stopped short.

Surely, I had noticed before that this was the religious studies section. But I came to this part of the library so often that the books themselves disappeared into the background. I had stopped noticing them.

But that night, I noticed them. Volumes of theology, Biblical studies, histories and hagiographies, all from a Christian perspective. I was surrounded. God was before me. God was behind me. God was to my left and to my right. It was as if, the whole time, without even knowing it, I had always been surrounded by God.

It occurred to me that if my life were a novel, I knew what the next development in the plot would be: I would become a Christian. I would acknowledge the miracles I had witnessed and participated in. I would acknowledge the fact that God had, for years, been weaving herself in and out of my life, making her presence known.

I was particularly struck by how much had happened to make that moment, in that library, in late November 2002, possible: I almost wasn't accepted at Wabash College, and I almost didn't go. I almost didn't meet the people who softened my stance toward faith. I might have never read the book that brought me closer to God. I almost didn't join the fraternity where I met the people who introduced me to Dani. I almost didn't date her. Julia decided to stay in Pennsylvania rather than attend the University of Indianapolis. Nothing came of my flirtations with Seth, Francisco, and Gabriela. The way had been cleared, perhaps by an unseen hand, to bring me to my evangelist. And there were the events of that fateful weekend—the anxiety, the pain, the prayer; the missed phone calls that caused Dani to spend the night; the visit to that Presbyterian church. It all seemed too intentional to be coincidental. God's authorship was all over my life, and the plot of the novel was inextricably clear.

At that moment, what I wanted was a book. Previous milestones in my spiritual journey had been marked by books. What I wanted at that moment was a book that could tell me why Christianity was reasonable, or how I could be an intelligent person and still adopt this faith. I wanted intellectual cover to justify the move I was about to make.

But then I realized that I didn't need a book. The evidence was all around me. The evidence was inside me. The story I was living was evidence enough for the narrative and its author. The story I was living was the book I had needed all along.

I closed my eyes. Using the evangelical language that was close to mind at that moment, I thought: *I accept Jesus Christ as my personal Lord and Savior. I believe in the God of the Bible.*

In a lot of ways, I wish my conversion had been more intellectual. I wish this story could be used as a tool to convince atheists that Christianity is fully rational, and that the right arguments will always lead to faith. But my story is not a completely intellectual one—it's an emotional one. I was guided toward faith by feeling, intuition, and relationships, and the intellectual framework would come later. The books I wanted in that final moment before surrendering—I would find them in due course. But even the best of those books, written with the clearest thoughts and deepest words, will most likely not be enough to convince a person to adopt Christian faith.

What's needed for faith is a variety of ways of knowing: rational thought, full-hearted emotion, and spiritual searching. What's needed is a whole and authentic human being, drawing closer to the real self God created at our genesis—with all the faculties of head, body, and heart willing to commit themselves to a mysterious God without knowing all the answers.

Our creative God feels for us as much she thinks for us. She created us with more than one way of knowing so we could engage the world as more than just a mind. We are more than thinking and rationalization and emotional distance. God created us so that the more we know ourselves, the more we know her.

Looking back, I wish I had been convinced by an idea and not a feeling. I wish I had been guided by philosophy rather than intuition. I wish, at the very least, that the miracles were grander and less ambiguous, that they were a clear, dramatic, undeniable testimony.

But I have come to accept that it was better this way. God does not submit to philosophical proofs. The Lord is not one more piece of empirical data. God cannot be contained or quantified or measured. God is not repeatable.

We have no way of testing our hypotheses about God, and even if we did, Lord help us if we tried! God is wild and unpredictable and relational. Our Creator cannot be contained in a clear argument—only hinted at in stories and metaphors that, no matter how hard an author tries, always fall short of the full reality.

In the end, God is a being who cannot be known—at least, not in the way that Newton's laws can be known. God, it seems, is a somewhat slippery, somewhat unsatisfying mystery. And so is the story of me becoming a person who knows himself and belongs to God.

15

Life Ever After

WHAT WAS THE MYSTERIOUS pain in my leg that night? I wish it had been something more dramatic, like a broken bone or a sudden wildfire, something less ambiguous and more verifiable and less weird to talk about. But it was what it was. Was it a psychosomatic aberration? Was it a lifetime of repressed nervousness suddenly shooting through my right leg? Was it the first hint of a chronic illness still latent in my body? Was some force of evil trying to prevent me from going to that Presbyterian church on Sunday morning? Was it a demonic attack?

I don't believe in demons, not the way some Christians do. Demons make for good devices in narratives, including Biblical narratives, but it is hard to imagine a just and loving God creating supernatural creatures who would become corrupt and malevolent, and then launch violent attacks on creatures who bear his image.

Besides, I think human beings are capable of enough evil on our own. We do not need supernatural encouragement. Our minds are powerful and can sometimes do inexplicable things—things that make us feel like a tangible force of evil is attacking us from the outside, capturing our bodies, minds, and souls. I think it is no coincidence that most people who report demonic possession also have a trauma history. In these events, I wonder if something that looked like demonic possession could have been the body and the mind unleashing a physical storm of trauma.

Our minds are capable of going to extraordinary lengths to protect us from danger. And from the outside, those extraordinary lengths may look like evil personified. But I think there is more than enough evil inside of us, both absorbed from other human beings and generated by our own sinful desires, to explain the evil we see in the world.

As for me and my right leg, I think it was psychosomatic. I think it was my body feeling emotions I had tried to keep inside. I think it was my body trying to stop me from feeling more pain, responding to my nervous anticipation of humiliation with a physical pain that would save me from the shame. As I said, the human mind is a powerful thing, and it may be motivated by trauma to protect us from trauma.

The miracle of that night was not the weird pain, but the prayer. I prayed to a God I didn't believe in and told him explicitly that I didn't believe in him. He answered my prayer all the same, and he made sure Dani got to my fraternity house, and he got us to that church on Sunday morning.

That night, and throughout my life, there was a larger hand guiding the story, an author whose brilliance becomes clearer over time. In the self-work I have done, exploring my own memories and the memories of others, I have found a story that reveals more depth with each reading, with each layer that is unpeeled.

Today, I am forty years old. I am married with two kids, ages eight and five. I am married to a woman—and she's not Dani or anyone else I've written about so far. My spouse and I are both Presbyterian ministers. I am a nascent counselor and part-time interim pastor, and she is a hospital chaplain. Our kids have to deal with our faith in God and our doubts about God—our joy, fear, and anger with our Creator. Please pray for them.

And please pray for us—as we continue to become who God made us to be—because the motion toward authenticity is a perpetual journey.

The story I have told in this book is a story of increasing self-realization, a story of *becoming* that one day led to Christian faith—an unorthodox Christian faith, to be sure, but faith nonetheless. Still, that story did not end at the moment of conversion. I did not become a fully authentic person at the age of nineteen in the basement of a college library. Carl Jung says a person cannot really work on self-realization until they are middle-aged or older. Before then, you do not really know who you are. I have found that to be true. Today, I am more myself than I have ever been, but I am sure the journey toward authenticity is not over.

I know my childhood defenses still exist, and that they try to form a protective layer around my authentic self. They tell me not to ask for help when I need it, because no one can help and no one will answer—because other people are unable or unwilling to help. My defenses tell me to duck down and take cover in my shell, to prevent others from seeing me and hurting me. They tell me to be ashamed of myself, and that it's all my fault, and that blaming myself for everything that goes wrong is somehow the way to redemption.

Those voices continue to exist in my head, but today, they are countered by other voices. I am loved, and I know I am loved. There are internal voices who encourage me to take social risks, to put myself out there, to live a less filtered life where more of who I am on the inside comes out and expresses itself.

Three years prior to this writing, in the fall of 2020, I had a crisis of confidence. I stopped believing I was loved—at least by my wife, Kari. I let the stress of our marriage weigh on me. I felt overwhelmed by the pandemic and young kids and God knows what else.

I took all the worst advice from the lowest impulses of my defense mechanisms. I ducked down and hid, so that Kari would not see I was a hurting person in need of help. I did not ask for help from anyone else, because I was sure that no one was willing or able to help. I decided that I was not in love. I decided that my wife was not really in love with me. This was the modern expression of all those ancient shames and doubts, felt by a kid left alone in his crib and then felt again when he was brutally hit in paradise.

In 2020, for months, I operated alone, analyzing our relationship, ruminating on my thoughts, and then finally telling her—the day after her birthday—that I wanted a divorce.

I didn't want to do it before her birthday, nor did I want to do it so soon after, but by that time, I was ready to burst and could not hold it inside any longer.

I said I was open to counseling. I could admit to a one-percent chance that I was wrong, and we might reconcile. At the very least, we might use counseling to negotiate a relatively amicable divorce.

But that was then, and this is now. Kari and I are still married—and happier than we have ever been. In fact, while I do not recommend precipitating a crisis in your marriage in order to achieve happiness, that happens to be what worked for us.

However, before I tell you about how we recovered our marriage and deepened our personal journeys toward authenticity, I want to tell you more about who we are and how we came to be a "we" in the first place.

As I said, Dani did not become my wife. She and I spent the fall semesters of our respective junior years abroad, me in Aberdeen, Scotland, and her in Salamanca. While in Aberdeen, I developed a crush on another girl. Laura was a student in my study abroad program and came from a college in Michigan. She was a liberal Christian, a swimmer, and a writer of science fiction. She was beautiful inside and out.

One night, my crush and I had a romantic-comedy moment. We had just seen *Love, Actually* in a theater with a group of friends. We laughed and talked about the movie all the way back to the dorms, as we often did, and I walked her back to her room. She had opened her door with a set of keys and left them dangling in the keyhole while she sat down at her desk.

As we said goodnight, we continued talking. I must have looked mischievous, because she could tell I was up to something; she said so, and she assured me she could not be pranked. I nodded. We said our final goodnight, and as I turned to leave her room, I snatched her keys and ran down the hallway. She laughed, chased after me, and took me down with a full-body tackle. We were both laughing hysterically. I wanted nothing more than to caress her blond, curly hair and kiss her. But I couldn't betray the relationship I was in.

Before we had parted ways for the semester, Dani and I agreed that we would be totally honest and tell each other about any crushes we developed. Under the pressure of distance and travel and hormones, we agreed that whether we wound up staying together or parting ways, we would at least be honest.

Dani and I had been dating for a year and a half at that point. I had been a Christian for around a year We were talking about marriage and life choices and how we would raise our kids. Still, there were some sticking points. I was still a long-haired hippie, and she was sometimes concerned that I did not have the conventionally masculine attributes required of a head of household. And for my part, I wasn't sure I wanted to be the head of anyone's household. I wanted to be the equal partner of someone with an independent spirit. I was starting to realize that I wanted to be with someone like Laura.

The weight of all this was too much for that fragile college relationship to bear. I told Dani about my crush on Laura. I didn't tell her about our almost kiss, or how deep the fault lines of longing went. Dani could forgive the small sliver of truth I gave her, but our relationship was already cracked, and this crush was enough to crush us.

We tried to keep the relationship alive. We met in Barcelona when our respective semesters were over, to begin our previously planned end of term travels. Spain is in love with public displays of affection, and we were happy to take advantage of their social etiquette by making out all over the city. However, as we struggled to decide what to do with ourselves, Dani had a thought: The kissing was getting in the way. It was preventing us from thinking clearly about our relationship and its future.

On the night of December 23, 2003, we took an overnight train from Barcelona to Paris. We had read in our travel guides that if you were traveling with another person, a hotel room was comparable in price to two beds in a hostel, and was certainly more secure and convenient, so we booked a room in an old building in the heart of the city. Under other circumstances, it would have been romantic.

But on the morning of December 24, we argued through the streets of the City of Lights. We argued about what to eat for breakfast. We argued about where the hotel was. We argued about how to navigate public transportation. Finally, we found the hotel and settled into our room.

We were both relieved to finally be there. From the balcony of our room, we had a beautiful view of the historic city, with bakeries and coffee shops lining cobblestone streets. It was incredible. It was gorgeous. Dani broke our kissing moratorium and kissed me.

But at that moment, we both knew our relationship was over. We felt nothing.

We broke up on Christmas Eve in Paris.

Later romantic adventures would lead me to Ruth, Sheila, and Benjamin, with a variety of other crushes and false leads along the way. But before we get to the true love of my life, Kari, I need to tell you about how I got to the place where I met her. We went to the same seminary in the suburbs of Atlanta, Georgia. But the journey there was not a straight and narrow path.

Toward the end of college, my career aspirations were changing. More than anything, I had wanted to be a creative writer, and maybe a literature professor at a school like Wabash, so I could pay the bills while also doing something I loved. In college, I received some encouragement in creative writing. I was published in our school's national, undergraduate literary journal, where my poems, creative nonfiction pieces, and short dramas were selected over excellent works by students at Susquehanna and DePauw.

Shortly after graduating, a poem of mine was published in a professional literary magazine. They misspelled my name and didn't pay me anything, and I felt that was a pretty accurate statement about the quality of my writing. Upon graduation, I was accepted to an MA program in creative nonfiction at Ball State University. I was offered a teaching assistantship and everything. At that point, I felt thrilled to be offered the princely sum of $10,000 a year in exchange for teaching introductory writing and dreaming about seeing my name in print.

But I didn't wind up going to Ball State. I didn't pursue creative writing as a first passion. I had a relentless sense that God had something else in mind for me.

During the summer between my sophomore and junior years, I had a spiritual experience with Anselm of Canterbury. Do you remember Saint Anselm, from my college search? When I read about that little college in New Hampshire with the black-robed Benedictine monks wandering the mall?

I met Anselm again during the summer between my sophomore and junior years at Wabash. I was on campus for an internship at a liberal arts think tank hosted by my college. We were researching short-term study abroad programs and how they fit within an overall liberal arts framework. I was looking forward to my upcoming semester in Aberdeen.

One night, after work, I was praying in my room and a name came into my awareness: Anselm of Canterbury. I was befuddled by this—and curious. I remembered the name from that long-ago college search, but surely there was nothing more to it than that.

But my curiosity led me to do a little research on Anselm. I discovered that he had been a monk, a theologian, and the Archbishop of Canterbury. I wondered what God could be trying to tell me, if anything, about this figure. When I visited Europe that fall, should I go to the ruins of his old monastery? As a student, should I read his theology? Or was this just a matter of a random name from a random moment in the past appearing in my mind at a random time?

The next day, when I was headed to my internship site, I stopped at a different academic building to get a soda, going to the one vending machine on campus that had Mello Yello. As I was walking out of the back door of that building, my eyes grazed a bulletin board and I noticed a call for papers for an academic conference on Saint Anselm, to be held that following spring at Saint Anselm College in New Hampshire. I was freaked out, but also amazed.

Yes, it could have been a coincidence. It's possible that I had seen this sign before out of the corner of my eye, that the name registered with my memory on a subconscious level, and that it simply appeared again during a quiet moment of personal prayer. But I would argue that all those mechanisms of coincidence and consciousness can be the means by which God works. Either way, I believe it was still a message from God, that it was still miraculous.

That summer, I went to see Bill Placher, the religion professor and Wabash graduate whom I had interviewed about the campus response to the Kent State shootings in 1971. Dr. Placher was a lifelong Presbyterian, so I was drawn to him as a teacher. Soon after my conversion, I connected with the local Presbyterian pastor, and he was guiding my first steps into faith. At the same time, I took on a religion minor to learn more about my new religion, and Dr. Placher became an important professor for me. It was not just his Presbyterianism, but also his kindness, patience, and intellectual humility. I knew that Presbyterianism pumped through my veins, and I knew that the local Presbyterian church was my church, though I never formally joined. For all those reasons, I knew he was the professor I needed to see.

I told Dr. Placher about my recent experience with Anselm, and he agreed to guide me in an independent study on Anselm the following spring. The timeline was likely a little short for me to write a conference-worthy paper for that year's conference at Saint Anselm College, but I could at least explore the man and consider the possibility.

That spring, after I broke up with Dani on Christmas Eve in Paris, I studied Anselm of Canterbury with Bill Placher in Crawfordsville.

Anselm's theology is interesting. His writing is less dry and pedantic than a lot of medieval theology, but it is still medieval theology. And I was more engaged by his biography than his theology. As a young man born to an Italian noble family, he had childhood visions of himself as a monk. He tried to enter a monastery at the age of fifteen, only to be denied because he did not have his father's permission. The family would have liked him to inherit the family estates and lead the next chapter of their nobility.

But Anselm had other ideas for himself. After suffering a psychosomatic illness over the weight of his disappointment, he spent years wandering Europe. He considered becoming a scholar, but the schools of the day were not religious enough for him. Meanwhile, the monasteries were more ascetic than scholarly and did not make much room for intellectual pursuits. He felt sure his calling was a religious one. He wanted to devote his life to serving God. But where could he find the right meeting of the spirit and the mind? Finally, he came to the monastery at Bec, which was searching for a schoolmaster. There, he could be both a brother and a scholar. There, he found the place where it all came together.

I could identify with all this. There was pressure from one's family and psychosomatic illness. I could relate to that. I could also relate to Anselm's sense of religious calling. When I first became a Christian, I began thinking about ministry.

On one hand, before I had settled on creative writing, I had considered becoming a teacher, a social worker, a non-profit director, a community organizer, or a counselor—basically, if there was an overstressed, underpaid position that served people and communities, I had considered it. Still, it occurred to me that a pastor does all of those things.

But weren't all these thoughts like running before I was walking? How arrogant was it to consider becoming a minister when I was so new to the faith? And anyway, I was such an introvert. I remembered how red my face got while giving speeches on the speech team in high school. How could I, of all people, become a pastor? Besides, I was drawn to academics. I wanted to teach, and write, and have Dead Poet's Society moments where all my students stood on desks and shouted lines from Walt Whitman.

I tried to let thoughts of ministry rest, but those thoughts persisted. Soon enough, I no longer knew what to do with myself.

And then Anselm came along—a man whose vocational crisis had resonance with mine, and who had resolved his own crisis by finding a mix between scholarship and monasticism.

When I discovered that, I knew the answer, deep in my heart and soul. Why had this name come into my mind? Why had I been drawn to this independent study? What did I have to learn from this ancient figure's writing and teaching and life?

I had learned that his monasticism was essential to his scholarship. The experience of monastic life profoundly shaped his theology, and his theological insights would be even less well-known today if not for the unique contributions of monasticism. For Anselm, the dual natures of his calling were inextricably intertwined.

I felt sure that it would be the same for me, and that this was the message from God I had been seeking. I wasn't sure exactly where it would lead. Anselm was an eleventh-century Catholic and I was a twenty-first century Protestant, so there are vocational roads that made sense for him but not for me. Still, I was convinced that some combination of social services, ministry, and literature would define the shape of my calling.

After graduating from Wabash in 2005, I returned to the shining metropolis of Fort Wayne, Indiana. I worked for two years at a social service job, joined a Presbyterian church, and waited for further word about the next steps. I felt the urge, more and more, to go to seminary. Whatever my Anselmian combination would wind up being, I was sure that the place to explore it was this kind of graduate school.

In 2007, I arrived at Columbia Theological Seminary just outside of Atlanta, ready to explore my vocation. I was also ready for love. I was sure that this was the place where I would meet the liberal Christian of my dreams, the rare person who could accept the combination of my strong faith, my sexuality, and my progressive politics. Kari, for her part, came to seminary ready to explore the world. She wasn't looking to be tied down to anyone. She was not quite ready for me, but we found each other all the same.

Interestingly, bisexuality is part of how we came together. I was a big LGBT activist on activist. She saw me in classes and public forums articulating an inclusive point of view. She liked how I advocated for inclusion passionately but not reactively, how I balanced intellect and emotion. During our first year, she didn't know that I had noticed her and was impressed with her, as well. She was deep, insightful, and bore the aura of a person who had really experienced something in the world. I was intrigued by her.

Kari was dating the guy who lived across the hall from me. When she passed the open door to my room, she often heard cool, indie music resounding from my speakers, but she also saw my giant Star Wars poster and thought, "What a nerd."

After she and her boyfriend broke up, I looked for ways to get to know her better. We ate our meals at the school cafeteria, which we called the refectory, and that was a good place to sit close to her and engage her in conversation. I was trying to figure out whether she was the one I was looking for. She just thought it was neat that the friend of her ex-boyfriend didn't hate her.

Some key context: In the wake of their break-up, I took her ex under my wing. He hadn't developed much of a social life on campus beyond her. He needed some support. I remember asking him if he wanted to grab a drink and talk about the break-up, and he was nonresponsive. Then I asked him if he wanted to grab a drink and talk about anything else, and he thought that was a great idea.

Anyway, back to Kari. One night, we had a spring dance, and it was awkward to the max. It was middle school. The boys were on one side of the room and the girls were on the other. People stood around drinking punch and eating Chex Mix, complaining about the loud music they felt too awkward to dance to. Still, several people dressed up for the event, and Kari was wearing a dress that highlighted all her best physical features. I was very motivated to talk to her. That night, we had a deep conversation, one of those conversations of a lifetime where you reveal who you are to another person who very much wants to know you.

The discourse got so deep that Kari eagerly accepted my invitation to talk in a quieter place. We found some quasi-comfortable seating in the lobby of an academic building. There, we shared our life stories. Her traumatic childhood. My traumatic childhood. How she was going to conquer the world after seminary, and how I was going to do the same.

For me, there were echoes of another wild night of conversation on an academic campus. There were visions of Kari as the hero of my dreams, the woman on the white horse who would liberate me from my intellectual prison. But more than that, there was just her, this person who seemed to understand me on a deep level, and who I seemed to understand, as well.

I was ready to burst with desire for her!

But there was a challenge: the ex. My friend. I approached him and asked if it would hurt him if I asked her out. He said it would. I reluctantly honored his wishes. But then a couple of days later, he knocked on my door and said, "You know what? Go ahead." I was thrilled.

That night, Kari and I both ate dinner in the school refectory. As I often did in those days, I sat close to her and tried to be impressive. I attempted to catch her after the meal, to ask her out then and there, but wound up being delayed by another conversation. Steeling my nerves, I was determined that this night would be the night I asked her out. I went to her room and knocked on her door. She was surprised to see me. I told her I liked her. I asked, "Would you like to go out to dinner sometime?"

She was silent for a moment. She had been quite oblivious to all my machinations, and she was surprised that I was interested in her in that way. At that moment, Kari uttered the immortal words we laugh about to this day: "Um... uh... like... how?" I said, "In my car," and then trailed off, unsure of what to do with that response. Eventually, she recovered her senses and told me she would think about it.

From there, I found her on AOL Instant Messenger. We chatted on that familiar platform, which I hadn't used in some time, but I dusted it off for her. We got to know each other even better. We made arrangements to study together. I tried to be present and distant all at once. Following the advice of an underrated movie, *The Tao of Steve*, I made sure to not be around at times when she was expecting to see me. I wanted to create an air of mystery.

One night, we watched the movie *Once*, and we kissed.

And the rest, as they say, is history.

I asked her to marry me in July 2009, and we were married by August of that same year.

Kari was planning to go to Toronto that year, to pursue a second master's degree and prepare for PhD study in Old Testament. I was going to stay in Georgia and finish my third year of seminary. The original plan was that we would get married in the summer of 2010.

The problem was that Kari's mother needed help. She had lost her job just before the economic crash of 2008, and then suddenly found herself in a tough job market as a person who was too old to hire and too young to retire. By the summer of 2009, my future mother-in-law's savings were running out. One day, I happened to be with Kari when she was on the phone with her sister. Her sister said, "Someone has to do something about this," and the sister wasn't the someone. Kari was the someone. At that point, we were already engaged. So we decided to get married early, to have her move back to Georgia and abandon Toronto and her PhD dreams, so we could take care of her mother together.

For three years, we sent Kari's mother $500 a month, bridging the gap between an annuity she could draw on and her expenses. We helped her get to the age of early eligibility for Social Security. We weren't making a lot ourselves, but we made do and got it done.

Still, our marriage began under the strain of her mother's weight, and it almost ended in the same way. In 2017, we celebrated our eighth anniversary by inviting Kari's mother to come live with us. She had early-onset Alzheimer's. I don't know how much you know about Alzheimer's, but the early-onset variety tends to be more severe. With this disease, Kari's mother made a rapid descent into dementia and all that comes with it: forgetfulness, strange behavior, irritability, and rage. Our son was three when she moved in. Our daughter was born a few months later. We had two young children and a bizarre adult who was subject to constant temper tantrums, and that was our life. For two years.

This whole situation was harder for Kari than it was for me. She saw her mother lose her sense of herself, experienced the sharp words that flew from her mouth, and cared for her physically in ways that wounded and traumatized them both. Kari shouldered more of the burden of direct care for her mother than I did. In addition to all this, she was a hospital chaplain, encountering situations that reminded her of her own life and feeling all the fierce emotions that came with those moments. She had no escape from loss and grief.

Still, for my part, our situation was difficult, as well. To maintain my mother-in-law's safety and prevent her from wandering out of the house, I had to adjust my work schedule to stay home with her. My work as a congregational minister suffered as a result. I had to deal with the stress of my church being unhappy with me, and churches are not always kind about their unhappiness.

Meanwhile, we did not have an equal partnership with the kids. I took the lead more often, as Kari needed to be free to care for her mother, and I wanted to give her time to rest. I took care of Kari and helped her deal with her emotions, and I tried my best to calm the waves of a stormy sea at church. In the midst of all this, I was lost.

Eventually, after a long struggle, we were able to enroll Kari's mom in Medicaid in the red state where we currently live, and we were able to find a placement for her in a Medicaid-eligible memory care unit.

Then, as soon as that was accomplished, a global pandemic set in. Kari was and still is a hospital chaplain. She was coping with the stress of serving in a hospital during a profound healthcare tragedy. I was a congregational pastor, and I was coping with the stress of reinventing church and caring for my community in those strange times.

Meanwhile, because I had the more flexible schedule between the two of us, I was home with the kids most of the day. Daycares were closed. Playgrounds were closed. We had no physical contact with friends or grandparents. All the places we might have gone to achieve relief from each other were not available to us. I had to balance a two-year-old, a five-year-old, and a full-time job that had suddenly become much more complicated. For my vocation, I worked early in the mornings before everyone woke up and late at night after everyone went to bed. In the afternoon, while one kid napped and another watched TV, I made phone calls to check in on people. I was absolutely fried—and unequipped to say a word about my feelings or my needs.

Is it any wonder, then, that by the fall of 2020 I was ready to burst? Yes, I had grown emotionally over the course of my adult life. But I hadn't grown enough to meet the challenge of all this.

In the face of these stressors, I reverted to who I had been as a child: I became emotionally frigid. The whole planet was going through a trauma, and I reverted to my trauma response. I cut myself off from emotions because they were too dangerous to feel. I didn't want to access my sadness, my grief, my rage. I didn't want to have to deal with the depression. I just needed to survive. To cope. To get through this day. To get through the next one.

Rather than dealing with my emotions directly, I channeled them into fantasies of escape: Divorce. A new job. A new life. I would take the kids and leave the rest of the mess behind.

Rather than talking about these feelings with anyone else, I turned them over and over in my mind. I felt unloved. I knew that Kari appreciated the things I had done for her, but for someone to love me, they would have to know me, and I felt unknown. I was spending so much time and energy turned inward on myself, hiding my true thoughts and feelings—how could anyone know me? I was hiding from my partner, and I felt hurt that she was not doing more to come and find me.

Living into the patterns I learned as a child, I decided that either no one could help or no one would. So I tried to work it out by myself, and I felt increasingly alone—as grief, fear, suspicion, and a desire to disconnect festered in my mind.

By the fall of 2020, I was ready to burst. My long-repressed emotions exploded on my wife, revealing a longing for divorce that shocked her to the core.

With my one percent willingness to see a counselor, I sat with Kari doing the most pandemic of things: virtual marriage therapy. We hid in a room in the church while dear friends watched the kids. I said out loud so many of the things I would previously say only to myself. To my shock, Kari affirmed that she was my partner and my person. She angrily asserted that she did love me, that she wanted to reestablish our partnership and make more room for me to be present. Throughout the process, we dealt with me holding back and her holding back. We found ourselves and found each other. With our therapist, we discovered the beginning of who we had the potential to be.

I could not have offered my part in that without a good therapist who helped me dig deeper, express myself more, and process more from my childhood. Through years of therapy and through the therapy of writing this book, I can be present as the person I authentically am—the person God created me to be.

This inner work has made all the difference not only in keeping me bonded to the love of my life, but also making me a better father, pastor, counselor, and friend. Today, I am fully present here and now, in all the places where I am called to be.

Over the years, I have been many things to many people.

To my mother, I was the good kid, the one she didn't have to worry about as much. I was also the one who was hurting in ways that he could not communicate and she could not see. Today, we have a good relationship. She was a rolling stone when she was a young adult, and one of the fruits of that is her respect for freedom and individuality. As I have grown, she has given me room to grow, and she has helped me in a number of ways along the way.

To my sister, I was also the good kid, but that meant something different to her. I was the one who needed to be protected, who needed to be saved from the blows that came my way. I was the one who could leave our harsh experiences relatively unscathed, grateful to her for saving me, and worried about her as I saw her walk a different road. Today, I see her as a woman who protects others, who welcomes vulnerable kids into her home, who will go out of her way to help anyone. We may not have walked the same road in life—but I am proud of her, and she is proud of me.

To my wife and kids, I am a good husband and a good dad. It was not inevitable that I would become either of those things. It has taken a lot of personal work; a lot of care, grace, and acceptance from them; a lot of therapy; and a lot of love. I am grateful that they are the people I get to love.

To my high school self, I was a future poet. I was going to become a big-city writer living in a ratty apartment, nurturing a fevered heart for literary activism. I did not become that man, but my creativity is woven into my sermons, and my activism is an authentic part of who I am. Back then, I thought I needed to go to New York to find my tribe. Today, I know there are weird and wonderful people everywhere, looking for the locations where they can let down their guard and be themselves.

To my college self, I was a future literature professor. I was a natural teacher who would one day walk the quad to the neo-classical building that housed my office, where I would meet with students and guide their young lives and intellects, and then write poetry in the arboretum.

Of course, I did not become a literature professor, but the Bible is a great work of literature, spanning dozens of authors and many genres and three ancient languages. And I have faith in those ancient words, that they can inspire people to embrace a new vision of who God calls us to be—as individuals and as a church. Today, I still get to be a teacher, for people of all ages, and I get to do that without answering to administrators or giving out grades.

In the end, the only grades that matter are the ones we get from God. And in her eyes, we've already passed the test. We passed the test the moment we came into existence. We gained all the approval we will ever need from God simply by being created in her image. In her view, that's all we ever needed to be. At the same time, she invites us to grow. She wants us to be whole, to completely be the person we were made to be. As people who are loved, approved, and forgiven by God, we are free to find, talk about, and live as our full, authentic selves.

Still, no matter how much or how little we grow, God accepts us. No matter what we believe or how we live or how much we become who we are, we are welcome in the Kingdom of Heaven.

Today, I am a universalist. If I could find my fourth grade atheist self and have a friendly debate with him, I would say, "Yes, it's unfair for all the people who believe in a particular religion to go to heaven while everyone else goes to hell. And yes, if God set up a system like that, she would be unjust. But that's not my reading of Scripture. When I read Scripture, I see a tent that grows wider with each turn of the page. I see, in the Book of Revelation, a city that comes down to earth from Heaven, where the gates are never closed by day and it is never night. Moreover, I see in Matthew 25:31–46 that it's possible to be close to God and not know you are, even as it's possible to think you're close to God and not really meet him. What all this tells me is that there are many ways to get to where God is, and the gate is always open, ready for all people to come in."

And to bring every part of who they are. Every part. I don't think my fourth grade self would be convinced, but we would have an interesting conversation all the same.

Epilogue

Being Yourself at Church

THE FINAL QUESTION IS: How can churches support people in journeys toward deeper authenticity? How can a church make room for all its people to be who they are, without attempting to inhibit them or laying undue expectations on their shoulders?

There is an authentic self at the core of us. That authentic self was created by God, reflects the image of God, and represents the best part of the divine living within us. Our authentic selves are not free to do whatever they want and hurt whoever they want. A person who goes through a genuine process of self-realization will emerge more Christ-like. The most authentic version of you is both more like you and more like Jesus than who you are right now.

It's a paradox. Jesus said, "For those who want to save their life will lose it, and those who lose their life for my sake, and for the sake of the gospel, will save it" (Mark 8:35). A person who is walking the road of authenticity is confident enough in who they are to step aside and make room for others. They are fulfilled on their own terms, so they can be themselves and find joy in others doing the same.

Perhaps the difficulty with the church is that it is often not fulfilled on its own terms. On the one hand, you find evangelical megachurches acting out their insecurities—attempting to control others with tight regulations on what is and is not acceptable in the eyes of the self-styled representatives of God. They see the world in black and white, and they believe that if more people saw the world as they do, all would be well.

Other churches, especially the mainline Protestant ones, profess more tolerant theologies, but have to deal with their own insecurities and lack of fulfillment. According to their words, they want you to be who you are, but according to their actions, they want you to fit inside a box. They are worried about their declining budgets. They are worried about their aging membership.

They are so worried that they would prefer that you not stand out too much. "We're supportive of LGBT people, but we can't have a gay pastor," they might say. If we did, all our new members would be gay, and then we'd become a gay church!" First of all, honey, you should be so lucky. I can't tell you how many churches I've met who were afraid of becoming "a gay church," as though it would be a terrible thing to be inundated with creative and talented people who model authenticity to the world.

"We can't make our single-use bathrooms gender-neutral."

"We can't put a statement on our website saying that LGBT people are welcome. What about other people? How will they know that they're welcome, too?"

When churches demonstrate a clear affirmation of queer people, they show that they are a welcoming space for all people. When people in non-traditional families (such as single dads and their kids), see rainbow signs outside of a church, they know that this is a space where they and their odd little group are welcome. When people with tolerant and open views of any kind see that you are not like the evangelicals, and you're willing to shout it on the mountain, they know there is space for their families in your church.

But many mainline Protestant churches are inhibited. They profess tolerant theologies, but they do so quietly, hoping no one will notice. In the meantime, they hide the aberrant people in their communities. The tattooed, the people with blue hair, the people who are intellectually disabled—they're welcome, but we're not going to display them on the chancel. We don't want their presence to turn off attractive heterosexual couples with young children. After all, if people start thinking of us as a freak show, how will we grow?

Many mainline Protestant church members have this fantasy: that young, nuclear families will find the church en masse, that they will bring with them enough money to restore all the programs and staff members they have lost to declining budgets, and enough energy to carry the church's beloved ministries on their shoulders—and enough children to provide life, love, and laughter, but only at appropriate times during the service.

Instead of accepting and embracing who the church authentically is, they spend their lives longing to recapture a past that met the needs of decades ago but doesn't reflect where people are now—if it ever did. Are you sure, church, that those memories of past glory aren't exaggerated a little bit? Are you sure that the needs of the people—*all* the people—were met back then?

In my experience, mainline Protestant churches are often consumed with maintaining their image and striving to be who they think they're supposed to be. But I believe God is inviting them to relax and simply be who they are, and to make room for their members to be who they are, as well.

As Kari and I have had our adventures together, I wish we had been part of churches who welcomed us as who we authentically are. I wish we had opportunities, earlier in life, to grow into the people God intended us to be, and to build ourselves up for the challenging days ahead. I wish we had been part of churches who were committed to authenticity. The churches we have been part of would probably say that they were exactly that. But in reality, they all had their own inhibitions and expectations. They all had their ways of wanting us to be less or more of who we were.

For example, there was Harmony Presbyterian Church. This is the church I joined in 2005, after graduating from college, when I moved back to my hometown and took a job in social services. I couldn't decide between grad school in English or grad school in religion, so I found a job and learned a little about life instead.

There were a couple of churches near me that were explicitly LGBT-affirming, but they were big, downtown churches. I liked that Harmony was a smaller, neighborhood church. They also had a decent-sized community of young adults. They seemed like as good a place as any to continue to explore my newfound faith—and to discern a potential call to ministry.

I remained quiet about my bisexuality there. No one ever told me I should. I don't remember any anti-LGBT sermons from the pulpit. It never came up. And I didn't force the issue. At that point, I was simply learning how to be a member of a church. I wasn't equipped to try to be my whole self in one.

Harmony Presbyterian ordained me into leadership as a deacon. They offered me opportunities to serve, allowing me to teach Sunday School classes for kindergarteners and teenagers. They endorsed me for our denomination's ordination process and cheered as I went off to seminary.

At Columbia Theological Seminary in Georgia, I met other queer Christians. I recognized that I'd had a relatively easy coming-out experience because I didn't grow up Christian. As a teenager, I was privileged to able to accept myself without a body of people telling me that God would not love me if I affirmed my identity.

Today, my denomination—the Presbyterian Church (USA)—is more accepting of LGBT people than it was in 2007. We still have a road to travel on inclusivity, but we're better now than we used to be. Back then, during that first year of seminary, I knew that one way I could help the cause would be to tell the people at Harmony who I am. I could tell them, "Look! You know and love someone who has a queer identity. Could that influence you to expand your minds?"

I started my campaign around Thanksgiving 2007. I called my pastor before I left for home. I gave her an opportunity to veto my coming out to the church, if she felt that the church wasn't ready, or that in some other way it was the wrong decision. At the time, I discovered that she was opposed to LGBT inclusion in the life of the church universal. In 2007, the denomination was making moves toward affirming ordination for LGBT people, and she'd given a speech against it at a denominational meeting. She'd posted the speech on Harmony's website. It turns out that Harmony, under her leadership, was not harmonious for all people.

Still, in her conversation with me, she reasoned that I was an adult and could do what I like.

So I headed home to eat turkey and talk turkey. To keep me entertained on the drive from Georgia to Indiana, my boyfriend at the time, Benjamin, burned me a CD (for older readers, this is the younger equivalent of a "mixed tape;" for younger readers, this is the older equivalent of a "playlist"). It had Cher and the Village People and other gay standards. It also had the beautiful Tracy Chapman anthem, reminding me that "talkin' about a revolution / sounds like a whisper." It was just what I needed to steel my nerves for coming out to this church.

This would have been hard enough—even harder, in its own way—if I had grown up in this church and had deep relationships with these people. But they hadn't known me until two and a half years prior to this. So when I began telling people, individually, about my identity, they didn't know what to do with that news. They didn't hug me and say, "Congratulations for coming to terms with yourself," or, "I don't understand this, but I love you all the same." They just shrugged and continued cleaning the fellowship hall. I tried again on a few other trips home, but my news still did not elicit much of a reaction.

Finally, when I came home after the school year in May, my pastor asked me to preach on two successive Sundays. I was glad to do so. The first sermon was preached on Trinity Sunday. I talked about unity in the midst of diversity and diversity in the midst of unity—in the context of the Trinity and the context of us. I referenced the denomination's debate over LGBT ordination, and said, "I hope, as a bisexual person and a candidate for ministry, that we can find a way to disagree with each other and remain unified, to be a group of people who have different views but who can still come together and worship the same Triune God."

Those words, apparently, were egregious enough for me to be exiled by the church. I was not allowed to preach a second time. The elders met "in executive session" to decide what to do with me. In their "executive session," they decided to revoke their endorsement of me, to kneecap my bid for ordination by taking away this necessary seal of approval. They did this soon after my sermon, but they didn't tell me about it for a month.

I went back to the church a few times after that. Any one of them could have talked to me. Any one of them could have asked me directly about my identity and the issues surrounding it. Any one of them could have told me about the decision they made. None of them did.

To them, I was not a person to love, but a threat to be neutralized. I was a person whose existence might imperil the life of the church, because my authentic existence might convince wealthy donors to go elsewhere.

When I finally found out about their action, the day before I met with a denominational ordination committee, I was furious. As with past betrayals, there was part of me that laughed. There was part of me that expected nothing more than silent abandonment and uncaring treachery, and that part of me could only laugh at people doing what people do. But there was also part of me who had grown up enough to know that this was wrong. How could they do this without at least talking to me first? How could they hide it for a month, failing to tell me personal information that was vital to planning my life and career?

Still, I persisted in the ordination process.

I talked to my college pastor and Bill Placher, who affirmed that my connection to the Presbyterian church ran deeper than Harmony. I gathered comfort from my friends at seminary, including Kari, who saw me as a person with gifts for this calling. I also spent many long nights in the seminary chapel, praying in the dark, expressing my fury and wondering if I should not abandon this path altogether, but God kept affirming that I was called to ministry.

I joined a small LGBT-friendly church in Atlanta that just happened to be in the neighborhood where my mom and sister lived in the '70s. This also became the church where Kari and I got married, and where I was ordained to ministry. This is the closest I have ever come to an ideal church—a place where I was supported, encouraged, and empowered to be my full self.

But even here, there were all the institutional questions. Where would a small church like this find the money to keep going, to maintain its building and pay its small staff? If the church figured out how to grow, how could it do so without losing the familial qualities that made it special to the people who called it home?

As a minister-in-training, I assisted in ministry at this church, and I wanted to help it innovate. I thought that new forms of preaching and teaching could help us take advantage of our small size—and maybe even attract new members looking for something different. But many of the people of the church were not open to innovation. They wanted their church to be what it had always been—just a little bit bigger and more financially viable.

In this space, I was free to be myself as a person, but not to be myself as a minister. For them, the fragile sense of family they had found required adherence to tradition. Anyone who wanted to be their minister would need to remain in a well-defined box.

After graduating from seminary in 2010, I worked for a couple of years as a chaplaincy resident in two hospitals in Atlanta. In 2012, Kari and I moved to Connecticut, where I earned a second master's degree—a one-year degree designed for those seeking further preparation for PhD study. While earning this degree, I learned that PhD study was not my cup of tea.

Instead, I felt God was calling me to become the pastor of my own church. I wanted to preach, care for people, and lead them in mission. I wanted to help a church become what God had called it to be. With this in mind, in 2013, I became the pastor of a quirky, semi-rural church in a red state.

At that time, Kari and I had been married for three-and-a-half years. We were no longer financially supporting her mother, but we still faced challenges, as any couple does. The act of truly opening yourself up to another person, and fully receiving that person in return, is hard. Most people begin marriage not really knowing how to do this.

I loved Kari. We were good partners. We were deeply compatible. We were happy. There was part of me that wouldn't allow anyone to fully love me—part of me that was born out of childhood fear and abandonment, part of me who tried to protect the rest of me by not letting anyone else in. But Kari was as close to me as I could allow another person to be. I was as sure of her as I could be of anyone.

And given our marriage, I decided not to tell the churches that considered hiring me about my bisexuality.

I thought about it this way: Bisexuality is weird. Even a lot of gay people don't understand it, especially when you're in a relationship with someone of a different gender. If I were in a same-sex relationship and claimed my bisexual identity, that would be easier for many people to wrap their heads around. But if you're a man married to a woman, why say you're bisexual? Just because you're the one who cooks and she's the one who fixes things, does that really mean anything? After all, doesn't 'bisexual' mean that you have an open marriage and you're looking to screw anything that moves?

I said to Kari, "If I just choose not to talk about it, I'll have a wider range of churches to choose from. If I talk about it, I'll be locked into progressive churches that are already LGBT-friendly, and I'm definitely open to a church like that. But if I choose not to talk about it—if I present as a straight ally of queer people—then I can serve in different places. Moderate places. Purple churches. Places where I could sneak in and be a voice for inclusion."

Basically, I chose to censor part of myself. I did this because of my understanding of how intolerant churches can be, and because I wanted to be a person who helped make them more inclusive. I chose influence over authenticity.

In so doing, did I underestimate the churches? Would they have taken me just as I am, without one plea? The stories I hear from others would indicate not. LGBT people have a hard time becoming pastors of churches, even in inclusive denominations. They're welcome to serve as chaplains and social workers and counselors, or in any kind of ministry that truly values diversity. But churches have images to maintain. They have stately brick facades to manage. They have a vision in their mind of the ideal pastor, and it looks a lot like the person who was their pastor in the 1950s: a straight, white male with a genial smile who's active in the Chamber of Commerce and spreads his winning charm all over Sunday morning.

If you asked these churches, they would say that they do not discriminate, that they are open to all people and love all people. But in reality, they have their limits. They want their pastor to be a pillar of their community; to be broadly attractive to the young, straight families they hope to attract; and to inspire confidence in the church.

I didn't think that I fit that expectation, with my weird-looking face and nerdy glasses and thick, red lips. But I would be a bit more marketable if I pretended to be straight.

And just like that, I was called to a quirky little church in a semi-rural area with a 1970s eye for interior design and a fog machine and laser lights in their sanctuary. Every December, they put on a Trans-Siberian-Orchestra-inspired Christmas show. They were lovely people. The main challenge of my call was that they really couldn't afford a pastor, even at the three-quarters salary to which we agreed.

Could I have been myself there? A prominent member of the church had a daughter who was a lesbian. When we arrived in town, Kari was asked to officiate the wedding of his daughter and her future-wife. These were welcoming people, and they considered their church to be an inclusive church. At the same time, there were members who voted against accepting me as their pastor because I had LGBT-friendly views; we were in a semi-rural area, after all. Having a bisexual pastor would have been an oddity.

Besides, they gave me a lot of indications that they couldn't accept me in other ways. I was an intellectual liberal with the taint of the east coast. They criticized my high-brow word choices and what they saw as a lacking work ethic (but which was really a combination of social anxiety and a commitment not to work for more hours than I was being paid).

I was told by one member that financial giving had dropped in the church because I did not fit in to the culture of the town, and people were reluctant to support my part-time salary. In their eyes, my hands were too smooth and my words were too slick; I was full of myself and arrogant. And they were right. I was arrogant in some ways. I still am. But I'm also riven with insecurity. Could I have talked about that with them?

Maybe they could have accepted a bisexual pastor who was not odd in the other ways I was odd, one who fished and drove a motorcycle and fit with the culture of that town. But for me, with all my supposed liberal elitism, I think 'bisexual' would have been a bridge too far.

My next stop was a mid-sized suburban church. This was a more cosmopolitan, intellectual congregation. These were well-educated, middle- to upper-class people. They had high expectations for their pastor. They wanted a glad-handing moderate who was uncontroversial, well-regarded in the community, and socially affable.

I tried to be as socially affable as I knew how to be. I learned more as I went—how to be open to them and their gifts, how to be emotionally expressive with them, how to let them know that I loved them.

But my heart was always for the marginalized people. For the hidden homeless, living in their cars in the parking lots of the suburbs. For the traumatized, for the young, for the people who were aging faster than they could stand. For the people whose wild personal stories made them misfits in the vast suburban landscape.

For the people who were physically, socially, and emotionally bleeding, I was the right pastor at the right time.

But for those whose marginality was more hidden, for those who tried to conceal that they had ever known exclusion, rejection, and pain—for them, ministry was harder for me.

I'm a person who wants to live with my wounds on the surface, with my vulnerability visible for all to see. With people who want to hide their vulnerabilities, who want to project an image of confidence, who wish to assert that everything is great and me and my loved ones always fit in—I don't know what to do with that.

I spent eight years with this church, and I learned how to pastor the people who were challenging for me. As I grew into the person I was becoming, I became more confident personally and professionally. On one hand, there were many times when I felt stifled by the church, stifled by the images they were protecting and facades they were maintaining, and stifled by the image they wanted to have of me. On the other hand, the more I experimented, the more I acted like myself, the more they met me where I was.

When I shared stories of childhood trauma and abuse, I inevitably heard other stories of childhood trauma and abuse. People thanked me for naming these things out loud and helping them to be comfortable sharing their own stories.

When I shared my love for people on the margins, church members rose to the challenge and looked for new ways to love people on the margins.

When I shared my wounds and vulnerabilities, they thanked me for my openness, or at least some people did.

The younger members, and a few of the older ones, came to see church as a place where they could be honest, vulnerable, and authentic. These people changed and grew. They embraced the vision of crafting a church of authenticity, where we all embrace even the marginal parts of ourselves, as we create a site of welcome for the marginalized and centralized alike.

With these members, we started an innovative new worshipping community. We tried bold experiments in mission. For a year and a half, we housed a woman in the church's youth room. She had been homeless, and we walked beside her for a year and a half. We helped her recover from trauma and rebuild her confidence. We gave her a chance to rest physically and recover emotionally from the rigors of homelessness. We launched her into a new life with her own apartment. More importantly, we got to know her. We learned from her. Through her determination, optimism, and good humor, she had a lot to teach us. We were privileged to walk beside her.

These are only some of the extraordinary things this congregation did while I was pastor there. This is a sign of how much they accepted a vision of authenticity, universal love, and reaching to the margins.

But the vision was not universally accepted. Some people complained that I talked too much about my childhood experiences. They complained that the church was taking too many risks to help people. They complained that too many things were changing, but they couldn't name the changes. They didn't realize, or didn't verbalize, that the primary change was me not fitting the ideal image of the suburban pastor. I was leading the church to embrace a Christian vision of holiness through weakness, of fullness through marginality (1 Corinthians 1:26–31), and that didn't fit with their vision of what they wanted the church to be.

Through my ministry, I was asking them to shift their vision of a successful Christian: less a well-dressed member of a burgeoning church with a stately facade, and more a homeless wanderer who walks from town to town, collecting donations, preaching, and healing.

Some of them did live into this vision. They shared more of themselves. They took risks to help others. Could these people have accepted me as a bisexual person? Absolutely. Those people could have.

But there were others who couldn't, people who were never on board with this program. They regarded me with suspicion and held me at a distance. For my part, I will admit that I was far from perfect with them. At first, I didn't know how to love them, and they felt unloved by me, and it is hard to follow someone if you do not think they care about you.

If I had been a better pastor from the beginning, could they have accepted me as a bisexual? No, I do not believe so. As an openly bisexual person, I would never have been hired to be their pastor.

Once, I tried to convince the church's board to write a statement of explicit welcome for LGBT people on the front page of our website. From my feigned perch as a straight ally, I tried to convince them that young people of all orientations look for statements like these as indications of the kind of church you are. One of our leaders, a single mother, said that statements of LGBT welcome made her feel welcome as a person in a non-traditional family.

She and I tried to convince the others that a statement like this was needed in order for us to reach LGBT people, who too often hear "all are welcome" from churches where they are not really, fully welcome. For them, a clear statement of inclusion would demonstrate that our welcome mat was genuine. For others, it would declare that we were opening our arms to all people. No one would feel excluded just because we made it clear that the LGBT community is welcome.

But the church board didn't want to do it. They didn't believe me or the other leader. They feared that non-LGBT people would be driven away. They contended that "all are welcome" ought to be enough. Besides, they said, they didn't want to be a "gay church."

This church was afraid. Their previous pastor had left under a cloud of controversy, and many members left in response, either because they felt repelled by him or repelled by the controversy. While they were getting smaller, they were also riven with debt. In 2004, they took on $3.5 million in mortgage debt for a building expansion, which they hoped would make them look even more successful and sophisticated. But many of the people who could help pay this debt left when the former pastor did.

Even still, the church had been losing members before that. Beloved staff members were leaving for other opportunities. Youth were graduating and families were moving. Long-time pillars of the church were feeling alienated by the church's theological rigidity, and this in turn drove them away. People got tired of hearing things like: "No, we cannot play a Johnny Cash song at your mother's funeral." "No, we cannot allow photographers to move around during your son's wedding, because it's a worship service." "No, we cannot baptize your grandchild, because his parents are not members of the church."

By the time I came, the church was mired in debt, upset about losing members and friends, and angry that the church was changing in ways they did not expect and did not choose. They were, in turn, hopeful that the glory days might someday return, and not yet ready to embrace a new vision that didn't look to them like the glory days.

Scripture says, "God chose what is foolish in the world to shame the wise; God chose what is weak in the world to shame the strong; God chose what is low and despised in the world, things that are not, to reduce to nothing things that are, so that no one might boast in the presence of God" (1 Corinthians 1:27–29).

During my time at this place, I tried to convince the church to embrace its weakness—to accept that it was smaller than it used to be, less grand and less outwardly attractive. We could instead be a place of vulnerability, as a site and as a people, a place where we are open about our weaknesses because we know they make us strong in our faith.

And again, some people embraced that vision with love and wonder, while others could never stop longing for the good old days—and blaming me for not bringing them back.

During what became my final year there, I thought I might want to tell them about my bisexuality. I thought I might want to do more to model the authenticity I had been preaching about for years. So I tried telling a few people. It was clear that they had a hard time accepting me, that the prospect of my announcement made them afraid for the future of the church. They were nervous that too many people would not understand. They were anxious that resistant people would leave in the wake of my words. Of course, these resistant people would take their money and time with them—and then where would we be?

In the end, I had pushed them far enough, and they would go no further. Once again, accepting me as a bisexual person was a bridge too far. Even in this place that was boldly learning authenticity and bravely embracing vulnerability, I could not be myself.

The question is, then, can we be ourselves anywhere? Can any church accept leaders and people for who they are? Can any church be a place where you can tell a story like mine and be your whole self the whole time. Or will institutional concerns always get in the way?

Will the image the church wants to have always reflect our individual fears and insecurities? Will the money invested in the pastor always be a hard limit on how authentic church professionals can be? And what about the rest of the people? Is there room for them to be themselves in the mortar of that facade?

I have hope that that there is.

In my career as a congregational minister, I have served two congregations as their solo pastor, and I served the second one for eight years. I did not feel fully able to be myself in either church, but I will try again in the next one. I will try to be my full, weird, creative, vulnerable, intellectual self. I will look for a church that is already known for being accepting, and I will do my best to trust them. I will try not to let my own insecurities get in the way.

I may not have found the answer yet, but I have faith that a place like that is possible, and I have confidence that becoming that is what Jesus wants us to do. With that in mind, I'll continue searching. And if I can't find a place like this that already exists, I'll create one.